# Outdoor Learning Ac the Curriculum

Following the acclaim for *Learning Outside the Classroom* in 2012, this latest book more deeply explains how well constructed outdoor learning experiences can benefit children and young people's academic development and health and wellbeing.

*Outdoor Learning Across the Curriculum* outlines the theory and practice to enable preservice and experienced primary and secondary school teachers to systematically incorporate meaningful outdoor learning opportunities into their daily teaching activities, in a range of environments and with diverse groups of students. Six of the chapters are substantially re-worked versions of the 2012 book, two are completely re-imagined, and four are entirely new. Topics for developing learning and teaching outdoors include:

- Inclusive educational design.

- Learning for sustainability.

- Community-based learning.

- The role of student curiosity and wonder.

- Evidencing learning.

- Developing a whole school approach.

- Place-responsive education.

- Integrating digital technology.

With practical and engaging chapters containing aims, case studies, and guidelines for practice, this timely book provides teachers the tools with which they can integrate outdoor learning into their daily timetable. It will also be a valuable resource to other professions which use the outdoors for educational purposes.

**Simon Beames** is Professor of Friluftsliv at the Norwegian School of Sport Sciences in Oslo.

**Peter Higgins** is Professor of Outdoor, Environmental, and Sustainability Education at the University of Edinburgh.

**Robbie Nicol** is Professor of Place-Based Education at the University of Edinburgh.

**Heidi Smith** is a Lecturer in Outdoor Learning at the University of Edinburgh.

Teaching outdoors is both a necessity and a challenge. In *Outdoor Learning Across the Curriculum* the necessity is underlined by research-based evidence, thus equipping stakeholders arguing for an inclusive pedagogy in the outdoors. The book addresses both overarching issues concerning an inclusive pedagogy with both curriculum based-, adventure- and sustainability-perspectives on the educational process, as well as a modern and critical standpoint on the educational practice today. Moreover, the book can be used as a practical tool in the implementation of outdoor learning, as it includes experience-based and thorough practical advises, e.g. for the use of digital technologies in the outdoors, classroom management and safety issues. We certainly need to continuously develop the aims of the education, but also the pedagogy, and *Outdoor Learning Across the Curriculum* adds a valuable contribution to this.

*Karen Seierøe Barfod*
*Docent, VIA University College, Denmark*

When introduced to the idea of outdoor learning, most teachers understand intuitively that, given the state of the world, it makes good sense. But they also want to know how to do it and to see that it can be done. Most importantly, they need practice integrating outdoor learning into the classroom and school in a comprehensive way, and articulating to themselves and others the significance of this work. This book is simply the best field guide to the theory and practice of outdoor learning that I've ever seen. The authors have carefully built a curriculum for learning that is responsive to the current historical moment and that is based on decades of experience with the craft. This will be my go to book on the theme for the foreseeable future.

*David Greenwood*
*Professor of Environmental and Holistic Education,*
*Lakehead University, Canada*

The Covid pandemic has provided ample motivation for teachers and students to spend as much time out of doors as possible, and the timing of this book could not be better! The justification for learning outdoors, and learning for the long game of sustainability, is articulated in a clear and inclusive way in this book. But then it takes it to the next level by providing a roadmap with the logistics of how to get your students out of doors. This takes outdoor learning from the philosophical to the logistical—something that school-based practitioners who work directly with students rarely see in educational literature. If you want to get your students away from the screen and into an interdisciplinary classroom without walls, where curiosity and wonder drive learning, this book is for you!

*Tom Drake*
*Principal, Crossett Brook Middle School, Vermont, USA*

Clear, insightful and inspiring—this book offers a refreshing and progressive take on outdoor learning and its critical role in the holistic education of future generations of learners. It is a comprehensive handbook which offers useful ideas. Each chapter contains objectives, a case study, and suggested guidelines for practice which educators would appreciate. It is poignantly persuasive in nudging each of us to educate for a socially and environmentally just planet. For me, it is the kind of book that has the potential to inspire and transform lives.

*Susanna Ho*
*Lead Outdoor Education Specialist,*
*Ministry of Education, Singapore*

This book is a must-read for anyone seeking to broaden their horizons and gain a deeper understanding of teaching modalities to incorporate outdoor learning experiences into their lessons. Collectively, the authors' writing style is engaging and thought-provoking, and makes complex topics enjoyable to read and digest. The pearls of wisdom shared in this book will stay with you long after you've turned the last page.

*Tonia Gray*
*Professor, School of Education,*
*Western Sydney University, Australia*

UNESCO, OECD, and other shapers of education systems are calling for a huge undertaking by nations: the transformation of their education systems; to address future sustainability challenges; to include experiential learning with exposure to realities; to build deeper, knowledgeable connections with issues; and create empathic connection to those affected by global realities resulting in informed action. In answering this call, I strongly suggest you read *Outdoor Learning Across the Curriculum* to begin the journey and keep it by your side as you rise to the challenge of the undertaking that is so desperately needed.

*Charles Hopkins*
*Professor and UNESCO Chair in Reorienting*
*Education towards Sustainability, York University, Canada*

Especially in times when children, through their education, are continuously seduced to go back to their screens for entertainment and quick answers, the risk of becoming disconnected from the natural world in both urban and rural environments is greater than ever. How to restore biophilia and a sense of place in the Anthropocene? This timely book provides some answers by taking the outdoors as both a starting point and a context for relational forms of learning that can reconnect young people with their local environment and, ultimately, will help heal the Earth.

*Arjen Wals*
*Professor of Transformative Learning for Socio-Ecological*
*Sustainability and UNESCO Chair, Wageningen University, The*
*Netherlands/Norwegian University of Life Sciences, Norway*

# Outdoor Learning Across the Curriculum

## Theory and Guidelines for Practice

Simon Beames, Peter Higgins,
Robbie Nicol and Heidi Smith

Routledge
Taylor & Francis Group

LONDON AND NEW YORK

Designed cover image: John R Evans

Second edition published 2024
by Routledge
4 Park Square, Milton Park, Abingdon, Oxon, OX14 4RN

and by Routledge
605 Third Avenue, New York, NY 10158

*Routledge is an imprint of the Taylor & Francis Group, an informa business*

First edition published by Routledge 2011

*British Library Cataloguing-in-Publication Data*
A catalogue record for this book is available from the British Library

*Library of Congress Cataloging-in-Publication Data*
Names: Beames, Simon, author. | Higgins, Peter J., author. | Nicol, Robbie, author. |
    Smith, Heidi, 1973– author.
Title: Outdoor learning across the curriculum / Simon Beames, Peter Higgins,
    Robbie Nicol, Heidi Smith.
Other titles: Learning outside the classroom
Description: Second edition. | Abingdon, Oxon ; New York, NY : Routledge, 2024. |
    Revised edition of: Learning outside the classroom. 2012 | Includes bibliographical
    references and index.
Identifiers: LCCN 2023012447 (print) | LCCN 2023012448 (ebook) |
    ISBN 9780367819323 (hardback) | ISBN 9780367819330 (paperback) |
    ISBN 9781003010890 (ebook)
Subjects: LCSH: Outdoor education. | Place-based education.
Classification: LCC LB1047 .B37 2024 (print) | LCC LB1047 (ebook) |
    DDC 371.3/84—dc23/eng/20230517
LC record available at https://lccn.loc.gov/2023012447
LC ebook record available at https://lccn.loc.gov/2023012448

ISBN: 978-0-367-81932-3 (hbk)
ISBN: 978-0-367-81933-0 (pbk)
ISBN: 978-1-003-01089-0 (ebk)

DOI: 10.4324/9781003010890

Typeset in Melior
by Apex CoVantage, LLP
Printed and bound by CPI Group (UK) Ltd, Croydon, CR0 4YY

# Contents

# Preface

As you read through these pages, you will soon come to the big open secret about this book: It is not just about outdoor learning; it is about learning and teaching more generally. There is simply no way that the wide range of experiences learners need to stimulate intellectual and physical development, and effective opportunities for educating for a socially and environmentally just planet can take place solely indoors. That is our belief. If you don't believe that, we aim to persuade you to take a step beyond the four walls of your classroom. This book offers guidelines for outdoor learning teaching practices, along with their theoretical underpinnings.

All chapters include aims, a case study, and most finish with guidelines for practice. There is no specific order in which we advise reading this book. While we have deliberately arranged the chapters in a certain structure, feel free to read them in any order you like.

The book you are now reading is not a second edition of *Learning outside the classroom: Theory and guidelines for practice*, but neither is it completely new. Six of the chapters are substantially re-worked versions of the 2012 volume (1, 3, 4, 7, 10, and 11), two are completely re-imagined (5, 6), and four are entirely new (2, 8, 9, and 12).

The first chapter provides an overview of what we consider outdoor learning to be, for the purposes of this book. Next, four zones of learning—covering the school grounds to overnight trips—are explained. The chapter then delves into some of the most pressing issues of our time (e.g., climate and nature crises, pandemics, systemic inequalities, health, and wellbeing) and positions these as rationales for inclusive educational design—outdoors, indoors, and online. The chapter concludes by discussing outdoor learning as a pedagogical approach for all abilities, peoples, and communities.

Chapter 2 examines the origins of our thoughts, beliefs, values, and teaching practices. We have positioned this chapter early on, as our intention throughout this book is to invite you to reflect upon the sources of, and influences on, your own worldviews. As authors, we cannot know who you (the reader) are—where you might live, work, socialize, and spend time. Nor can we assume to know your backgrounds, life experiences, thoughts, and practices. We cannot possibly write in a way that speaks to all circumstances and contexts in which you may be thinking about developing or extending your outdoor learning practice, if indeed it is even your intention to do so. This chapter asks readers to consider their own positions and explore how the differences, similarities, and intertwining of their worldviews with those of others, help to more deeply understand how we think, feel, and act in the world—particularly when they might reproduce social and environmental inequalities.

Chapter 3, learning across the curriculum, explains how rather than outdoor learning being regarded as an infrequent, recreational disruption to learning, it can be seen as an extension and complement to the indoor and online classroom. Outdoor learning content is usually found within national and official curricula, and as with life in the real world, it is inherently interdisciplinary. Outdoor learning is positioned as an important means to address the inadequacies of curricular areas, such as geography, mathematics, language, arts, science, and history, which are traditionally taught separately from each other. This chapter discusses how the inherent interdisciplinary nature of the outdoors lends itself to these subjects being understood in relation to one another.

Learning for sustainability is arguably the most important educational enterprise in human history. It is also the hardest to define and integrate into teaching. Crucial to learning for sustainability is understanding how all life is interdependent and inextricably linked to the Earth's physical and biological systems. By helping pupils understand our planetary systems, learning for sustainability can foster a deep connection to the natural world and awareness of our personal environmental decisions. Chapter 4 outlines a range of principles and approaches that can help with integrating environmental and sustainable development education into lessons that take place inside and outside the classroom, and online.

Place-responsive education is the focus of Chapter 5. This approach to education involves students learning about the history, culture, natural environment, and landscape in which they go to school or are travelling through. This approach to learning can be fuelled by student curiosity, broadened by their own research, and the knowledge gained can be creatively shared with others through a variety of media. Broadly speaking, learning in, with, through, and about place involves coming to understand the sociocultural, geophysical, and ecological phenomena of a given landscape—ideally through direct interaction with it. Crucially, place-responsive education is firmly located in authentic, real-world contexts. Approaches to sharing one's places with others through technology are also discussed.

Curiosity, when combined with child-centred, experiential approaches to learning can be a powerful motivation for teachers to encourage and direct learning outdoors. Educational systems that are driven by performance, measurement, and standardized outcomes have, however, limited teachers' capacities to use curiosity as a pedagogical tool. In Chapter 6, we introduce the concept of wonder as something freer and less tightly defined than curiosity. Wonder builds on a learner's "desire to know" by affectively exploring the limits of what we know through engaging with love, mystery, and the search for deep knowing and meaning in a changing world. This chapter suggests that outdoor places are characterized by openness and unpredictability, and by approaching them with a deeper sense of wonder, they can provide endless experiential and spontaneous learning opportunities.

Chapter 7 focuses on community-based learning, where schools and outdoor programmes can work with individuals and organizations to promote the well-being of all residents and the local environment. Special emphasis is placed on acknowledging, respecting, and understanding issues relating to age, ethnicity, race, and economics. Crucially, members of the community become regarded as co-educators. Partnering with voluntary organizations can provide pupils with authentic opportunities to experience and learn about what it means to be an active citizen and contributor to democratic society. It is through creating opportunities for pupils to work within more diverse education settings more caring and mutually sustaining social networks between individuals, community organizations, and local businesses can be fostered.

In the last decade, the ubiquity of mobile device use has become staggering, as the advent of touchscreen phones has dramatically changed childhood. Indeed, research shows how many of today's young people spend an alarmingly high amount of their waking time interacting with their mobile devices. Educators of all kinds are now forced to make decisions about whether to ban the use of mobile devices during class time, tolerate them, or deliberately and creatively put them to educational use. Chapter 8 provides guidance on how educators can decide when and where to integrate mobile device use into their lessons, particularly outdoors—and how this can enrich learning.

In Chapter 9 we return to the concentric circles model we introduced in Chapter 1. While this places the school as the epicentre, it is intended to encourage teachers and their students to move naturally between the zones when their educational purpose and intention demands it. First, we introduce some mapping techniques to enable everything from local neighbourhood learning activities to full-day excursions. Next, we turn to residential outdoor educational experiences and explore different programmes on offer, including those featuring adventurous physical activities, as well as those concentrating on field studies to support curricular subjects such as biology and geography. Finally, we refer to a body of increasingly rigorous research that points to the educational value of residential outdoor education experiences and the importance of developing robust partnerships between schools and residential outdoor centres. In particular, high-quality, long-lasting educational provision depends on enabling these centres providing a clear progression of experiences and learning, connection to the curriculum, and relevance, where possible, to students' home communities.

All teachers are capable of enhancing their pupils' learning experiences by systematically and progressively incorporating ventures outside the classroom into their lessons. Chapter 10 argues that almost all learning outdoors does not require specialist equipment and expert instructors, nor does it require complicated risk assessments. Learning is enhanced by pupils having clothing and footwear that will keep them comfortable in most conditions. "Blanket consent" forms, completed at the start of the year, can pave the way for spontaneous and frequent journeys to places near the school. General risk assessments for being in the school playground and walking/taking the bus to places in the local neighbourhood can be put in place, and more detailed risk assessments for specific events can be completed as required. Perhaps most importantly, we suggest that students should undertake their own benefit/risk analysis and come up with appropriate management strategies before each journey outside the school grounds. Chapter 10 outlines how educators can put together their own thorough risk management plan.

The outdoor learning environment can provide as much (or as little) structure as an educator needs. Being outdoors with students requires specific people-management skills that are often in contrast with those needed in the classroom. This is particularly the case for those who work with students with Additional Support Needs as outlined in Chapter 1 and in Chapter 11. More generally, just as do indoor teachers, teachers working outside the classroom need to be mindful of the different ways students learn, and their aptitudes. They are likely to need other tools, such as strategies for overseeing groups moving from one location to another (in urban and rural contexts), keeping track of who is where, managing students' primary needs (e.g., food, water, warmth, toileting), and addressing groups in a variety of environmental conditions, such as bright sunlight or in the wind and rain. Chapter 11 offers an array of tips and strategies that can be employed to effectively manage students outdoors.

The final chapter focuses on developing and implementing a whole school plan. There are a number of elements central to the success of integrating outdoor learning into conventional classrooms and online teaching. The first of these is embedding learning outside the classroom into the school's culture. When this is done well, it involves having a progressive plan that starts in the first year of school and finishes in the last, with each year building on the skills and competencies that were learned the year before. This chapter outlines considerations for developing enduring schoolwide approaches to combining outdoor, indoor, and online pedagogies. Chapter 12 continues by exploring how student learning can be evidenced in ways that are explicitly linked to assessment criteria. Considering ways to demonstrate how curricular learning outcomes can be achieved effectively through outdoor pedagogies is central to this chapter.

We conclude the preface with the perhaps self-evident statement that we authors bring our own particular backgrounds, interests, knowledge, skills, and biases to this project. This cannot be helped. That said, we are highly mindful of our positions and privileges, and have taken every precaution to write as inclusively as we can, to as broad an audience as possible. Part of this effort includes chapter drafts being sent to 17 different external reviewers for critique. While we come to this book with over 140 years of combined practitioner and researcher experience in outdoor learning and in education more broadly, our own thinking evolved as we wrote, read, debated, and edited our way through this manuscript.

We believe that the planet—humans and the more-than-human—need us, now more than ever, to educate in ways that address the biggest social and environmental challenges of our times. If you, like us, you are interested in exploring how this kind of educational enterprise can be made more possible, engaging and effective through teaching outdoors, alongside indoor and online spaces, then read on!

# Acknowledgements

We wish to thank the following people for offering critiques and suggestions on individual chapters. This book is much stronger for the insights you have offered us.

Karen Knamiller, Ruth Prince, Joyce Gilbert, Bob Barton, Roger Greenaway, Brendon Munge, Imre van Kraalingen, Jennifer Broughton, Julia Childs, Sam Harrison, Roger Scrutton, Scott Taylor, Mary Higgins, Alison Lugg, Lewis Stockwell, ML White, and Zoé Robertson.

Special thanks to Beth Christie for her valuable contributions to the project.

# Foreword

My mentor and friend Yale University Psychology Professor Seymour Sarason used to say that if you dedicate your life to changing schools, you deserve God's blessing. Those of us who have spent long enough trying to change teaching and learning in school, often feel like we're pushing an elephant up the stairs. Most schools today look very much like the schools you and I went to many years ago, where the most common learning environment was the classroom. There are many people today who believe that the time has come for that traditional learning environment to change.

This is not the first time people have thought there is another way to achieve more inspiring ways to educate. There have been numerous efforts during the past centuries, where formal schooling has challenged conventional educational culture. Some pioneers have tried to bring teaching and learning out from school classrooms to the real-world, emphasizing work-related and community-based learning. Then there have been those who have championed transforming schools and classrooms, so they feel and look more like the world outside the school gate.

I am writing this Foreword in Australia, which is home to the oldest continuing civilization in the world. Over the past 60,000 years, generations after generations have successfully educated their young to live in harmony with each other and with the land. A significant part of that long educational tradition has involved learning to connect with nature and then to grow from it. First Nations Peoples around the world have done the same—outdoor learning is not a new idea! We have a lot learn from our past.

While digitalization is part of almost everything we do these days, outdoor learning is having a renaissance. Surprisingly, it is only now that we are beginning to really understand that outdoor education is a pedagogy for achieving formal intended learning goals. Too often, however, we continue to debate why we should teach our students more outdoors. Research and systematic evidence during the past decade alone are convincing and strongly suggest our students would benefit from purposeful outdoor learning.

Some of my own recent research with colleagues involved conducting a detailed systematic analysis of 147 high-quality studies on outdoor learning. The focus of these studies ranged across outdoor adventure education, school gardens, field trips, and traditional school subjects taught in natural environments. The benefits of learning in outdoor settings included increased student engagement and owner-ship of their learning, improved academic achievement, development of social and collaborative skills, and better self-concept factors. Besides the growing evidence from around the world, experienced educators know that outdoor learning can and should be incorporated into every child's school experience with reference to their local context.

If Seymour Sarason was among us today wondering whether schools will change or not, he might conclude: If not now, when? Digital technologies, the global pandemic, and increasing uncertainty and insecurity are wake-up calls for policy-makers, educators, and parents to be brave and bold in thinking about what school could be. It is in this unprecedented time in our lives that *Outdoor Learning Across the Curriculum* brings much-needed promise and hope. It is a book for times like these, written for all of us who care about how our young people can be better prepared to deal with some of the biggest issues of our lifetimes.

In transforming schools, we are all in it together. Today, educators around the world are looking for new ways to teach and learn. There are many ways to do that. Of these, outdoor learning clearly has potential to change schools for the better. The evidence presented in this book is abundantly clear, and provides a roadmap for educators to take learning outdoors.

**Pasi Sahlberg**
*Professor of Educational Leadership*
*Melbourne Graduate School of Education*
*University of Melbourne*
*Australia*
*pasisahlberg.com*

# Education to address the planet's big challenges

## Chapter aims

- Articulate what outdoor learning is and is not.

- Illustrate how outdoor learning can take place in four main contexts.

- Understand how the rationale for outdoor learning lies in the need to tackle the educational, social, and environmental issues of the time.

- Recognize how outdoor learning is for people of all abilities.

Outdoor learning (OL) practice has grown steadily in the last ten years—within schools, in particular. While largely sporadic, more universities are incorporating OL into their teacher education programmes; large empirical research projects have been conducted (TeachOut in Denmark, Natural Connections in England); extensive continuing education programs have been rolled out (British Council "Connecting Classrooms" in Scotland); national outdoor learning networks have been established (Italy); and rigorous research is taking place in countries such as Taiwan, Malta, Singapore, and Bangladesh, as well as the nations where there is already a well established tradition (e.g., UK, North America, Australia, New Zealand, and a range of European and Nordic countries). These indicators show us that, increasingly, the questions educators are asking is not "why should we teach outdoors?", but "how do we teach outdoors?", and even "what does the research tell us about the best approaches to teaching outdoors?"

## What is outdoor learning?

While this is not the place to get into a long discussion on the history of OL, it is important to lay out some parameters about what outdoor learning is for the purposes of this book. First, in many cases, OL has to do with delivering the officially sanctioned curriculum of your country, state, or province. This is not to say that activities done after-school, on the weekends, or during holiday periods, cannot be considered OL; indeed, all kinds of rich learning might take place during a school gardening club or on a climbing trip. The important distinction here is that education involves having stated aims and objectives and oversight from an educator (Roberts, 2012).

Second, outdoor learning is not curriculum; it is pedagogy, which, in its simplest terms, is about how we teach to intended—and remain open to unintended—learning outcomes. Here we use the popular meaning of "pedagogy", rather than its stricter roots, which have to do with teaching children specifically. Outdoor learning can, and does, involve people of all ages.

Norwegian scholar, Arne Jordet (2002), explains that learning outside the classroom builds bridges between the school and the students' worlds, and between class subjects and everyday life. Following Jordet, and drawing from the UK's Institute for Outdoor Learning (IOL, 2021, para 3), we define outdoor learning as *an educational process that allows a learner to develop knowledge, skills, attitudes, and behaviours through direct engagement with outdoor environments, and which provide the learner with a range of personal, educational, and social benefits, which may have wider value for society and the planet.*

The final feature of OL that we will add is that, ideally, it should foster in students the capacity to think critically about their place in the world and how they might be able to positively shape themselves, their communities, and the ecosystems they inhabit. Together, these features of OL are broad and inclusive enough to serve as a platform upon which educators from around the world can discuss for themselves what OL means for them in their own life experiences.

It should be noted here that just because this book is about OL does not mean that we are against indoor learning. As readers will see, our chief concern is to advocate for and support excellent teaching that will maximize student learning wherever it takes place: Outdoors, indoors, and online. However, we believe that maximizing student learning cannot be accomplished solely within the four walls of a classroom. Doing this means breaking down the outdoor/indoor binary and viewing the outdoors as an extension of the classroom, while incorporating mobile and online approaches as appropriate (see Chapter 8).

As we write this in 2022, it is becoming increasingly evident that this outdoor/indoor binary of which we are so critical, is actually much more complex. Accelerated by the impact of the Covid-19 pandemic, online learning has shifted from an independent way of finding out about things that interest us, to a mass form of formalized education. While this ongoing transition has been pragmatic, it can also serve to further separate many learners from direct and even indirect engagement with the tangible and social world of learning. Hence, while we see the value in learning in all three "places" (outdoors, indoors, and online), learning outdoors helps to redress deficits brought about by disproportionately high levels of online and solitary learning, and helps redress some kind of educational balance in the ways that people learn about the world they inhabit.

Thus, we advocate a skilled blending of outdoor learning with face-to-face and online learning. A teacher needs to be able to decide the best methods to help students learn specific parts of the curriculum, at the right time in their developmental journey, and in the most suitable place.

## The range of contexts for outdoor learning provision

The provision of OL can be thought of as taking place within concentric "circles": Four "zones", with the school grounds placed firmly in the centre. Beyond the school grounds is the local neighbourhood, which can be explored on foot or by using public transport. Day excursions ("field trips") often take place a little further away and usually require some kind of group transport. Residential outdoor centres, cultural visits, and expeditions that involve being away from home overnight, comprise the fourth "zone" and have their own obvious logistical challenges. This is a conceptual model, and so the "zones" are of course not circular, there are no "hard" boundaries, and such as they are, these can overlap and merge one into another.

All landscapes have cultural and ecological stories, including school grounds, of course. The land upon which the school sits has tremendous relevance in the lives of the students, as this is the place where the majority of their formal learning takes place, and for many children, their principal site of unstructured, informal outdoor play and learning.

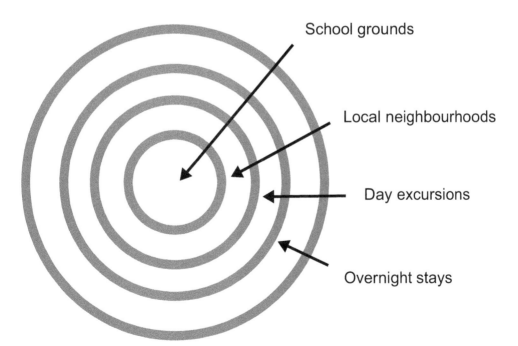

**Figure 1.1** The range of contexts for outdoor learning.
*Source:* (adapted from Higgins & Nicol, 2002, p. 44)

While we do place the school grounds at the centre of the model, all four contexts have tremendous potential for eliciting all kinds of learning. We strongly believe, however, that students must first have an understanding and appreciation of those places that are closer to home, before organizing trips to far away places, simply because that is where the majority of their formal education takes place. Of course, in order to maximize the potential to learn about a given topic, it may be entirely logical to travel some distance in order to experience, for example, a specific ecosystem, historic site, or different culture. There will also be value in students "bringing home" learning from further afield and comparing this to their local places. Still, before venturing with students beyond their immediate surroundings, we advise exploring the myriad of ways in which local issues, stories, laws, buildings, organizations, flora, and fauna, provide authentic contexts in which curricular aims can be met.

## The global context

The reason for listing all of these issues, problems, and social phenomena is that they are all "signs of the times". We believe the role of education is to give young people the tools to understand, thrive in, and, where appropriate, to transform the places in which they live. In our own practices, we aim to better connect our teaching to the most pressing issues of the day. After all, these issues are inevitably cross-curricular and can be addressed by learners of all ages and abilities. For the most part this is about a process of becoming aware and developing the wherewithal to "act". Moving towards these lofty aims will involve becoming experts at seeking reliable and trustworthy sources of information to inform what we know, how we think and feel, and what we can do.

## The climate and nature emergencies

The impact we have been having, and continue to have, on the planet has become ever more evident. The urgency of our need to respond is indicated by, for example, the term "climate change" generally being replaced with "climate emergency" or "climate crisis". Further, the global loss of biodiversity (sometimes used interchangeably with "nature") and its impact on climate change (and *vice versa*), has become ever more apparent—leading commentators to refer to the "biodiversity crisis" and, indeed, more dramatically, the "sixth great extinction" (or "extermination"). The positive corollary is that it is now apparent that efforts to address the climate and biodiversity crises are inextricably linked. Dealing with both in tandem will go some way towards stabilizing our planet's "support systems". Nonetheless, the scientific community is clear that this is the biggest issue of this or any generation, and that we must not exceed "planetary boundaries" (Rockström et al., 2009; Ripple et al., 2019) relating to climate, biodiversity, oceans, freshwater, and forests, which would destabilize planetary systems and result in catastrophic mutually reinforcing impacts.

These profound and accelerating changes, driven and exacerbated by a range of socioeconomic factors such as increased use of fossil fuels, consumption, and population growth, have led authors to argue that we are now in a new geological epoch that should be referred to as "the Anthropocene" (Steffen et al., 2011)—a period when a single species (*Homo sapiens*) has irreversibly changed the Earth's biogeochemical systems, global ecosystems, and climate.

The situation has prompted increasingly urgent calls and practical suggestions for action. For example, in 2017, Ripple and colleagues and over 15,000 signatories from 184 countries, issued the *World Scientists' Warning to Humanity*, which, among its 13 major recommendations to counter global threats to sustainability and biodiversity, urges "increasing outdoor nature education for children as well as the overall engagement of society in the appreciation of nature" (p. 3). This view has been supported by the globally significant Dasgupta Review (2021) on the economics of biodiversity, which has emphasized the role of nature in building personal sustainability values, alongside health and wellbeing:

> We rely on Nature to provide us with food, water and shelter; regulate our climate and disease; maintain nutrient cycles and oxygen production; and provide us with spiritual fulfilment and opportunities for recreation and recuperation, which can enhance our health and wellbeing.
>
> (p. 1)

The Review goes on to state that "(e)nabling the changes we need will also require collective and sustained action to transform the systems that underpin our engagements with Nature, above all our financial and education systems" (p. 4). While we are not setting out to transform financial systems, it should be plain that we are trying to shift policy and practice in education to support and equip learners to develop the attitudes, values, and skills to address these global challenges. There is growing research evidence demonstrating the importance and effectiveness of the role of outdoor learning in this process, specifically in studies emphasizing relationships with the natural world, and positive orientations towards sustainability (see for example, Christie & Higgins, 2020; Kuo et al., 2019).

## Mental health and well-being

There is a growing body of knowledge pointing towards increasing mental health challenges for young people (McGorry & Mei, 2018). Young people's mental health is inseparably tied to the powerful and unsettling developmental challenges they encounter—socially, physiologically, emotionally (Siegel, 2015). Research from Australia highlights how—apart from the pressure to achieve good grades—students' biggest challenges include navigating loneliness, isolation, and supporting friends who have been bullied through social networks (McCrindle Research, 2021).

Unsurprisingly, decreasing levels of youth mental health are being connected to increasing levels of mobile phone and social media use. These are, of course, enormous and integral parts of most young people's lives (boyd, 2014)—so much so that three quarters of Australian young people's time out of school is spent in front of a screen (McCrindle Research, 2020). In the US, teenagers have been reported to use "entertainment screen media" more than seven hours a day (not including schoolwork or homework) (Rideout & Robb, 2019). Twenge's (2017) research shows that it is common for American youth to use their phones while in bed and then sleep with them close at hand. The steadily increasing incidences of depression, eating disorders, and stress-induced illnesses (Twenge, 2017; McGorry & Mei, 2018) and increased prescription of antidepressants (Jack et al., 2020) among young people is alarming. This situation is only likely to have become exacerbated by the Covid-19 pandemic and the resulting lockdowns around the world (e.g., Barnardo's, 2020).

The peer-reviewed literature on the relationship between health and wellbeing and time spent in nature is very robust. Indeed, the first sentence from a 2019 paper from the acclaimed journal *Nature*, states that a "growing body of epidemiological evidence indicates that greater exposure to, or 'contact with', natural environments (such as parks, woodlands, and beaches) is associated with better health and well-being" (White et al., 2019, p. 1). Given this supporting evidence, even if teachers don't feel 100% confident in their outdoor teaching skills, they are doing right by young people simply by getting them outdoors into green spaces.

Teaching and learning outdoors thus has an important role to play in addressing decreasing levels of mental wellbeing in children and youth. Educators can draw on psychological literature that explains how programmes that help to boost levels of optimism, self-awareness, mastery, self-esteem, and social support, help individuals to better handle life stressors (Hooley, Butcher, Nock, & Mineka, 2017). While this has led to arguments for "nature therapy" and prescriptions of a "nature-dose", for example, commentators such as Lord and Coffey (2021) warn against a "technological drift in nature exposure and health . . . that reduces nature to a resource for human use" (p. 110). In essence, they argue that the separation of ourselves from nature is the real problem. This offers a clear message for outdoor educators: Get kids outside, even if there are not educational or therapeutic aims, as it will benefit them anyway. The evidence of direct educational benefits from learning outside the classroom is steadily increasing and is outlined in Chapter 3.

## The global Coronavirus pandemic

One new "reality" for us all is, of course, the global Coronavirus (Covid-19) pandemic, that began in early 2020. It has been hugely disruptive to almost all forms of education in most parts of the world—not least for outdoor learning (Quay et al., 2020). These impacts have been felt in schools, colleges, and universities, where outdoor learning for curricular subjects such as biology and geography have lost practical fieldwork courses. Residential outdoor education centres and expedition-focused providers have been particularly disadvantaged, as many in the UK, for example, were closed for well over a year, at the peak of the pandemic. A number of these organizations have closed permanently. However, there have been some positive changes as a result, with many governments and education authorities advocating for learning outdoors due to the lower likelihood of spreading the virus, and increasingly recognizing the positive benefits of such a strategy for both academic learning and health and well-being.

While the educational implications of the pandemic will take time to be fully revealed, some academics have begun to reflect and consider the longer-term implications (see Quay et al., 2020)—specifically in relation to how humans can explore new ways of living more social and environmentally just lives. It is tempting to think that, once the Covid-19 crisis is over, we will be able to return to previous ways of working. In our view, this is hazardous as it ignores an important opportunity to reflect, to consider the consequences for OL, and to (re)imagine and implement ways of learning and teaching better in the future.

We believe, however, that the following is important to bear in mind that there is convincing evidence that this pandemic is not a "one off". In 2015, the World Health Organization and Secretariat of the Convention on Biological Diversity established that similar diseases (e.g., HIV/AIDs, the SARS Coronavirus and Ebola) originated from animal populations under severe environmental pressures, and that most emerging infectious diseases are driven by human activities (see p. 140). Given the fact that we are continuing to destroy habitats and biodiversity, there seems a high likelihood that we will encounter other highly transmissible diseases in the years to come.

Further, as is evident from the World Health Organization and Convention on Biological Diversity (2015) report, there is a deep relationship between environmental and social justice issues such as poverty, equity, and health, and their role as both contributing factors and symptoms of this wider crisis in the natural world. Related to this, it seems that air pollution has a significant impact on mortality, and this is a particular issue for people in lower socioeconomic neighbourhoods in our cities, many of whom come from Black, Asian, and minority ethnic (BAME) communities (Wu, Nethery, Sabath, Braun, & Dominici, 2020).

The way in which learners learn was already changing pre-Covid, but the trend to more online and blended learning has accelerated and is likely to continue to do so. Policy makers, educational structures and systems, teachers, facilitators, and instructors will need to respond. What is undeniable is that all of the abovementioned circumstances have influenced our sociocultural, political, environmental, and educational worlds. How could they not? *So, how do we respond?* We believe our work needs to be relevant to these challenges, and this requires that we constantly reflect on what, how, and where we teach. It is here that outdoor educators can play a valuable role by connecting learning to concrete issues of the times, using novel and creative approaches in teaching, and working alongside surrounding communities. This requires flexibility, creativity, and enterprise.

## The need for curricular reform

In view of all the above, it should be clear that educational systems have to reform to deliver a curriculum in accord with present and future demands. Failure to do so risks the fate of the students subjected to Harold Benjamin's famous "Saber-Toothed Curriculum" (1939). Benjamin, who went by the pseudonym J. Abner Peddiwell, imagined a Stone Age society where children were taught how to grab fish, club woolly horses, and scare saber-toothed tigers with fire. They needed these skills to sustain themselves, to get food and protect themselves from danger. This was all fine until the climate changed and a great glacier advanced down the valley. The tigers disappeared and the bears that came in their place weren't afraid of fires and couldn't be scared away; the waters became so muddy that the fish could no longer be seen and caught with bare hands. But schools still continued to teach the arts of tiger-scaring and fish-grabbing. Benjamin's central argument was that education systems need to have one eye on the present and the other on the future.

However, the lack of willingness of policy makers (and society) to undertake significant educational reform is still as evident today as it was in Benjamin's time. Outdoor learning has been on the margins since education, with its curricula and assessments, became formalized in Western nations in the latter half of the 19th century (Ogilvie, 2013) through legal requirements for children to be educated in schools. It is our firmly held contention that all educators should be asking themselves how their teaching can meaningfully respond to the current and future challenges facing society. Can educators respond to these massive societal changes through an education that only takes place indoors and online? We authors don't think so. Beyond actual teaching, our task is also one that involves seeking evidence of approaches and convincing policymakers to embed progressive, developmental OL experiences in the educational journeys of all learners.

Many educators may feel like they do not have enough time to focus on anything but preparing and delivering lessons in their subject areas and curricular lesson plans. Our view is that all of this needs to be done under the overarching aims of social and environmental justice—and take fullest advantage of the affordances from teaching spaces that are outdoors, indoors, and online. These educational imperatives ought not be regarded as "extras" to be squeezed in to an already packed curriculum: They need to be central to the curriculum.

## A book for people of all abilities

We have given a great deal of thought to the issue of how, in this book, we might address OL for those with additional support needs (ASNs—our preferred term), special educational needs, and disabilities. It will be evident from these terms that this is a terminologically complex area, and one that varies internationally. Even use of the term "disabilities" requires careful consideration, as while some insist that they do have disabilities and that society must recognize that they are consequently disadvantaged, others argue that this brings a social stigma.

The complexities of terminology are dwarfed by those surrounding what these terms actually mean as "descriptions" of those with such needs or disabilities. As examples, autism is often referred to as a "spectrum"; the needs/disabilities a learner may have can be mental or physical or both; and how do we as teachers/facilitators acknowledge, without intrusion, that significant behavioural responses may result from these or may be a symptom of personal or social difficulties? Further, do we include those with significant psychological issues or long-term physical injuries? What level of "need" or "disability" constitutes one for which "additional" educational support (in the classroom or outdoors) is beneficial? Who makes decisions on these issues, and how and on what criteria do they do so? Our purpose here is to highlight that each learner is unique, and that these are issues for the teacher/facilitator to consider, with the involvement of the learner, their family/carers, and other professionals. This is especially true when working in an outdoor context.

These issues have been the focus of an enormous amount of debate, academic research, and often conflicting policy development. One particular consideration in formal education has been, and continues to be, that of inclusion: Namely, whether young people with ASNs/disabilities are best taught (fully or partly) alongside their peers who do not have ASNs. If so, what is the purpose of this? Is it for the benefit of the young person, or to increase awareness and acceptance among their peers and society? As leading academics in the field, Ainscow and Miles (2008) argue, while globally there is considerable debate on the policy and practice of "inclusive education", this too is a concept that is interpreted differently in many countries.

In some countries, inclusive education may "still be thought of as an approach to serving children with disabilities within general education settings" (Ainscow, 2020, p. 9), whereas in others, following the UNESCO (2001) approach, it is considered "more broadly as reform that supports and welcomes diversity among all learners" (Ainscow & Miles, 2008, p. 16). UNICEF (2021) considers disability as "the single most serious barrier to education across the globe" (para 3), and has firmly located its advice on inclusive education as the removal of barriers to education for "children with disabilities". The organization highlights that "children with disabilities are often overlooked in policy-making, which limits their access to education and their ability to participate in social, economic and political life" (UNICEF, para 2).

While an extended discussion of this topic is clearly beyond the scope of this book, we take our position from Ainscow and Miles (2008) who argue that:

> a common sense of purpose around inclusive education, together with a consistent use of language, is essential if Education for All (EFA) strategies are to become more inclusive. This does not require the introduction of new techniques; rather it involves: collaboration within and between schools, closer links between schools and communities, networking across contexts, and the collection and use of contextually relevant evidence.
>
> (p. 17)

It is that shared sense of purpose and pragmatism guides our work here. We are not specialists in the areas of inclusion and education for those with ASNs, but there are those who are, and we recognize, as we outline below, that a substantial amount of OL provision does take place in schools for people ASNs and specialist outdoor centres.

It will be apparent that a particular question arises in the context of this book, and that is, "What is the difference between guidance we might offer for educators working with those with ASNs and those who do not?" Before attempting to fully address this, it is important to point out that there are many schools, residential outdoor education centres and other care or educational establishments worldwide that work outdoors, specifically with such individuals and groups. Such provision may be state-funded, through charities or commercial ventures, and may mirror the mixed-economy approach to "mainstream" provision of learning outdoors. In some cases, the outdoors is used more extensively for those with ASNs than for those in mainstream education (Beames & Polack, 2019). This then raises a further question: "Is OL provision for people with ASNs more or less effective than OL where specific consideration for people with ASN is absent?"

These questions are difficult to address due to the paucity of research evidence. This is unsurprising considering that compared to formal education, OL has received very little research attention—research on OL with learners with ASNs far less. Very few such studies are empirical and these understandably often rely on teacher/facilitator reports. However, Szczytko and colleagues (2018), using a quasi-experimental design drawing on reports from teachers and students, found that outdoor environmental education was at least as effective for children with emotional, cognitive, and behavioural disabilities.

Research with such young people is particularly complicated due to a range of ethical, moral and access considerations, and due to methodological difficulties related to communication, for example. There should be no real need to elaborate on this here; simply imagining oneself designing and conducting such studies will make some of the complications evident. This lack of attention is evident in a significant recent systematic review on nature-based learning by Mann and colleagues (2021), which makes no mention of ASNs, "disabilities" or their synonyms.

However, there have been a few notable doctoral studies on OL for those with ASNs (e.g., Crosbie, 2014), and a few published articles. Of these, quite understandably, some studies focus on proxy issues such as the perceptions of the effect of a programme on family quality of life (e.g., Petersen, Rogers, Togneri, Lee & Quinto, 2020), or on work with students who have moderate rather than severe needs. For example, Szczytko, Carrier and Stevenson (2018) studied a curricular outdoor science programme that took place over four to ten full-school days across the year. The findings revealed that "teachers perceived students had significantly improved attention spans and decreased disruptive behaviours when learning outdoors" (p. 1). One notable study on an outdoor adventure programme for children with autism found statistically significant "improvement in social-communication . . . social cognition, social motivation, and autistic mannerisms' compared to the control group" (Zachor et al., 2017, p. 550). While not research-related, there is a recent practical guide to outdoor practice and children with autism (James, 2018).

It is notable that the relatively small amount of literature on the outdoors and people with ASNs lies in contrast to the growing range of publications relating to those with social, emotional, and behavioural difficulties (e.g., Price, 2015) and "outdoor therapies" (e.g., Harper & Dobud, 2020). In terms of curricular learning, while there is a range of studies that report more positive impacts of learning outdoors compared to indoors (see Chapter 3), there are very few that could be construed as relevant to learners with ASNs.

So here, we return to our core question and reflect on the purposes of providing OL for people with ASNs. In our thinking we are persuaded by Crosbie's (2015) argument (quoting Richardson, 1986, p. 45) that people with and without ASNs "participate in outdoor adventure activities not for their therapeutic benefits but for the same reasons" (Crosbie, 2015, p. 378).

In an effort to be true to our approach to inclusion, we keep those with ASNs in mind throughout our teaching practice and in the writing of this book. There are, however, additional specific considerations, techniques, and skills that the outdoor learning ASN specialist will need beyond those required by other practitioners. Rather than elaborate these here, we have included them in Chapter 11, where we discuss managing groups outdoors.

For the reasons above, we feel that a comprehensive review of the ASN field is beyond the scope of this book. However, it is a core dimension of our work that we believe demands academic attention, research, and a broader published review. This is not simply to inform the practice of ASN outdoor learning specialists, but also because we believe their work is at the cutting edge of our field and has much to teach those working across OL settings.

## The state of outdoor learning research

Research written in English in the world of OL has seen not only plenty of activity over the last decade, but a marked shift in content. Three very general areas at the centre of this shift include: Women's perspectives, Indigenous and international voices, and research methods and scale.

One marker of the state of knowledge in a given field of study is large edited "handbooks" on a broad topic that are produced by established publishing houses. In 2016, Humberstone, Prince, and Henderson's, *Routledge International Handbook of Outdoor Studies* was published. In 2018, Gray and Mitten's 62-chapter volume, *Palgrave International Handbook of Women and Outdoor Learning* was released, and in 2019, Humberstone and Prince's *Handbook of Research Methods in Outdoor Studies* has added further to the field.

While outdoor education researchers across the globe continue to build a body of knowledge on the effectiveness of OL—most of which is published in research journals for that community—there has also been growing research interest among mainstream social scientists, educational psychologists, philosophers, and others who recognize the potential of OL and regard it as a vastly under-researched area. The Handbook of Research Methods highlights how the actual nature of research itself has developed, through showcasing the broadening range of methodologies that embrace the full gamut of those used in the social sciences—from autoethnography to empirical studies, from mobile methodologies to arts-based research from case studies to comparative studies Whether it is conducting research outdoors or capturing the meaningfulness or outcomes of events that have taken place outdoors, the unique challenges of undertaking empirical inquiry in our field are becoming more clearly problematized and more helpfully addressed. The last decade has also witnessed several large-scale, longitudinal, funded research projects, such as TeachOut in Denmark, Natural Connections and Brilliant Residentials in England (which were all mentioned in the chapter's opening paragraph), and the research-informed Connecting Classrooms professional development programme for Scottish teachers.

Another transition in the English language OL literature has been the emergence of voices and perspectives that have historically been systematically marginalized and erased on the international stage. Some of these voices include Black, Indigenous, and People of Colour (BIPOC) from Canada, the United States, Australia and New Zealand, and empirical inquiries in Bangladesh, Malaysia, and Malta. While research projects in Scandinavia, the UK, North America, Australia, and New Zealand continue to dominate the English language literature, the increasing proportion of authors writing from outside of these countries should arguably be much more strongly supported by the more prolific research centres (e.g., UK, America) that have been so influential up to this point.

Finally, as noted above, OL research continues to grow globally, and as reviews by Mann and colleagues (2021) and Christie and Higgins (2020) highlight, the body of OL literature increasingly supports the argument that the outdoors is not just an effective place to learn, but is often more so than indoors.

# Summary

Besides OL taking place (largely) outdoors, it is not markedly different to indoor learning. It involves an educator, ethically driven learning outcomes and giving learners the tools with which they can thrive as individuals, contribute to their communities, and live lightly on the planet (Beames, 2017). We outlined four contexts for learning outdoors, which feature the school (and its grounds) at the centre, and then extend to the local neighbourhood, day trips, and overnight stays.

Education needs to be based upon our individual and collective responses to the most pressing issues of the day, such as the twin climate and biodiversity emergencies, mental health, pandemics, and rising inequality, rather than reproducing decontextualized lessons that were conceived at another point in history.

Considerations for practice when working with people with additional support needs were also offered, with ASN outdoor learning specialists highlighted as sources of best practice for those working in mainstream OL settings. Finally, an overview of the changing state of outdoor learning research was provided, noting how it is becoming more internationalized and more inclusive.

# Guidelines

- Ensure that outdoor learning sessions are designed with clear connections to specific learning outcomes held in curricular documents, while remaining open to unintended learning opportunities that present themselves.

- Identify ways that lesson design can be based on aspects of today's biggest societal and environmental challenges.

- Endeavour to give students plenty of time in natural, green spaces as a way to boost their mental health and wellbeing.

- Provide concrete opportunities for students to critically examine their biases, privileges, roles, and responsibilities within society.

# References

Ainscow, M. (2020). Promoting inclusion and equity in education: Lessons from international experiences. *Nordic Journal of Studies in Educational Policy, 6*(1), 7–16. https://doi.org/10.1080/20020317.2020.1729587

Ainscow, M., & Miles, S. (2008). Making education for all inclusive: Where next? *Prospects, 38*, 15–34.

Barnardo's. (2020). *Mental health and covid-19: In our own words*. Essex: Barnardo's.

Beames, S. (2017). Innovation and outdoor education. *Journal of Outdoor and Environmental Education, 20*(1), 2–6.

Beames, S., & Polack, N. (2019). *School inspection reports and the status of outdoor learning, residential experiences and adventurous activities in Scottish schools.* https://beamingsimon.wordpress.com/2019/06/14/scottish-school-inspection-reports-and-outdoor-learning/

boyd, d. (2014). *It's complicated.* London: Yale University Press.

Christie, B., & Higgins, P. (2020). *Educational outcomes of learning for sustainability: A brief review of literature.* Edinburgh: Scottish Government.

Crosbie, J. (2014). *The value of outdoor education for people with disabilities: An in-depth case study of the Calvert Trust.* Unpublished Doctoral Thesis, University of Edinburgh, Edinburgh.

Crosbie, J. (2015). Disability and the outdoors—some considerations for inclusion. In C. Henderson, B. Humbersone, & H. Prince (Eds.), *Routledge international handbook of outdoor recreation* (pp. 378–387). London: Routledge.

Dasgupta, P. (2021). *The economics of biodiversity: The Dasgupta review.* London: HM Treasury. www.gov.uk/government/publications/final-report-the-economics-of-biodiversity-the-dasgupta-review

Gray, T., & Mitten, D. (2018). Nourishing terrains: Women's contributions to outdoor learning. In T. Gray & D. Mitten (Eds.), *The Palgrave international handbook of women and outdoor learning* (pp. 3–18). London: Palgrave Macmillan.

Harper, N., & Dobud, W. (2020). *Outdoor therapies: An introduction to practices, possibilities, and critical perspectives.* New York: Routledge.

Higgins, P., & Nicol, R. (Eds.). (2002). *Outdoor education: Authentic learning through landscapes* (Vol. 2). Kinda Kunskapscentrum. www.education.ed.ac.uk/outdoored/resources.html

Hooley, J., Butcher, J. N., Nock, M. K., & Mineka, S. (2017). *Abnormal psychology* (7th ed.). London: Pearson.

Humberstone, B., & Prince, H. (Eds.). (2019). *Research methods in outdoor studies.* London: Routledge.

Humberstone, B., Prince, H., & Henderson, C. (Eds.). (2016). *Routledge international handbook of outdoor recreation.* London: Routledge.

Institute for Outdoor Learning. (2021). *About outdoor learning.* www.outdoor-learning.org/Good-Practice/Research-Resources/About-Outdoor-Learning

Jack, R. H., Hollis, C., Coupland, C., Morriss, R., Knaggs, R. D., Butler, D.,. ., & Hippisley-Cox, J. (2020). Incidence and prevalence of primary care antidepressant prescribing in children and young people in England, 1998–2017: A population-based cohort study. *PLoS Medicine, 17*(7), e1003215.

James, M. (2018). *Forest school and autism: A practical guide.* London: Jessica Kingsley.

Jordet, A. (2002). *En case-studie om uteskolens didaktikk.* Notat nr. 5. Lutvann-undersøkelsen. Prosjektbeskrivelse—Teorigrunnlag.

Kuo, M., Barnes, M., & Jordan, C. (2019). Do experiences with nature promote learning? Converging evidence of a cause-and-effect relationship. *Frontiers in Psychology, 10,* 305.

Lord, E., & Coffey, M. (2021). Identifying and resisting the technological drift: Green space, blue space and ecotherapy. *Social Theory & Health, 19,* 110–125. https://doi.org/10.1057/s41285-019-00099-9

Mann, J., Gray, T., Truong, S., Sahlberg, P., Bentsen, P., Passy, R., . . . & Cowper, R. (2021). A systematic review protocol to identify the key benefits and efficacy of nature-based learning in outdoor educational settings. *International Journal of Environmental Research and Public Health, 18*(3). https://doi.org/10.3390/ijerph18031199

McCrindle Research. (2020). *Understanding the future consumer: Generational insights to inform future strategies towards 2030.* https://mccrindle.com.au/wp-content/uploads/reports/Analyse-Australia-2020-Understanding-the-Future-Consumer.pdf

McCrindle Research. (2021). *The future of education: Insights into today's students and their future expectations.* https://mccrindle.com.au/wp-content/uploads/reports/Education-Future-Report-2021.pdf

McGorry, P. D., & Mei, C. (2018). Tackling the youth mental health crisis across adolescence and young adulthood. *British Medical Journal, 362*, k3704.

Ogilvie, K. (2013). *Roots and wings: A history of outdoor education and outdoor learning in the UK.* Lyme Regis: Russell House.

Peddiwell, J. (1939). *The saber-tooth curriculum and other essays.* New York: McGraw-Hill.

Petersen, G., Rogers, E., Togneri, M., Lee, C., & Quinto, A. (2020). The impact of outdoor adaptive play and leisure on quality of life for youth with disabilities. *American Journal of Occupational Therapy, 74*(4), 74115051801. https://doi.org/10.5014/ajot.2020.74S1-PO6206.

Price, A. (2015). Improving school attendance: Can participation in outdoor learning influence attendance for young people with social, emotional and behavioural difficulties? *Journal of Adventure Education and Outdoor Learning, 15*(2), 110–122. https://doi.org/10.1080/14729679.2013.850732

Quay, J., Gray, T., Thomas, G., Allen-Craig, S., Asfeldt, M., Andkjaer, S., . . ., & Foley, D. (2020). What future/s for outdoor and environmental education in a world that has contended with COVID-19? *Journal of Outdoor and Environmental Education, 23*(2), 93–117.

Richardson, D. (1986). Outdoor adventure: Programs for the physically disabled. *Parks and Recreation, 21*(11), 43–45.

Rideout, V., & Robb, M. B. (2019). *The common sense census: Media use by tweens and teens.* San Francisco, CA: Common Sense Media.

Ripple, W., Wolf, C., Newsome, T. M., Barnard, P., & Moomaw, W. (2019). World scientists warn of a climate emergency. *BioScience, 70*(1), 8–12.

Ripple, W., Wolf, C., Newsome, T. M., Galetti, M., Alamgir, M., Crist, E., . . ., & 15,364 Scientist Signatories from 184 Countries. (2017). World scientists' warning to humanity: A second notice. *BioScience, 67*(12), 1026–1028.

Roberts, J. (2012). *Beyond learning by doing: Theoretical currents in experiential education.* New York: Routledge.

Rockström, J., Steffen, W., Noone, K., Persson, Å., Chapin III, F. S., Lambin, E., . . . & Foley, J. (2009). Planetary boundaries: Exploring the safe operating space for humanity. *Ecology and Society, 14*(2), 32.

Siegel, D. J. (2015). *Brainstorm: The power and purpose of the teenage brain.* New York: Penguin.

Steffen, W., Persson, Å., Deutsch, L., Zalasiewicz, J., Williams, M., Richardson, K., . . . & Svedin, U. (2011). The Anthropocene: From global change to planetary stewardship. *AMBIO, 40*(7), 739. https://doi.org/10.1007/s13280-011-0185-x

Szczytko, R., Carrier, S., & Stevenson, K. (2018). Impacts of outdoor environmental education on teacher reports of attention, behavior, and learning outcomes for students with emotional, cognitive, and behavioral disabilities. *Frontiers in Education.* https://doi.org/10.3389/feduc.2018.00046

Twenge, J. (2017). *iGen: Why today's super-connected kids are growing up less rebellious, more tolerant, less happy—and completely unprepared for adulthood.* New York: Simon & Schuster.

UNESCO. (2001). *The open file on inclusive education* (ED.2003/WS/34 REV). Paris: UNESCO Digital Library, 146pp.

UNICEF. (2021). *Inclusive education.* www.unicef.org/education/inclusive-education

White, M. P., Alcock, I., Grellier, J., Wheeler, B. W., Hartig, T., Warber, S. L., . . . & Fleming, L. E. (2019). Spending at least 120 minutes a week in nature is associated with good health and wellbeing. *Scientific Reports, 9*(1), 1–11.

World Health Organization and Secretariat of the Convention on Biological Diversity. (2015). *Connecting global priorities: Biodiversity and human health: A state of knowledge review.* www.cbd.int/health/SOK-biodiversity-en.pdf

Wu, X., Nethery, R., Sabath, B., Braun, D., & Dominici, F. (2020). Exposure to air pollution and COVID-19 mortality in the United States: A nationwide cross-sectional study. *Science Advances, 6*(45).

Zachor, D., Vardi, S., Baron-Eitan, S., Brodai-Meir, I., Ginossar, N., & Ben-Itzchak, E. (2017). The effectiveness of an outdoor adventure programme for young children with autism spectrum disorder: A controlled study. *Developmental Medicine & Child Neurology, 59*(5), 550–556.

# 2 Encouraging students and teachers to explore worldviews, ethics and their own responsibilities

**Chapter aims**

- Identify why treating the individual as the sole focus of learning may be problematic.

- Describe how worldviews influence the way people think, feel, and act.

- Understand how different methods such as *Inquiry as Stance* and *Critical Pedagogy* can transcend individual learning to become political, moral, and cultural learning and teaching practices.

- Explore ideas for educational activities which may enable students to take on the perspective of the "more-than-human".

## Problems that can arise when the individual becomes the sole focus of learning

Students taking responsibility for their own learning was a key theme in the earlier edition of this book where we argued that teaching was not to be found at one end of a polarized continuum and learning at the other (Beames, Higgins, & Nicol, 2011). Instead, student-centred learning is characterized by a complex set of interpersonal relationships that can provide creative *frisson* between teachers and students. We noted that students taking responsibility for their learning could be nurtured both indoors and outdoors. However, the outdoors provides multidimensional spaces and places that present different opportunities, challenges, and decision-making processes than learning indoors. We referred to seminal learning theories such as Vygotsky's (1978) *zone of proximal development* and the associated concept of *scaffolding* (see Wood, Bruner, & Ross, 1976; Rotella, 2011).

Essentially, we were theorizing this relationship through the lens of educational psychology to support teachers as they plan ways to maximize learning opportunities

DOI: 10.4324/9781003010890-2

outdoors. In doing so we wanted to show how experiential approaches to learning place much more responsibility on students to learn for themselves (Loeber, van Mierlo, Grin, & Leeuwis, 2009). We were following the cues of Lewin (1967), Piaget (2002), Rogers (1983), Vygotsky (1978), and many others—all of whom posited the theory of individual difference and how students learn at different paces. We were also convinced by researchers like Pramling (2011), who stated that in addition to ideas associated with "age and stage", that teachers "supporting children to be *participants* in their own education, is to a large extent related to interaction and communication . . . [and that teachers should] . . . trust in children's capabilities to express themselves and take responsibility" (p. 113).

However, one of the limitations of theorizing with a specific focus on the individual in this way is that there is no guarantee that knowledge, values, and behaviours learnt in one educational setting will endure as the individual moves from one place to another. Further, students will be influenced by the social settings they inhabit, such as family, social media, various peer groups, clubs, and a diverse range of broader sociocultural values (Kasser, 2011). Finally, while individual centred learning depends on rich interactions between the student and teacher, these interactions are not in themselves sufficient for anyone to know how to live and act in the world.

## The learner in society

Thorburn (2018) provides a helpful distinction between methods of inquiry, such as experiential approaches to learning as discussed above, and applied ethics. In this chapter what we are interested in examining is how teaching and learning might interact more effectively with applied social and environmental ethics in order to explore worldviews. To do this, one needs to move beyond educational theories of individual learning and include philosophical thinking that integrates moral deliberation, knowledge construction, and curricular engagement with learning outdoors.

This approach builds on the three-way pedagogical relationship involving *students, teachers,* and *outdoor places,* by adding a fourth dimension: Applied *social and environmental ethics*. To be clear, this does not mean that the teacher has to teach ethics through imparting the detailed level of theoretical information that requires them to be a moral philosopher. In keeping with experiential approaches to learning, it is much more about finding ways to explore how teachers and students manage their moral lives through mutual responsibility. This will require new ways of thinking about responsibility and an exploration of how teachers may navigate a range of values, behaviours, and multiple worldviews.

## Methods of inquiry

The first point to note is Thorburn's (2018) view that there is no toolkit available to do this moral and ethical work. Or, perhaps more accurately, there are toolkits available, but they are limited to the three-way pedagogical relationship (students, teachers, and outdoor places) that we described above. In Chapter 6, we focus on the need to generate curiosity and wonder in students. If students are genuinely curious and full of wonder through their direct experiences outdoors, then, we believe, there is a fundamental necessity to direct that curiosity and wonder towards the fourth dimension of applied social and environmental ethics; that is to say, "how to live well in the world". Doing this successfully requires employing methods of inquiry that purposefully link the experiential and the local with the abstract and global.

One effective way of doing this is through what is called *Practitioner Inquiry*. We use this term here to mean when teachers engage in systematic inquiry into their own practice and their students' learning. This is something long-term and not like a topic or project that can be picked up and set aside when completed. It is more about an open-ended form of pedagogy that we may continue to return to throughout our lifetime. It is also a way of overcoming transmissive approaches to teaching, such as the passing on of facts and knowledge that hallmark what Paolo Freire (1968/1996) called "the banking model" of education. As world leaders in practitioner inquiry, Cochran-Smith and Lytle (2009) call for teachers and educators to "ally their work with others as part of larger social and intellectual movements for social change and social justice" (p. viii). They introduced the term *Inquiry as Stance* to describe a specific:

> worldview and a habit of mind—a way of knowing and being in the world
> of educational practice that carries across educational contexts and various
> points in one's professional career and that links individuals to larger groups
> and social movements intended to challenge the inequities perpetuated by
> the educational status quo.
>
> (p. viii)

The key to success is understanding that teachers, parents, support groups, and community initiatives—groups that Cochran-Smith and Lytle (2009) call "practitioners"—are central to school change and educational reform. In other words, it is not the responsibility of teachers and schools alone because success lies in partnerships (see Chapters 7 and 9 on Community-Based Learning and Residential Outdoor Education for more discussion on this). The lived experience of many teachers can be one of "subjugation", which involves teaching a curriculum someone else invented, teaching to the test, preparing students to work in a knowledge society, dealing with politicians who think they know best, coping with the allocation of resources that never seem to be enough, being treated like a social worker, and so on (see Hursh, 2006; Ross & Gibson, 2006). Experiences such as these can serve to alienate teaching staff from broader communities of interest, and externalize power and authority (i.e. it is someone else's fault that things are the way they are). However, these issues of power, authority, and inequality can also ignite reactions from teachers and students in their everyday education settings and inspire those who want to do something and "speak truth to power".

## Worldviews and critical pedagogies

Valk (2021) has highlighted that "'beliefs are the building blocks of a worldview" (p. 10). To understand issues of power, authority, and inequality it is important to recognize how worldviews, and differences between and within them, define how people come to think, feel, and act in the world. The worldviews of individuals, groups, communities, and societies are very likely to be the result of what Evernden (1985) has referred to as unexamined assumptions. By this he means that the thinking which sustains worldviews might not make much sense if it is not explicitly stated or voiced. The danger of holding such unexamined worldviews is the manifestation and perpetuation of unconscious biases that come from a lack of critical thinking. For example, would racists perceive of their views as being that of discrimination, prejudice, and "presumed" supremacy? Why do some racists justify holding these views by claiming them as a legitimate worldview? Talking about the long history of racism and sexism Morton (2018) states, rather pointedly, that:

> it has taken a lot of time and effort from a lot of different people to make obvious the types of patterns of thought, assumptions and behaviour that underlie prejudice and even make people think it's OK.
>
> (p. 7)

From this very brief description it can be seen that teaching about worldviews to and by people who may have been socialized into holding entrenched moral and political positions is very challenging work. At the same time, it would seem perilous for education and educational practices not to take or cultivate a critical stance, particularly if some worldviews allow people to ignore, or even justify, all sorts of inequalities. It is therefore our firm view that students, their teachers, schools, curriculum designers, policy makers and governments across the world need to find better ways of teaching and developing a diverse array of worldviews that help all to develop inclusive pedagogies that enable people to flourish and tackle human suffering.

## Criticality in teaching worldviews

If the problems associated with unexamined assumptions and unconscious biases are to be avoided, then the teacher has to begin by critiquing their own worldview(s) to understand their own biases, assumptions, and perspectives. Pashby and Sund offer an excellent guide to support teachers in how to go about doing this.[1] This guidance helps the teacher to consider not just their orientations *towards* belief patterns, such as good and bad, facts and values, thinking, knowing, and feeling, but the discrepancies, disputes, and inconsistencies within these, which if not examined can be unknowingly perpetuated. For example, someone living in the so-called "western world" may well have been taught about worldviews as if they were simply a history of ideas from the ancient Greeks through *The Age of Enlightenment* to the present (for a thorough review of this history see for example Russell, 1979). It is not possible in such a short chapter to discuss the geographical reach of worldviews that emerged and morphed into one another throughout this time-frame, but we have mentioned *The Age of Enlightenment*, sometimes known as *The Age of Reason*, because within the emerging industrialized nations it dominated the world of ideas from the 17th to 19th centuries (Russell, 1979). The Enlightenment was born from the idea that all human beings share the same basic needs and, as such, should enjoy the same rights and privileges. Enlightenment philosophers believed that human reason, rationality, and benevolence would lead to the natural progression of society and the betterment of life on Earth (Russell, 1979).

The reach of the Enlightenment has also been extensive to the point that many contemporary scholars insist that its dominance and legacy remain the defining worldview of the modern world—and this is troublesome. For example, Marshall, Coleman, and Reason (2011) have shown that the Enlightenment has set in train views, actions, and events that have shaped the current global economy. This means there is an interconnected worldwide trade in goods and services that affects everyone on the planet through patterns of communication, financial markets, trade, transportation, migration, immigration, and so on. This legacy has provided an enormous improvement in terms of human welfare in some societies. However, as Giddens (2009) has explained, the Enlightenment thinkers viewed these ideals as benign, but, as we know now, these ideas simultaneously unleashed massive destructive forces on the environment and cultures. Valk (2021) has shown how modern capitalism and consumption has led to socioeconomic injustices and oppression, while Santos (2014) has pointed out critically that the Enlightenment at its heart promotes the superiority of Western-centric European culture. Cajete (2015) has written in support of Indigenous education: First, because of the ways in which colonialism has brutalized Indigenous communities; and second, to reclaim thinking and knowing which places Indigenous ethics at the heart of teaching practices.

With increased attention rightly being given to inclusive education it is important to consider how worldviews and multiple perspectives are being raised, discussed, critiqued, and taught. These types of conversations have at their heart the search for social justice and a flourishing world. One way to deal with this is through our four-way pedagogical model of relationships where we extend the three-way information sharing relationship (between students, teachers, outdoor places) to include social and environmental ethical stances that interrogate the way we live and act in the world. This is much more complex than simply teaching ideas and theories *about* worldviews in the classroom; it is also why learning cannot simply be about individuals acquiring knowledge. Instead, Giroux (2020) argues for drawing on critical pedagogies that transcend individual learning to become political, moral, and cultural educational practices. The emphasis on critical pedagogy being about *practices* supports our position that it is not enough to learn about theories that illuminate inequalities or how existing power structures habitually reinforce them. Rather, students and their teachers need to actively question and challenge systemic social structures and their means of oppression.

## A more-than-human worldview

The greatest failure of the Enlightenment was its humanistic endeavour, which did not account for the fact that human beings are part of, and utterly dependent on, ecosystems and biodiversity for their own survival.

The Global Education Monitoring Report (2016) states that:

> Individual and collective human actions have put immense strain on the planet and the life forms it supports. Since humanity is clearly contributing to environmental degradation, rapid biodiversity loss and climate change, its actions must also provide the solutions to these challenges.
>
> (p. 11)

In his book, *The spell of the sensuous: Perception and language in a more-than-human world*, Abram (1996) coined the term *more-than-human* to draw attention to alternative worldviews to that of the Enlightenment. Abram's (2020) encouragement towards deeper self-knowing is to understand that:

> we have no autonomy, no integrity as a species separate from the other species of this world, no collective existence as a creature apart from the animate Earth. We can understand ourselves, and feel what it is to be human, only through our interaction and engagement with all these other, nonhuman beings with whom our lives are so thoroughly tangled.
>
> (para 16)

It is essential to highlight that for a very long time now, many educational systems around the world have failed to include the relationship between human beings and the more-than-human world in school, college, and university curricula. The story of the Enlightenment is a story of division, where humanity was deemed to be separate from nature, the mind separate from the body, teachers in some way separate from their students, and schools separate from society. This simply supports a form of human superiority, something "unmistakably" obvious, where one type of human being has dominance over another, and all human beings prioritize their own needs over the more-than-human.

Abram (1996, 2020) does not separate the human species from everything else, but instead advances a more-than-human worldview in which everything is related. As educators, it follows that we need first to reject the Enlightenment framing of the natural world as something distinct from humans. We then need to accept that as humans we *are* nature, as are all our creations. And so, cities are no less "communities" within a global ecosystem than are forest communities within a continent. Smyth (1998) simplified this complex philosophical discussion and provided a definition of nature as something "physical and biological, human and non-human, natural, cultivated and constructed, social and political, cultural and aesthetic, and temporal with a past and future" (p. 1). The frequent use of the conjunction "and" is intended to encourage reciprocity, not separation.

The trouble is that guidance like this can be as abstract as the problems it seeks to solve. So how do we move from transmissive teaching approaches, as we are doing here with our readers, to the experiential approaches we advocate above? We refer to the four-point epistemology introduced in Chapter 6 as a reminder that we are currently engaged in what we defined as propositional knowledge—in this case, the sharing of ideas and theory through writing. Theories are largely fact-based generalizations and help us think about phenomena at a macro level. While theory is an indispensable part of making sense of phenomena, at the same time it is not necessarily epistemologically diverse. To be more epistemologically diverse we need to explain how to work with these worldviews experientially. But, before we can do this, we need to ground our theories in places of practice. As Gruen-wald (2003) reminds us, places are a good starting point because social, economic, and environmental issues are interwoven with those places of common habitation, such as schools and communities. Also, McCoy, Tuck, and McKenzie (2016) show how "land" provides the background and basis for historical and cultural debates within communities as a way of avoiding European universalism. That is to say, first, places are not merely abstract ideas to be discussed through theory; and second, they are locations in which to develop practices of love and care that involve the more-than-human. Clearly, learning opportunities will vary from rural to urban settings, given the range of ecological, geographical, historical, and philosophical parameters outlined by Smyth above. The following case study illustrates how worldviews can be put into pedagogical practice through learning alongside the more-than-human.

## CASE STUDY: The Council of All Beings

Ainsley teaches a class of first-year secondary students in one of Singapore's state schools. She recently attended a Ministry of Education CPD (Continuing Professional Development) course and one of the workshops included an activity called "A Council of All Beings". Ainsley had been particularly looking forward to this workshop, having first read about it in Macy, Brown, and Fox's (1998) book *Coming back to life: Practices to reconnect our lives, or world.*

The workshop followed Macy and colleagues' guidance "to step aside from our human identity and speak on behalf of other life-forms" (p. 161). This guidance follows an eight-stage process through description, invocation, being chosen, mask-making, moving, and speaking as the life-form, gathering in Council, three stages of the Council, and finally the ending.

At the workshop, Ainsley learned that Councils of All Beings could include up to 100 participants of all ages and so she was keen to experiment with her class of 33. She knew that Councils of All Beings had been held in a variety of outdoor settings, even indoors, and this suited Ainsley, whose school had no green areas and was located within a large city that was among the most industrialized on the planet. Ainsley was reassured at her workshop that she did not need to be an expert in ecology or outdoor learning.

When she got back to school, Ainsley briefed her class that they were to go into the school grounds and walk around and think about something in the natural world that they cared about. This could be a place, an object or something living (each referred to from now on as a "life-form"). They were told that they did not need to know a lot about their life-form, but just to "listen" to whatever "speaks" to them as they think and walk. Afterwards, the students were told they would gather in a circle and speak of their life-form. This ended the "description", the first of the eight stages. They then set off outdoors to continue with their first Council of All Beings. What happened next?

Anyone wanting to find out what happens next will have to read more about how to run such a session and then take the plunge. There is much information freely available on the internet that can be found through a search for "Council of All Beings". There is no one way, or right way, to run this workshop and various structures are offered. It is important to remember that the structures are just an aid to setting up the workshop and need not be followed in every detail; the outcomes cannot be prescribed in advance. It is partly about letting go of control and trusting the process, while allowing for spontaneity.

We have found that some people will connect deeply with their life-form and others will take a more light-hearted and playful approach. It is almost inevitable that some students will be disruptive, but that is no different from classroom disruptions that happen indoors. When to intervene is a matter of judgement, and teachers will need to explore their own tolerance levels and degrees of control, while remembering that the levels deemed acceptable indoors are not easily transferred outdoors where spaces and places are different. As students take on their life-forms, some will want to share their experiences with others as they seek to be heard at Council. Through this sharing, the teacher will be able to detect any movement from the human to the more-than-human (and back again) as the various life-forms speak and interact with each other. However, some may not want to share, and that is perfectly acceptable, as it is not always fruitful to insist that everyone speaks. It is important to note who is speaking, and what they are saying—as well as who is not speaking—so that follow up activities can be pursued in keeping with Dewey's (1938/1963) concept of *continuity* described in Chapter 6.

Some of the guidance on running "Councils" refers to them as "rituals". We would urge caution in the use of the word "ritual", as it has a range of connotations that are difficult to resolve in the context of experiential approaches to education. Our preference would be that this process is teacher-led and co-constructed with students where appropriate; place-specific, in both rural or urban areas (see Chapters 5 and 9); and not prescribed by sequences and rules to deliver activities in "ideal" places. It is important to experiment and take some chances to find out what works, what does not, and under which conditions. If we are to truly engage in and embrace pedagogies and worldviews of the more-than-human, we need to find new ways of working.

This activity and others like it, foster opportunities for students to view the world from different vantage points. In terms of Heron and Reason's (2008) four-point epistemology, (more fully developed in Chapter 6), experiential and presentational knowing will already be evident to the teacher through what the students have experienced and shared after running a Council of All Beings. Dewey's concept of continuity (as described in Chapter 6) might now involve working with propositional knowing to extend students' knowledge of ecological theory, such as how humans are a part of nature. It is also through propositional knowing that we might better understand the need for multiple and intersecting worldviews. As explained above, Cajete (2015) has called for the development of a vision for Indigenous education, which is a worldview based on community needs—communities that include the more-than-human, and not universal principles such as those of the Enlightenment. Also, as we have stated, multicultural and multi-faith classrooms are increasingly the norm and so it is by leaving the classroom and interacting with community places that multicultural and multi-faith life experiences become real, in terms of their materiality and cultures. Therefore, we have argued for the importance of promoting a four-way pedagogical relationship involving students, teachers, outdoor places, and applied social and environmental ethics. This is because the fourth point (social and environmental ethics) precisely matches Heron and Reason's (2008) practical knowing and taking action for and with the more-than-human.

The history of the Enlightenment, and the enormous destructive forces it has unleashed on the planet, our home, is the rationale for teachers needing to help students interrogate their own worldviews, understand multiple perspectives, and promote critical pedagogies of love, hope, and care. This is not the sole responsibility of educators, but they do need to take responsibility within their own spheres of influence. This is why we have introduced the work of Cochran-Smith and Lytle (2009), who have paved the way for activist teachers with their idea of *Inquiry as Stance*. Taking stances and following a process of critical ideological analysis is the soul and lifeblood of change. Please go and run a Council of All Beings, or something like it, and then write to us and share your experiences. Through us sharing our ideas and practices with you and you sharing with us, and all of us extending our influence, we can begin to change the world.

## Guidelines

- Move beyond learning that only concerns knowledge being acquired by individual learners.

- Use experiential activities such as the Council of All Beings to give students opportunities to take on the roles of experiencing other cultures and the more-than-human in different school and community contexts.

- Facilitate opportunities for students to question the rules, norms, laws, and accepted practices in their places and in others.

- Experiment with the four-way pedagogical relationship involving students, teachers, outdoor places, and applied social and environmental ethics to explore different worldviews, and worldviews from different perspectives.

## Note

1  www.mmu.ac.uk/media/mmuacuk/content/documents/esri/projects/teacher-resource-project/Ethical-Global-Issues-English.pdf

## References

Abram, D. (1996). *The spell of the sensuous: Perception and language in a more-than-human world.* New York: Vintage.

Abram, D. (2020). In the ground of our unknowing. *Emergence.* https://emergencemagazine.org/essay/in-the-ground-of-our-unknowing/

Beames, S., Higgins, P., & Nicol, R. (2011). *Learning outside the classroom: Theory and guidelines for practice.* New York: Routledge.

Cajete, G. (2015). *Indigenous community: Rekindling the teachings of the seventh fire.* Minnesota, MN: Living Justice Press.

Cochran-Smith, M., & Lytle, S. L. (2009). *Inquiry as stance: Practitioner research in the next generation.* New York: Teachers College Press.

Dewey, J. (1963). *Experience and education.* London: Collier-Macmillan. (Original work published 1938)

Evernden, N. (1985). *The natural alien* (2nd ed.). London: University of Toronto Press.

Freire, P. (1996). *Pedagogy of the oppressed.* London: Penguin. (Original work published 1968)

Giddens, A. (2009). *The politics of climate change.* Cambridge: Polity.

Giroux, H. (2020). *On critical pedagogy* (2nd ed.). London: Bloomsbury.

Global Education Monitoring Report. (2016). *Planet: Environmental sustainability.* https://gem-report-2016.unesco.org/en/chapter/planet-environmental-sustainability/

Gruenwald, D. (2003). The best of both worlds: A critical pedagogy of place. *Educational Research Association, Educational Researcher, 32*(4), 3–12.

Heron, J., & Reason, P. (2008). Extending epistemology within a co-operative inquiry. In P. Reason & H. Bradbury (Eds.), *The SAGE handbook of action research: Participative inquiry and practice* (2nd ed., pp. 366–380). London: SAGE.

Hursh, D. W. (2006). Marketing education: The rise of standardized testing, accountability, competition, and markets in public education. In E. W. Ross & R. Gibson (Eds.), *Neoliberalism and education reform* (pp. 15–34). Cresskill, NJ: Hampton Press.

Kasser, T. (2011). Cultural values and the well-being of future generations: A cross-national study. *Journal of Cross-Cultural Psychology*, *42*(2), 206–215.

Lewin, K. (1967). *Field theory in social science: Selected theoretical papers*. London: Social Science Paperbacks in Association with Tavistock Publications.

Loeber, A., van Mierlo, B., Grin, J., & Leeuwis, C. (2009). The practical value of theory: Conceptualising learning in the pursuit of a sustainable development. In A. Wals (Ed.), *Social learning: Towards a sustainable world*. Wageningen: Wageningen Academic.

Macy, J., Brown, M., & Fox, M. (1998). *Coming back to life: Practices to reconnect our lives, our world*. Gabriola Island, BC: New Society.

Marshall, J., Coleman, G., & Reason, P. (2011). *Leadership for sustainability: An action research approach*. Sheffield: Greenleaf.

McCoy, K., Tuck, E., & McKenzie, M. (Eds.). (2016). *Rethinking pedagogies of place from Indigenous, postcolonial, and decolonising perspectives*. Abingdon and Oxfordshire: Routledge.

Morton, T. (2018). *Becoming ecological*. London: Penguin Random House.

Piaget, J. (2002). *The language and thought of the child*. London: Routledge.

Pramling, I. (2011). Why we should begin early with ESD: The role of Early Childhood Education. *International Journal of Early Childhood*, *43*(2), 103–118.

Rogers, C. (1983). *Freedom to learn: For the 80s*. London: Merrill.

Ross, E. W., & Gibson, R. (2006). Introduction. In E. W. Ross & R. Gibson (Eds.), *Neoliberalism and education reform* (pp. 1–14). Cresskill, NJ: Hampton Press.

Rotella, B. (2011). Scaffolding. In S. Goldstein & J. Naglieri (Eds.), *Encyclopedia of child behavior and development* (pp. 1286–1287). Boston, MA: Springer.

Russell, B. (1979). *A history of western philosophy*. London: Unwin.

Santos, B. S. (2014). *Epistemologies of the south*. Oxon: Routledge.

Smyth, J. (1998). *Learning to sustain*. Stirling: Scottish Environmental Education Council.

Thorburn, M. (2018). Moral deliberation and environmental awareness: Reviewing Deweyan-informed possibilities for contemporary outdoor learning. *Journal of Adventure Education and Outdoor Learning*, *18*(1), 26–23.

Valk, J. (2021). *Worldviews. A comprehensive approach to knowing self and others*. Fredericton, NB: Palgrave Macmillan.

Vygotsky, L. (1978). *Mind in society: The development of higher psychological processes*. Cambridge, MA: Harvard University Press.

Wood, D., Bruner, J., & Ross, G. (1976). The role of tutoring in problem solving. *Journal of Child Psychology and Psychiatry and Allied Disciplines*, *17*(2), 89–100.

# 3 Learning across the curriculum

## What is "the curriculum"?

The heart of the learning and teaching experience at any school involves teachers and students interacting with one another with the central aim of acquiring certain knowledge, understanding, skills, and values. The "curriculum" is generally thought of as the subjects and content comprising a course of study, and as such, is a key interface between the educational establishment, the teacher, and the student.

DOI: 10.4324/9781003010890-3

Teachers take the curriculum as advised or prescribed by the state (or other educational body), make decisions regarding which specific elements of content to include, and then develop this into creative teaching sessions. Each student's task is to make sense of this content and place it into their own learning context. They will do so in relation to their interest, their perception of the personal relevance of the content, and what they already know.

While curriculum is generally prescribed and written down, the approaches a teacher might take and the resources and places they might use are usually left open. Such decisions are made on a pragmatic basis within the context of what is available to the teacher. So, for example, school teachers generally have classrooms; they have boards to write on and computers to project content; they may also use tablets, cloud based collaborative spaces, books, posters, laboratory facilities, and so on. Much of this changes if the teacher has access to an outdoor teaching space and chooses to take their class there. In doing so, the curriculum has not changed but the context has. In making this decision, the teacher has to be mindful that this experience should enhance student learning rather than distract or detract. This change of context is significant and will be discussed below.

The term "curriculum" is often used alongside terms such as "formal", "informal", "explicit", "implicit", "null", and "hidden". The use of such terms has come about because of a concern among educators that there are implied value-positions in the state's construction of curriculum and in the way a school, or individual teacher, delivers it. For example, the "formal curriculum" is what the state (and society) expects to be delivered, and a school's success in doing so is often monitored and reported on (by the state, parents/guardians, and the media). The high significance of achievement in formal subject areas is clear, and students, parents/guardians, and teachers respond to this. This type of curriculum is "explicit" in that it appears in documents that define and guide educational communities—the school, its teachers, and students.

However, a number of authors have explored and critiqued more subtle interpretations of curriculum. Eisner (1985) suggested we could think of curriculum as "explicit" (previous paragraph), "implicit" and "null". The "implicit curriculum" is what the students will "pick up" from the way a school is organized and the way teachers teach. For example, if an aspect of the formal curriculum is allocated limited teaching time, or is programmed so that it is an option competing with another subject, the implication is that it has less status. Similarly, the way a teacher sets up a classroom can, for example, imply either control or collaboration. The "null curriculum" is also important because, for example, when subject matter is left out, or an approach, facility or location is not used, it becomes part of a null (i.e. not visible or acknowledged) curriculum, and are perceived as such by students, staff, parents/guardians, and the wider public. This links directly to initiatives such as *Diversify your narrative* (2021), which seeks to make curricula more inclusive—and thus "explicit" rather than null—by addressing "the complex issues of more inclusive curriculum, teaching pedagogy, racial equity, educational disparities" (para 2).

The term "informal" is often used in conjunction with "learning", rather than curriculum, and tends to denote socially-mediated, semi-structured learning (e.g., at home and other social settings), which often occurs through conversations that take place away from formal educational environments (Jeffs & Smith, 2005). It is often taken to include language development, developing social skills, and gaining awareness of cultural norms. Although this informal learning tends to be less visible than formal aspects of the curriculum, such learning also takes place within a school.

Closely related to this is the concept of the *hidden curriculum*. This refers to various aspects of unintended or incidental learning (knowledge and attitudes) that students acquire from their time at school. According to Giroux and Penna (1983), it is the "transmission of norms, values, and beliefs conveyed in both the formal educational content and the social interactions within these schools" (pp. 100–121) that leads to an attitude or approach to living in society. This concept has been the basis of a number of critiques, such as Freire's (1968/1996) *Pedagogy of the Oppressed,* where he contemplates the subtle, and often negative, influence of the state, and Gatto's (1992) critique of American schooling, where it argued that "School is a twelve-year jail sentence where bad habits are the only curriculum truly learned" (p. 19).

Taken together, these definitional issues are of some significance for outdoor learning. There are aspects of the formal curriculum (e.g., Earth sciences, ecology) where the justification for outdoor learning is straightforward. Furthermore, outdoor settings have long been used for informal learning, especially in terms of personal and social education. In both of these contexts the outdoor environment will be perceived by students as valued by the education system, while in contrast, if the outdoors is not used for teaching or even if the teacher's decision to go outdoors is questioned (*why outdoors?*), this implies a lack of value (null curriculum).

All of this matters because it is an unquestioned assumption that schools operate indoors rather than outdoors (perhaps with the exception of certain field trips, to a local museum for example), and this message comes across in all aspects of a teacher's life—from selection for preservice teacher education through to possibly becoming a school principal. So, the onus is almost always on the teacher to justify the decision to take students outdoors, while in stark contrast, it seems unthinkable that teachers will ever be asked their rationale for teaching in a classroom (*why indoors?*). This aspect of the null curriculum has consequences for the way students perceive the outdoors, and for their potential to develop a connection with their local environment and a love of the natural world (see Chapters 4 and 5).

## Why is outdoor learning across the curriculum important?

The most obvious curricular benefit of outdoor learning is that it provides the opportunity to engage in an educational activity, to study an environment, a species, a place, a building, or even people as required by a curriculum—for geography, geology, ecology, biology, history, social sciences, or art. Here the outdoors is the material embodiment of the curriculum and this is explored in detail next.

However, there are less well understood benefits of outdoor learning, and these concern its relationship to academic development. While the anecdotal benefits of outdoor learning on improved ability to concentrate both while outdoors, and in class after spending time outdoors, and on improved academic achievement, have been noted by many, these observations are becoming increasingly supported by research evidence across a range of stages of schooling. For example, Hamilton (2018) compared outdoor learning in primary aged children with a control group and showed that individuals and groups learning outdoors performed better than those being taught exclusively indoors. Importantly, "the effect of the outdoor setting on underachieving pupils was particularly notable, improving their engagement, contribution and self-confidence to match that of their peers" (p. 1). The corollary was that indoor classrooms were less motivating in general, but "especially for children with learning difficulties" (p. 1) (see Chapter 1). The study concluded that a key factor of the outdoors was the influence of the natural richness of the settings.

Higgins, Thompson, & Rawcliffe (2018) have argued that there is growing evidence that learning outside the classroom boosts educational attainment. Some of this support comes from work by psychologists who have taken an interest in this area and joined educationalists in conducting a range of revealing empirical studies (e.g., Otte et al., 2019; Kuo, Barnes, & Jordan, 2018; Kuo, Browning, Penner, 2019). In a recent review of such studies, Kuo and co-authors (2019) argue that there is "converging evidence of a cause-and-effect relationship" (p. 1) of the impact of structured "class" time outdoors on academic learning, personal development, and environmental stewardship (p. 1). Similar support has come from a review of a wide range of international literature by Christie and Higgins (2020). It is important to emphasize that these studies and reviews are reporting the effect of being and learning outdoors *in general*, and *not specifically* the effect of studying particular content furnished by being outdoors. While mechanisms that lead to these academic benefits are unclear, a study of young people's perceptions of learning outdoors suggested that what they valued in outdoor experiences depended on the way three dimensions interrelated: The *context/place*, the *activity* itself, and the *social aspect* (Mannion, Doyle, Sankey, Mattu, & Wilson, 2007, p. 45). Similarly, a more recent empirical study by Dieser and Bogner (2016) concluded that "hands-on-centred" environmental education was significant for student learning. This supports the findings of Blair's (2009) review of literature which concluded that gardening can have a positive impact on both student achievement and their behaviour in school.

As with learning inside the classroom, learning outside should be planned in line with curriculum guidelines, in order to maximize the learning potential of these experiences. These guidelines tend to have common themes that consider the content of the curriculum alongside the developmental changes in young people through their years of schooling. Associated structural issues such as inclusion (addressing the educational needs of every child) and transitions (between pre-school, primary, middle, and high school) are also frequently prominent, as are aspirations to develop cross-curricular understanding, personal and social capabilities, citizenship skills, and informed values.

Around the world, there are a number of ways outdoor learning is related to the local curriculum and social context. For example, it can be:

- *Defined as a curricular subject in its own right.* For example, the Australian state of Victoria offers a high school Outdoor Environmental Studies course (Victorian Curriculum & Assessment Authority, 2016). Further, Outdoor Learning recently has been listed as one of seven "curriculum connections" in the Australian Curriculum (2021).

- *Located in a broader area of study within a specified aspect of the curriculum.* For example, in England's Key Stage 4 (upper high school) physical education curriculum (National Curriculum, 2013).

- *Regular curriculum-based outdoor teaching and learning* in schools, often at primary or early secondary level—such as Danish *udeskole* (see Bentsen, Mygind, & Randrup, 2009) and New Zealand's *Education outside the classroom* (New Zealand Ministry of Education, 2016).

- *Linked specifically to state-defined personal and social learning outcomes*, such as in Singapore's Character and Citizenship Education syllabus (2021).

- *Related to deeply rooted cultural traditions* of travel and subsistence, community, nationhood, and recreation. For example, in Scandinavian countries *friluftsliv* (literally "free air life") is the loose equivalent of outdoor learning and is embedded within schools to varying degrees (Gurholt & Haukeland, 2020).

- *Linked to formal curricula*, with many aspects of curricular subject areas delivered outside the classroom. This is a widespread practice, particularly for subjects such as geography and biology.

Each of these approaches has advantages and disadvantages in both the construction of learning experiences of the pupils and also in the potential for teachers and policy makers to justify outdoor learning in the school. The purpose of this book is not to choose between these approaches, but more generally, to support teachers in taking learning outdoors in a way that is compatible with their own curricular and local context. As implied above, while there are compelling arguments for doing so, establishing a justification for outdoor learning that gains acceptance and becomes established in a national policy context is not straightforward. As an example, the following section outlines efforts to do so in Scotland (see Higgins, 2019) for a more extensive commentary).

The national education framework for ages three to 18 in Scotland, called "Curriculum for Excellence" (Education Scotland, 2022), provides good opportunities to reflect on and critique the relationship between outdoor learning and the curriculum. It "offers an inspiring and widely supported philosophy of education" (OECD, 2021, p. 1) with an explicit central focus on the learning experience of the student. Since it was introduced in 2004, this focus has stimulated the development of various policy guidelines, resources, and teacher development initiatives. One of these is of particular significance to this book—"Curriculum for Excellence through Outdoor Learning" (Learning & Teaching Scotland, 2010), which sought to encourage and support teachers to deliver the curriculum outdoors (see below). Finally, in the past ten years, emerging research evidence emphasizing the role of time spent in the natural world in supporting learners' attitudes sustainability (Christie & Higgins, 2020), has supported its inclusion in curricular entitlements concerning "Learning for Sustainability" (see Chapter 4).

The central thrust of Curriculum for Excellence is that schools should focus on the development of students' personal capacities that will be valuable throughout life. Hence, curriculum design is based on the following key principles: Challenge and enjoyment, breadth, progression, depth, personalization and choice, coherence, and relevance. The principles apply to the curriculum in terms of organization (at national, education authority, school, and individual levels) and in all learning settings. The intended outcome is that all young people should become "successful learners, confident individuals, responsible citizens and effective contributors" to society (Education Scotland, 2021).

This approach prompted Beames, Atencio and Ross (2009) to argue that the Curriculum for Excellence challenges the "current emphasis in disciplinary specialism" and calls for schools to "place the nature of the educated person at the centre of curricular purpose, and to reduce the amount of de-contextualized subject content, and to promote real world experience" (p. 42). Government policies like Curriculum for Excellence serve to legitimize the kinds of flexible, cross-curricular, autonomous learning that may be offered by theoretically-driven educational opportunities outside the classroom. Beames and colleagues highlight that it is "hard to reconcile this with timetabled, indoor, subject-based, textbook classes" (p. 42). Seen this way, and in the context of the arguments outlined in later chapters, learning outside across the curriculum is a fundamental educational imperative and should be an entitlement for all children. While this principle is acknowledged in policy commitments in Scotland, the reality is that a range of other constraints (e.g., resourcing, staffing, timetables, training) limit the opportunities to discharge this commitment, and hence for young people to learn outdoors (Higgins & Nicol, 2018). The degree to which a meaningful "entitlement" can be expected in other nations will depend on the official curriculum of that country, but where there is a commitment to the development of "capacities" such as those above, the logic for "learning outside across the curriculum" should surely prevail.

This view is in accord with the Scottish Government, as outdoor learning is explicitly stated or implicit in a number of recent policy documents that culminated in the publication of *Curriculum for Excellence through Outdoor Learning*

(Learning & Teaching Scotland, 2010) and *Vision 2030+* (Education Scotland, 2016). The former was the first time in the UK that a specific policy document issued guidance on outdoor learning, and the latter was the first time guidance made an explicit link with attitudes towards sustainability (see Chapter 4). New Zealand's *Education Outside the Classroom* (New Zealand Ministry of Education, 2016) provides similar policy support and guidance for "curriculum- based learning and teaching that extends the four walls of the classroom" (p. 1). Both the Scottish and New Zealand documents illustrate much of this with reference to broader material themselves, together with curricular opportunities, detailed exemplification, advice on planning, suitable locations, health and safety, and sources of further support. Scotland's National Improvement Hub (n.d.) is an example of additional support that is available.

The emphasis we have placed on mainstream curricular planning is not accidental. If outdoor learning is to be respected and valued by the educational establishment, the justifications must be credible. Outdoor learning must be a benefit rather than a diversion or simply "fun", and must articulate properly with the school curriculum. The principles of Curriculum for Excellence have been used to develop local guidelines in Scotland, and these are now extensively used by schools, outdoor centres, and others, in explaining their approach to outdoor learning. In light of the increasing demands on schools to meet high academic standards, such explicit linkages are plainly necessary to maintain support for outdoor learning. One related concern is equity of provision: For example, certainly in Scotland, research has shown that curricular outdoor learning is relatively uncommon in low-income high schools (11–18 years) (Beames & Pollack, 2019), suggesting that the benefits of outdoor learning for all learners needs to be made evident, and that adequate resourcing is provided to support it.

## How can teachers incorporate outdoor learning across the curriculum into their teaching?

The following section provides a number of examples of ways in which teachers can make the most of their local outdoor environments in their teaching. Most of the subject matter here is "generic" in that it concerns subject matter that exists in curricula all over the world. However, there will be many region-specific variations of this subject matter and other local phenomena that will inspire teachers to use the outdoors creatively.

In considering what particular opportunities for learning (curricular or otherwise) a place/space offers, the term "affordances" is useful. Gibson introduced the term in 1979, defining it as what an environment "offers the animal, . . . provides or furnishes, either for good or ill" (Gibson, 2015/1979, p. 119). When understood in relation to education, affordances can be considered as "the particular relationships that can arise through the bringing together of the learner, the learning opportunity and the environment or contextual condition in which an educational experience takes place" (Christie & Higgins, 2020, p. 3). The practical implications of this concept as a way of thinking about both informal and curricular outdoor learning are evident in a range of settings.

The physical development of young people is an aspect of both the formal and informal curriculum throughout a student's school life. In early years provision around the world most nurseries, preschools, and kindergartens build outdoor play into the structure of the day. Such activities are generally unstructured, with children being encouraged to make use of playground equipment or the physical attributes of the play area. A well designed playground may provide many opportunities for physical and sensory development (see Goddard Blythe, 2004). However, more "complex" environments, such as the uneven ground, logs, trees, boulders, and rocks that may be found in local parks or natural play areas provide additional stimuli for developing activity and the movement patterns that can be transferred to other environments (in other words, they offer greater "affordances"). This approach to early childhood play is widely recognised in Scandinavia, as Fjørtoft (2004) and MacQuarrie and Nugent (2017) have discussed. As well as the place as a whole, even a stick or a stone will have multiple "affordances" to a creative young mind. The outdoor environment is also important for sensory development, as it can engage all the senses and multiple intelligences (Gardner, 1993) in an integrated fashion and in ways not possible in a classroom. This may have even greater significance for learners with additional support needs, particularly those with sensory impairments (see Chapter 1).

While physical activity through play tends to become stylized in the curriculum as physical education and team sports, the role of green spaces remains significant in providing informal opportunities for physical and social development, and personal reflection (e.g., Bell et al., 2008; Muñoz, 2009; Martin et al., 2020). Further, a broader area of green space research has emerged in recent decades relating to its developmental role and establishing it as a key factor in health and wellbeing. Historically significant work by Ulrich (1983), has been followed by empirical and review studies on health and wellbeing (e.g., Bird, 2007; Hartig, Mitchell, de Vries, & Frumkin, 2014; Bloomfield, 2017), and on the positive impact of nature on mental health (Lackey et al., 2019). There is growing evidence for the mental health benefits of landscapes where water is present ("blue spaces"), such as rivers, lakes, and the sea (see Gascon et al., 2015; Völker & Kistemann, 2011; White et al., 2019). The enhanced natural richness of such settings provides both wellbeing benefits and increased affordances for learning.

In their day-to-day work in classrooms, teachers use their theoretical knowledge to help students develop an understanding of subject content. Judicious use of the outdoors provides excellent opportunities to create innovative practices and experiments that can illuminate theory and provide real learning contexts for their students. Consequently, a key overarching message within this book is that the opportunities for *academic development* outdoors are extensive and can enhance almost any subject area in the curriculum.

For example, the basic skills of reading and writing are often developed from experiences and material drawn from nature. A quick look at the children's reading shelves in a bookshop or library demonstrates childhood interest in the outdoors as a place to encounter nature and adventure. Many teachers make use of this inherent fascination when they set creative writing tasks or bring outside material into the classroom.

History is, of course, concerned with people and place over time, and many aspects of local history are enlivened by visits to a local landscape. This theme is explored in detail in Chapter 5. Historical development is closely linked to the geography and geological past of the area, and it is here where, among the sciences, biology and ecology are most obviously enhanced through outdoor learning.

Studying habitats and ecosystems demands facilitated direct experience(s). While curricula may offer examples from internationally famous ecosystems (e.g., tropical rain forests, the great plains of Africa, oceans, the Arctic), few teachers can find these just outside their classroom. Nonetheless, the same principles apply around the globe in both terrestrial and aquatic ecosystems, and it is straightforward enough to find local examples of food chains/webs, adaptation, and competition, and then apply these principles globally. At an introductory level, studies of biodiversity through pond or stream sampling, or rock pools, seem to have an almost universal fascination. With the aid of magnifying lenses, an astonishing diversity of form can be examined, and life and death struggles may unfold in the sample tray alone. With a modest level of knowledge, the attributes that such organisms must have to enable them to live in these environments (such as mayfly larvae hatching to become adults for only a few days before they die) can be interpreted to fascinate the students.

Teaching mathematics outdoors may not spring so readily to mind, but of course, doing so provides opportunities for measuring length, distance, height, area, mass, volume, and angles, and limitless circumstances to make basic through to advanced calculations (see the Case Study below). Physics and chemistry are an important means of understanding, and to some extent predicting, the processes that define our physical world. Some aspects of physics, such as observations of weather and climate, astronomy/cosmology are obvious candidates. A simple walk can provide opportunities to construct experiments and discuss principles of matter and motion—mass and density of objects, gravity, balance, friction, momentum, collisions; energy flow (e.g., from the sun, or even the warmth of human bodies), absorption, and reflection. Similarly, an understanding of chemical processes can, for example, be developed through measurements of pH in rain, soils, and water bodies, or comparative studies of pesticides and organic gardening in garden beds in the school grounds. The concrete, bricks, mortar, and metals in our schools and other structures are all formed by chemical processes. These can be described and investigations conducted on the effects of water, heat, and pressure in causing them to decay over time.

An integrated science session on a river can be a means of developing understanding of the *relationship of the sciences* in a "real world" situation. For example, this can include aspects of biology (e.g., river ecology, adaptation, physiology), along with measurements of oxygen levels in water samples and measurements of stream volume and velocity. In turn, human dependence on water and water bodies, and human modification of aquatic environments (e.g., bridges, water turbines, pollution, and water treatment) can provide an entry point to utilitarian approaches to water use, and to a discussion of relative values. This can, of course, be juxtaposed with water's universal cultural significance, in terms of aesthetic and recreational appeal. Such an approach reflects the way in which knowledge must be applied across a range of subject areas to gain depth and contextual understanding.

Studies of community planning and development and other aspects of social studies benefit considerably from direct experiences outside the school (see Chapter 7 for more detail). For example, visits to local town centres or agricultural areas, community gardens, municipal agencies, and public facilities can all provide rich material for discussion and project development in class. The learning from these local spaces and organizations can lead to deeper understandings of civics, citizenship, social roles and norms, employment, and social equity, while developing a sense of place and identity. All of these possible outcomes involve learning that a child can contextualize as part of their lived experience.

One great strength of outdoor learning is that it is possible to provide opportunities for planning, decision-making, and responsibility-taking that transforms student learning into a more active enterprise. These aspects of what is often an "informal" personal and social education curriculum can be integrated with more formal curricular areas to provide stimulating integrated learning opportunities. For example, short journeys with or without maps of local areas where route-finding decisions are required can be used to develop knowledge of the local environment.

This approach finds support from "progressive education" philosopher, John Dewey (1973), who argued that the onus was on educators to place their students in "indeterminate situations" (p. 227) that necessitated critical and creative thinking, decision-making, and problem-solving to negotiate. In other words, Dewey believed that the educator's job was not to lead students "down a road", but to place students at "forks in the road", where they had to assess the benefits and pitfalls of a certain courses of action, and then act on their decision. Dewey's concept of the indeterminate situation is strongly connected to the way experiences are structured for learners, as it implies that educators need to coordinate learning environments where many different courses of action may be taken by the participant.

The potential curricular use of the outdoors is clearly considerable and by no means confined to the subject areas that we have discussed thus far. Carefully constructed outdoor learning experiences can demonstrate the relationships between many subject areas and disciplines that are simply not visible in classroom settings. Teachers of students at all ages and stages, and in most subject areas, can find inspiration and opportunities in the outdoors.

An increasing range of books exist to support educators as they take their teaching outdoors. For example, Sue Waite's (2017) *Children learning outside the classroom: From birth to eleven* and Juliet Robertson's (2014) *Dirty teaching* both provide excellent, illustrative examples of how a wide range of curricular areas can be taught outside. Excellent books exist in other countries, too, of course. With a little creative thought, teachers can move beyond the delivering of decontextualized parts of the curriculum towards the kind of integrated, interdisciplinary knowledge and understanding of the "real world" that is so valuable in life beyond school.

## CASE STUDY

The parking lot at Lakeview Primary School appears to be nothing special. It is a paved, rectangular space, with white lines, that is roughly the size of two tennis courts. Despite the school being in an area of the city without much greenspace, Nisha, a grade four teacher without a background in outdoor learning (OL), was determined to try and teach some of her mathematics, science, and history curriculum outdoors.

In her three-week foray into the world of OL, Nisha decided to focus on one curricular area each week. Mathematics was first. In groups, students were instructed to come up with their own questions around area, volume, and percentages, in relation to the car park. One group chose to figure out the total area, while another set about determining the volume of the covered bicycle shelter. A third group compared the number of adult bicycles in the bike shelter with the number of cars in the parking lot. The fourth group calculated the proportion of cars fueled by petrol, electricity, or a combination of the two. This sparked an interesting discussion on fuel sources for cars!

Week two featured the natural sciences, and flora, in particular. On one side of the parking lot there was a hedge; there was a big tree in the northwestern corner; the east side had a long flower box; and the backside of the boulder, near the fence, in the shade of the big tree, had some very furry moss. This time, the groups were given the task of trying to identify the different species, with both their common and scientific names.

The final week of Nisha's experiment focused on history. Again, she opted to have her students form their own questions about the parking lot, and, in pairs, they came up with a long list of things they wanted to find out. Topics included: When the parking was last paved, what asphalt is actually made from and how it is made, when the parking was first paved, what was on the land before it was paved, and how much it would cost to re-pave the parking lot. As a result of the lesson, one pair of students decided to draft a petition to the school administration and Parent Teacher Association to dig-up the parking lot and "re-green" it.

As we discuss in Chapter 5, learning in all landscape is cross-curricular. In the above case study, the parking lot was simply a "way in" to the curriculum. The opportunities to connect each aspect of our places to official learning outcomes are virtually endless.

# Key points for outdoor learning across the curriculum

In all forms of outdoor learning planning, it is vital to use the environment in an authentic rather than contrived or abstracted way (Beames & Brown, 2016), as this makes the learning appropriate to the context and place, and can thus demonstrate the interconnected nature of many aspects of the school curriculum (see more in Chapter 5 on Place). This provides an opportunity to distinguish between what Smith (2000) refers to as *process* and *product* models of curriculum. Here, the emphasis is on the *process* of becoming self-reliant "successful learners", rather than simply on the *product* orientation of learning aspects of knowledge that will be of instrumental value in higher education and employment. Clearly, both approaches to learning are necessary. However, if teachers focus on the *process* of learning when outside the classroom and encourage critical reasoning and reflection on these experiences, they will help their students develop the skills to become self-reliant and successful in learning throughout life. This does not, of course, rule out the potential for such learning to also have a *product* orientation.

As with most of our everyday lived experiences, outdoor learning is usually inherently interdisciplinary. There are multiple interpretations of this term and its various forms (e.g., multidisciplinary, trans-disciplinary—see Chettiparamb, 2007) and many definitions of it (e.g., Boix Mansilla, Miller, & Gardner, 2000; Areek-kuzhiyi, 2017). For the purpose of this discussion, we consider interdisciplinary learning to be taking place when learners draw on two or more disciplines to develop their overall understanding of a subject which itself extends beyond the boundaries of any single discipline.

As is evident, the very nature of the complex educational "arena" that is to be found outdoors—along with its affordances and serendipitous encounters with places, people, and the more-than-human—facilitates important ways of integrating curricula that, depending on age and stage, are often traditionally taught as separate subject areas (e.g., geography, literature, ecology, and history). There are clear benefits in teaching aspects of these subject areas in an integrated fashion (both indoors or outdoors), as this reflects the interdisciplinary nature of the world—the way we interact with each other and our planet.

## Guidelines

- For schools, the curriculum is the totality of all that is planned for students throughout their school years. Through this planning, subtle messages are conveyed (deliberately or inadvertently) about the relationships between subjects, the relevance of learning environments (e.g., the outdoors), and both personal and cultural values.

- Outdoor learning can provide an action context for the formal and informal curriculum, and can support physical, academic, personal, and social development.

- The opportunities for academic development outdoors are extensive. Although almost any subject area in the curriculum can be enhanced this way, most formal parts of the curriculum are ideally suited to learning outdoors. Additionally, the outdoors offer interdisciplinary learning opportunities in realistic contexts that are at once different and complementary to those available indoors.

- There should be no "competition" between indoor and outdoor learning. Both may be necessary to maximize students' learning opportunities. "Good pedagogy" is "good pedagogy", wherever the teaching takes place.

- In addition to curricular benefits, time spent outdoors in green spaces and gardens has been shown to improve classroom concentration, achievement, physical fitness, general wellbeing, and pro-environmental behaviours.

## References

Areekkuzhiyil, S. (2017). Emergence of new disciplines. *Edutracks*, *7*(4), 20–22.

Australian Curriculum. (2021). *Curriculum connections*. www.australiancurriculum.edu. au/resources/curriculum-connections/

Beames, S., Atencio, M., & Ross, H. (2009). Taking excellence outdoors. *Scottish Educational Review*, *41*(2), 32–45.

Beames, S., & Brown, M. (2016). *Adventurous learning: A pedagogy for a changing world*. Abingdon: Routledge.

Beames, S., & Pollack, N. (2019). *School inspection reports and the status of outdoor learning, residential experiences and adventurous activities in Scottish schools*. https://beam-ingsimon.files.wordpress.com/2019/06/carnegie-report_web.pdf

Bell, S., Hamilton, V., Montarzino, A., Rothnie, H., Travlou, P., & Alves, S. (2008). *Greenspace and quality of life: A critical literature review*. Stirling: Greenspace Scotland.

Bentsen, P., Mygind, E., & Randrup, T. (2009). Towards an understanding of *udeskole*: Education outside the classroom in a Danish context. *Education 3–13*, *37*(1), 29–44.

Bird, W. (2007). *Natural thinking*. www.rspb.org.uk/Images/naturalthinking_tcm9-161856.pdf

Blair, D. (2009). The child in the garden: An evaluative review of the benefits of school gardening. *Journal of Environmental Education*, *40*(2), 15–38.

Bloomfield, D. (2017). What makes nature-based interventions for mental health successful? *BJPsych International*, *14*(4), 82–85.

Boix Mansilla, V., Miller, W. C., & Gardner, H. (2000). On disciplinary lenses and interdisciplinary work. In S. Wineburg & P. Grossman (Eds.), *Interdisciplinary curriculum: Challenges of implementation*. New York: Teachers College Press.

Chettiparamb, A. (2007). Interdisciplinarity: A literature review. *The Higher Education Academy*. www.heacademy.ac.uk/ourwork/networks/itlg

Christie, B., & Higgins, P. (2020). Educational outcomes of learning for sustainability: A brief review of literature. *Scottish Government*. www.gov.scot/publications/educational-outcomes-learning-sustainability-brief-review-literature/pages/3/

Dewey, J. (1973). Experience is pedagogical. In J. J. McDermott (Ed.), *The philosophy of John Dewey* (pp. 421–523). Chicago, IL: The University of Chicago Press.

Dieser, O., & Bogner, F. (2016). Young people's cognitive achievement as fostered by hands-on-centred environmental education. *Environmental Education Research*, *22*(7), 943–957. https://doi.org/10.1080/13504622.2015.1054265.

Diversify Your Narrative. (2021). *Our mission.* www.diversifyournarrative.com/our-work

Education Outside the Classroom. (2016). *EOTC guidelines.* https://eotc.tki.org.nz/EOTC-home/EOTC-Guidelines

Education Scotland. (2016). *Vision 2030+: Concluding report of the learning for sustainability national implementation group.* Education Scotland. https://education.gov.scot/improvement/documents/res1-vision-2030.pdf

Education Scotland. (2021). *Curriculum for excellence.* https://education.gov.scot/education-scotland/scottish-education-system/policy-for-scottish-education/policy-drivers/cfe-building-from-the-statement-appendix-incl-btc1–5/what-is-curriculum-for-excellence/

Education Scotland. (2022). *Scotland's curriculum for excellence.* https://scotlandscurriculum.scot/

Eisner, E. (1985). The three curricula that all schools teach. In E. Eisner (Ed.), *The educational imagination* (pp. 87–108). New York: Macmillan.

Fjørtoft, I. (2004). Landscape as playscape: The effects of natural environments on children's play and motor development. *Children, Youth and Environments, 14*(2), 21–44.

Freire, P. (1996). *Pedagogy of the oppressed* (M. Bergman Ramos, Trans.). New York: Continuum. (Original work published 1968)

Gardner, H. (1993). *Frames of mind: The theory of multiple intelligences* (2nd ed.). London: Fontana.

Gascon, M., Mas, M. T., Martínez, D., Dadvand, P., Forns, J., Plasència, A., & Nieuwenhuijsen, M. J. (2015). Mental health benefits of long-term exposure to residential green and blue spaces: A systematic review. *International Journal of Environmental Research and Public Health, 12*(4), 4354–4379.

Gatto, J. T. (1992). *Dumbing us down: The hidden curriculum of compulsory schooling.* Gabriola Island, BC: New Society.

Gibson, J. (2015). *The ecological approach to visual perception.* New York: Psychology Press. (Original work published 1979)

Giroux, H., & Penna, A. (1983). Social education in the classroom: The dynamics of the hidden curriculum. In H. Giroux & D. Purpel (Eds.), *The hidden curriculum and moral education: Deception or discovery?* (pp. 100–121). Berkeley, CA: McCutchan.

Goddard Blythe, S. (2004). *The well balanced child: Movement and early learning.* Stroud: Hawthorn Press.

Gurholt, K. P., & Haukeland, P. I. (2020). Scandinavian *friluftsliv* (outdoor life) and the Nordic model: Passions and paradoxes. In M. B. Tin, F. Telseth, J. O. Tangen, & R. Giulianotti (Eds.), *The Nordic model physical and culture* (pp. 165–181). New York: Routledge.

Hamilton, J. (2018). *Outdoor learning: Closing the attainment gap in primary schoolchildren in Scotland.* Forestry Commission, 12pp.

Hartig, T., Mitchell, R., de Vries, S., & Frumkin, H. (2014). Nature and health. *Annual Review of Public Health, 35*(1), 207–228.

Higgins, P. (2019). Knocking on doors in the policy corridor—can research in outdoor studies contribute to policy change? A professional narrative on shaping educational policy and practice in Scotland. In B. Humberstone & H. Prince (Eds.), *Research methods in outdoor studies* (pp. 329–341). London: Routledge.

Higgins, P., & Nicol, R. (2018). Outdoor learning. In T. Bryce, W. Humes, D. Gillies, & A. Kennedy (Eds.), *Scottish education* (pp. 538–544). Edinburgh: Edinburgh University Press.

Higgins, P., Thompson, D., & Rawcliffe, P. (2018). Learning outside the classroom boosts educational attainment. *Scottish Natural Heritage Science Newsletter, 23*, 7–9.

Jeffs, T., & Smith, M. K. (2005). *Informal education. Conversation, democracy and learning.* Ticknall: Education Now.

Kuo, M., Barnes, M., & Jordan, C. (2019). Do experiences with nature promote learning? Converging evidence of a cause-and-effect relationship. *Frontiers in Psychology*, *10*, 305.

Kuo, M., Browning, M., & Penner, M. (2018). Do lessons in nature boost subsequent classroom engagement? Refueling students in flight. *Frontiers in Psychology*, *8*, 22–53.

Lackey, N. Q., Tysor, D. A., Mcnay, G. D., Joyner, L., Baker, H., & Hodge, C. (2019). Mental health benefits of nature-based recreation: A systematic review. *Annals of Leisure Research*, *24*, 379–393. https://doi.org/10.1080/11745398.2019.1655459

Learning and Teaching Scotland. (2010). *Curriculum for excellence through outdoor learning*. Glasgow: Author.

MacQuarrie, S., & Nugent, C. (2017). Considering children's opportunities for exploration of their local environment and engagement with nature. In T. Waller, E. Ärlemalm-Hagsér, E. B. H. Sandseter, L. Lee-Hammond, K. Lekies, & S. Wyver (Eds.), *The SAGE handbook of outdoor play and learning* (pp. 229–241). Thousand Oaks, CA: SAGE.

Mannion, G., Doyle, L., Sankey, K., Mattu, L., & Wilson, M. (2007). *Young people's interaction with natural heritage through outdoor learning*. Perth: Scottish Natural Heritage.

Martin, L., White, M. P., Hunt, A., Richardson, M., Pahl, S., & Burt, J. (2020). Nature contact, nature connectedness and associations with health, wellbeing and pro-environmental behaviours. *Journal of Environmental Psychology*, *68*, 101389. https://doi.org/10.1016/j.jenvp.2020.101389

Ministry of Education. (2021). *Character and citizenship education*. www.moe.gov.sg/-/media/files/secondary/syllabuses/cce/2021-character-and-citizenship-education-syllabus-secondary.pdf?la=en&hash=D41C87D627D3AA6CF52C14538121EA5E1B9E0B44

Muñoz, S. A. (2009). *Children in the outdoors: A literature review*. Forres: Sustainable Development Research Centre.

National Curriculum. (2013). *National curriculum in England: Physical education programmes of study*. www.gov.uk/government/publications/national-curriculum-in-england-physical-education-programmes-of-study/national-curriculum-in-england-physical-education-programmes-of-study#key-stage-4

National Improvement Hub. (n.d.). *A summary of outdoor learning resources*. https://education.gov.scot/improvement/learning-resources/a-summary-of-outdoor-learning-resources/

New Zealand Ministry of Education. (2007). *New Zealand curriculum for English-medium teaching and learning in years 1–13*. Wellington: Ministry of Education.

OECD. (2021). *Scotland's curriculum for excellence: Into the future. Implementing education policies*. Paris: OECD. https://doi.org/10.1787/bf624417-en

Otte, C., Bølling, M., Stevenson, M., Ejbye-Ernst, N., Nielsen, G., & Bentsen, P. (2019). Education outside the classroom increases children's reading performance: Results from a one-year quasi-experimental study. *International Journal of Educational Research*, *94*, 42–51. https://doi.org/10.1016/j.ijer.2019.01.009

Robertson, J. (2014). *Dirty teaching: A beginner's guide to learning outdoors*. Carmarthen: The Independent Thinking Press.

Smith, M. (2000). *What is curriculum? Exploring theory and practice*. https://infed.org/curriculum-theory-and-practice/

Ulrich, R. (1983). Aesthetic and affective response to natural environment. In I. Altman & J. Wohlwill (Eds.), *Human behaviour and environment* (Vol. 6, pp. 85–125). New York: Plenum.

Victorian Curriculum and Assessment Authority. (2016). *VCE outdoor and environmental Studies*. www.vcaa.vic.edu.au/Documents/vce/outdoor/2018OutdoorEnviroStdsSD.pdf

Völker, S., & Kistemann, T. (2011). The impact of blue space on human health and well-being—salutogenetic health effects of inland surface waters: A review. *International Journal of Hygiene and Environmental Health*, *214*(6), 449–460.

Waite, S. (2017). *Children learning outside the classroom: From birth to eleven*. London: SAGE.

White, M. P., Alcock, I., Grellier, J., Wheeler, B. W., Hartig, T., Warber, S. L., . . . & Fleming, L. E. (2019). Spending at least 120 minutes a week in nature is associated with good health and wellbeing. *Scientific Reports*, *9*(1), 1–11.

# 4 Outdoor learning and sustainability

**Chapter aims**

● Understand the concepts of "sustainability" and "sustainable development", the implication that all life on Earth is interdependent and inextricably linked to the Earth's physical and biological systems, and that individual and societal wellbeing is dependent on these.

● Recognize the relationship between sustainability and international and intergenerational environmental and social justice.

● Understand how the closely related concepts, "outdoor environmental education", "education for sustainable development", and "learning for sustainability" can help learners understand and appreciate the significance of "sustainability".

● Encourage awareness of the impact of our actions, and foster a values-oriented approach to personal environmental decisions relating to nature and society—both locally and globally.

● Outline a range of principles and approaches that can help in planning integrated environmental and sustainable development education lessons both inside and outside the classroom.

## Sustainability and sustainable development

The term "education for sustainable development" (ESD) will be familiar to many, while "learning for sustainability" (LfS) may be less so. Both share the premise that education can support learners as we (hopefully) move towards "sustainable" futures. Yet both differ over the terminology employed, so what do the terms "sustainability", and "sustainable development" mean?

DOI: 10.4324/9781003010890-4

The concept of "sustainability" draws in part on ecological principles relating to the long-term stability of relationships between organisms and both their immediate and global environment (biological, chemical, physical, and geological). As a guiding concept, it implies that our future depends on the stability of our relationship with the whole environment, and that the impact of our activities must not exceed the capacity of planetary processes to absorb, repair, and restore. This requirement must be met over the short-, medium-, and long-term to avoid irreversibly exceeding planetary boundaries (Rockström et al., 2009; Ripple et al., 2019) and destabilizing planetary systems, which will result in catastrophic impacts on life on Earth. It is obvious that our impacts on the planet's climate, biodiversity, and peoples are profound and accelerating—driven and exacerbated by a range of socioeconomic factors, such as population growth, global capitalism and increased consumption, and this has led authors to argue that we are in a new geological epoch: The Anthropocene (Steffen et al., 2011).

While there are limits to resources and hence to growth, the understandable aspiration that all communities will benefit from improvements in health, standards of living, and so on, leads to continued depletion of resources and places enormous pressures on ecosystems. This need to balance "development" with "sustainability" gave rise to the notion of "sustainable development" (SD). This is arguably one of the most significant concepts of our time, as in the long-term at least, our survival as part of a global community of all species *must*, by definition, become sustainable.

Although "sustainable development" is vague and commonly misunderstood or misconstrued, its original underlying fundamental premise was to balance the needs of society and economy with the protection of the environment. While there continues to be much debate about terminology and the contradictory nature of sustainable development (see Salas-Zapata & Ortiz-Muñoz, 2019), the discussions illustrate both the difficulty societies face (and in turn their education systems experience) in embracing the concept, and the central importance of sustained critical analysis of the term.

The origins of the concept can be traced back to work done in the 1980s by the International Union for the Conservation of Nature (IUCN, 1980) and its "World Conservation Strategy". Eventually, the World Commission on Environment and Development (1987) agreed on a working definition of sustainable development—"development that meets the needs of the present without compromising the ability of future generations to meet their own needs" (p. 43). That this definition is still widely used owes much to its clarity and human-centred message. However, it is also widely critiqued due to its anthropocentric focus, and because terms such as "development", "generations", and "needs" are open to interpretation and feel at odds with the degrowth and limits to growth approach that is needed (Selby, 2015), if some form of meaningful global sustainability is to be achieved.

Growing concern about human impact on the environment in general, and in turn, the impact on human communities (especially in areas vulnerable to climate change), led to the 1992 UN Conference on Environment and Development (UNCED) in Rio de Janeiro, Brazil (often called the "Earth Summit"). The ensuing report, Agenda 21 (commonly referred to as "The Rio Accord") (UNCED, 1992) was important for several reasons. By this time, climate change had become a major concern to many governments and individuals, and the conference was the first attempt by the international community to develop a universal, wide-ranging plan to address human impact on the planet. The report also emphasized the role of education, both throughout the document and in a dedicated chapter.

In the past 30 years or so, the scientific evidence has become ever clearer, with a series of reports from United Nations organizations such as the Intergovernmental Panel on Climate Change (IPCC) (n.d) and the Convention on Biological Diversity (CBD) (n.d) and others, which emphasize both the scale of our impacts and the increasing rate of change.

Many major international conferences have continued to highlight the issues, with perhaps the most significant being the 2015 United Nations Climate Change Conference (COP 21) in Paris. The goal of the resulting "Paris Agreement", a legally binding international treaty on climate change, agreed by the 196 countries participating, was to reduce global carbon output "as soon as possible" (UNCCC, 2015, para 3) and "to limit global warming to well below 2°C, preferably to 1.5 degrees Celsius, compared to pre-industrial levels" (para 2). Despite continuing and increasingly strident warnings from the IPCC (2021, 2022) it is clear that the Paris agreement is unlikely to be kept; with estimates suggesting current national commitments will lead to at least 2.4°C rise by the end of the century (see Masood & Tollefson, 2021; IPCC, 2022).

The already significant impacts of the current global temperature rise (~1.1°C since pre-industrial times) are predicted to be devastating if we exceed 2°C (IPCC, 2021, 2022). Further, the *combined* impacts of global heating and destruction of biodiversity are already having predicted impacts on the planet's "support systems" (Ripple et al., 2017, 2019). In essence, global heating is destroying biodiversity, and similarly the destruction of biodiversity is accelerating climate change.

However, the corollary is that the positive impacts of biodiversity, and in particular natural carbon sinks, such as forests, peatlands, wetlands, estuarine areas, and oceans (through their chemical, biological, and physical properties), in stabilizing the climate have become increasingly recognized. Indeed, many leading scientists (e.g., Ripple et al., 2020; Strassburg, Iribarrem, & Beyer, 2020) and commentators (e.g., David Attenborough, Greta Thunberg) argue that "nature-based climate solutions" and "rewilding" represent the only viable way of doing so. While such appeals are focused on national and international policy makers, the social media response and increased public awareness of such pressing global issues presents an important opportunity (and perhaps a duty) for educators to respond—to re-vision and re-focus aspects of their work accordingly.

The foregoing discussion has, because of its fundamental significance, focussed on the environmental dimensions of sustainable development. More recently, however, the broader social and economic context has gained considerable importance. The most recent and significant manifestation of this is through the United Nations *Sustainable Development Goals* (SDGs) (2015a) for the period 2015–2030. The 17 interlinked goals are a call to action by all countries and intended to be a "blueprint to achieve a better and more sustainable future for all". They signify directly the international community's broader and interrelated sustainability concerns—notably poverty, hunger, health, women's rights, and employment, as well as those with specific environmental imperatives, such as action to combat global climate change, and to conserve terrestrial and marine biodiversity and productivity. While education is considered to be a vital enabler of *all* the Goals, SDG 4 (Quality Education) seeks to "Ensure inclusive and equitable quality education and promote lifelong learning opportunities for all" (United Nations, 2015b, para 1). It also has a specific focus (SDG 4.7) to:

> ensure all learners acquire the knowledge and skills needed to promote sustainable development, including, among others, through education for sustainable development and sustainable lifestyles, human rights, gender equality, promotion of a culture of peace and non-violence, global citizenship and appreciation of cultural diversity and of culture's contribution to sustainable development.
> (United Nations, 2015b, para 8)

This again is a manifestation of that much broader view of sustainable development, and the role of education in achieving it.

## Education, environment and sustainability

As far back as the "Earth Summit" in 1992, there was agreement that "education should deal with the dynamics of both the physical, biological and socioeconomic environment and human (which may include spiritual) development . . . and should employ formal and non-formal methods" (UNCED, 1992, p. 221). This was essentially a call for learners to study the environment (i.e. environmental education) in the belief that such knowledge would lead to positive attitudes towards the environment and behavioural change in support of its conservation and protection. This was the focus of several further high-level conferences in the 1970s, leading to the 1977 Intergovernmental Conference on Environmental Education in Tbilisi, which made emphatic recommendations to governments on the key role of environmental education in sustaining our global environment, and published principles and guidelines for doing so.

Since then, there has been ever greater expectation that schools and other education providers embrace *education for sustainable development* (ESD) to support learners to both understand and encourage actions towards sustainable futures. In line with the broad concept of sustainable development and reflecting the approach of SDG 4, the most recent definition of ESD from the United Nations Educational, Scientific and Cultural Organization (UNESCO, 2021) focuses on self and society:

> Education for Sustainable Development (ESD) empowers learners with knowledge, skills, values and attitudes to take informed decisions and make responsible actions for environmental integrity, economic viability and a just society.
>
> Education for Sustainable Development is a lifelong learning process and an integral part of quality education. It enhances the cognitive, social and emotional and behavioral dimensions of learning. It is holistic and transformational, and encompasses learning content and outcomes, pedagogy and the learning environment itself.
>
> (UNESCO, 2021, paras 1 & 2)

While this broad focus is to be welcomed, it does represent a distinct shift from the earlier focus on the environment, potentially implicitly reducing emphasis on learning opportunities in nature. A Scottish education policy approach, *Learning for Sustainability* (LfS) seeks to redress this by including outdoor learning with a focus on sensitizing experiences in nature. As noted in Chapter 3, the evidence base for this approach was established in the early stages of policy development in 2012 and continues to be re-enforced by further Scottish and international research (Higgins & Christie, 2018; Christie & Higgins, 2020). Consequently, learning for sustainability brings together a traditional emphasis on ESD and global citizenship education with outdoor learning, and is defined as:

> a whole school approach that enables the school and its wider community to build the values, attitudes, knowledge, skills and confidence needed to develop practices and take decisions which are compatible with a sustainable and more equitable future.
>
> (Scottish Government, 2012, p. 8)

Learning for Sustainability was linked explicitly with the SDGs in 2016 (Education Scotland, 2016) and is now built into the structure of the Scottish national curriculum, becoming both an entitlement of all learners and a responsibility of all teachers and education professionals (Education Scotland, 2016). It has recently become a feature of the school quality inspection framework and is gradually being incorporated into the curriculum for school and college qualifications.

While these international and local developments are politically and structurally important, the specific role of outdoor learning warrants further consideration. An overarching term, "*outdoor environmental and sustainability education*" allows broad discussion of the rationale for outdoor learning, and its significance in both content (curriculum) and approaches (pedagogy) to sustainable development.

# Outdoor environmental and sustainability education

Through our evolutionary history, humans have depended on our knowledge of the natural world, its resources, and phenomena to survive and thrive. Consequently, learning how to live well outdoors, through (no doubt, primarily guided) experience, was an imperative—an early form of "outdoor environmental education". Such traditional ecological knowledge and skills, and related "educational" processes continue to be important in indigenous cultures in many parts of the world—from the high Arctic to the tropics. Whilst the roots of outdoor environmental education in "Western" cultures lie partly in "knowledge of the natural world", the formalization of such approaches, as detailed below (see also Higgins & Christie, 2020) became less related to "survival" than to broader concepts such as academic understanding of and care for the natural world, planetary cycles, and systems.

It is important to note that this, as with any such discussion, takes place in a particular cultural setting, which may be generalizable to others, but not all (see Chapter 2 on Worldviews). While this is particularly (and problematically) so of the terms "environment" and "nature", which are often viewed as entities, separate from ourselves as humans, they have both featured in educational content (curriculum) and both theoretical and practical approaches (pedagogy) through many decades, as "nature education", "field studies", "environmental education", etc. These approaches are evident in the delivery of both formally examined and other curricula in schools, through links with communities and related provisions (e.g., park services, countryside rangers), and in specialist residential environmental centres.

While such approaches "in" and "about" the environment are clearly vital for developing understanding, this rationalist approach has led to many educators (Ives et al., 2018; Pisters, Vihinen, & Figueiredo, 2019) to point out that it lacks the emotional/affective emphasis essential to support a caring and pro-active approach to sustainability. This emphasis was articulated by Geddes in the early 1900s in his evocation of education through "heart", "hand and head", which is elaborated by Higgins and Nicol (2011), and in Sobel's (2008), *Children and nature design principles*. Others have further argued that the outdoors is of central significance in providing opportunities, whereby all the elements of "sustainable development" can be meaningfully integrated into formal and informal education (e.g., Higgins & Christie, 2020).

From this basic introduction it will be clear that universally accepted definitions of sustainability and sustainable development are elusive and contested (see Selby, 2015 for more discussion). Similarly, educational approaches to "environmental and sustainability education" (both outdoors or indoors) have multiple purposes and pedagogies. Nonetheless, all have a coherent and generally uncontested purpose: Progress towards sustainable futures that accept the indivisibility of human survival and flourishing alongside the "'other than human" world

(Jickling & Sterling, 2017 and Chapter 2). Consequently, for the purposes of this discussion, we have adopted the concept that "sustainability" is more a direction of travel than a definition. This resonates with the approach outlined in the Earth Charter in 2000 (see Earth Charter, 2021), which aims to develop a "global society founded on respect for nature, universal human rights, economic justice, and a culture of peace" (para 1). This way, "environmental and sustainability education" and its variants can be viewed simply as education that aids us on our journey towards sustainability.

## Why is environmental and sustainability education important?

Developing an understanding of the global implications of our daily actions is conceptually challenging, and all the more so when extrapolated into a future that can only be predicted by scientific models, which are by their nature imprecise. Matters are further complicated by the influence of globalized economies, marketing, media, and politics—many facets of which inadvertently promote unsustainable behaviours (Kasser, Tricarico, Boyle, & Simms, 2020). This situation offers both challenges and opportunities for the teacher.

Many current national and international sustainable development policies rely on the concept of "societal choice". Although these choices are complex and often confusing, they must be considered in any debate on human responses to an environmental issue. Their importance, and the role that levels of awareness and education play in informing such choices, cannot be overstated when it comes to successfully implementing any policy (sustainability-focused or otherwise). Education occupies a delicate position in such contexts. While educators cannot and should not coerce their students to adopt certain behaviours, they do play a key role in helping young people develop informed values to allow them to make considered personal choices. Hence it can be (and has been) argued that we should not educate *for* sustainable development, and similarly that learning should not explicitly be *for* sustainability (e.g., Jickling, 1992). However, it is our view that on both pragmatic grounds (see IPCC and CBD reports) and philosophical grounds (e.g., it embodies the notion of social and environmental justice), that aspects of education must be *for* sustainable development. Indeed, the corollary—that education is *not* for sustainability—poses an even greater challenge to ethics.

Sterling (2001) takes the view that sustainable development is of such central significance that schools should orient their structures and curriculum to deal with it: An approach he calls "sustainable education". His argument is that, as most of current educational provision is instrumental (developing skills for an industrial/commercial society), it takes little account of the "increasing complexity, interdependence, and systems breakdown in the world" (p. 1). His work has led to calls for "transformational education", which requires understanding the "frames of reference in which educators are operating, being able to reflect on them while exploring new frames of reference, in which processes of deeper learning can evolve" (Odell, Molthan-Hill, Martin, Sterling, 2019, p. 11). These authors (and Sterling) argue that to achieve the SDGs, education institutions:

> must be bold with a strong future-facing vision that can shift current systems and values to not only prevent further deterioration and instability in ecological systems but shift us onto a path of regeneration and restoration to improve socio ecological resilience.
>
> (p. 10)

The evidence strongly suggests that this "systems breakdown" is occurring (see IPCC and CBD reports) and we are passing crucial planetary boundaries that define a safe operating space for human societies to survive and thrive (Rockström et al., 2009; Ripple et al., 2017). It should then be obvious that education for sustainable development is of crucial importance. While there are examples of efforts to transform national educational approaches to address sustainable development, like Finland's "Phenomenon-based Education" (Lähdemäki, 2018) and Scotland's "Learning for Sustainability" (Education Scotland, 2016), such efforts generally rely on individual educators working pragmatically and urgently within current educational structures. This work rests on helping students make personal decisions on the basis of a clear understanding of Earth systems and ecological principles, and with an ethic of social equity, inter*national* and inter and intra*generational* justice.

The question then becomes "why is *outdoor learning* important in education for sustainable development?" The most obvious reason is that it offers direct physical/sensory, intellectual, and affective ways of knowing the planet we depend upon for survival and developing our relationship with it. However, sustainability is a complex issue and much of both its conceptual difficulty and beauty lies in the relationships between parts of our planetary systems and the ways in which we interact with these. Capra (2007) argues that in order to conceptualize and move towards sustainable futures it is vital that we understand and respect complex systems (e.g. biogeochemical cycles). While outdoor learning cannot provide a complete understanding, it can play a vital part in developing knowledge of the broad interdependencies within the natural world. It can also nurture relationships young people will need to move towards a more sustainable future (see Taylor & Pacini-Ketchabaw, 2015).

Throughout our evolution and as we develop from birth, we have come to *know* the world through physical and sensory experiences. Although these "lived experiences" are fundamentally individual, they provide the basis of a common sensory understanding of our planet and an intellectual understanding of how it functions (Kollmuss & Agyeman, 2002; Chawla, 2020). Engaging with the natural world (outdoors) is central to this "knowing", as it involves building a *connection*, understanding the *consequences* of our actions and developing an ethic of *care* (see the

"Six Cs model" in Higgins & Christie, 2020). As Sobel (2008) notes, a bottom-up approach to sustainability involves direct experience and interaction: "Talking to trees and hiding in trees precedes saving trees" (p. 19), and he suggests, from his perspective, that as educators we should be interested "in figuring out how to cultivate relationships between children and trees in their own backyards" (p. 19). It is of course, not just about "trees"—as the cultivation of such kinship or relationship with the natural world will likely require diverse nuanced starting points across and within contexts, countries, and curriculums.

An *intellectual* understanding of the environment through "field studies" is a long-established outdoor learning tradition, certainly in the "Western" world, and continues to make an important contribution to education for sustainable development (Burt & Thompson, 2020). Being able to see a geophysical or biological process, develop an understanding of form and function, and then potentially collect and analyze data offers a means of understanding that process. Significantly, this is also important training in the scientific method. While not confined to the natural sciences, the scientific method is a unifying principle that helps us understand the world, and indeed, our capacity to modify and thrive in it. As our scientific knowledge has developed, it has brought many advances that benefit society (e.g., in medicine and technology) and, arguably, some that do not (e.g., nuclear and biological weapons).

In a similar way that a sense of wonder at the natural world does not solely rest on scientific understanding, embracing the inherent elegance and beauty in basic scientific laws and principles, as well as in the complexity of our planetary systems can be significant for learners. Some examples include: The importance of gathering and analyzing empirical evidence; what constitutes a "fair test" in an experiment; that "being wrong" is just part of working towards a better understanding; that science is about uncertainty, and while theories and models are about using good evidence towards making the best predictions these can't be expected to be "right". Without some understanding of these laws, principles, and complexities, we are at risk of failing to appreciate our complete dependence on and our intrinsic "one-ness" with our home planet. Furthermore, we are inclined to misjudge the consequences of both our own actions and important predictions, such as those relating to global climate disruption. It is also the scientific method that allows us to examine the quality of the science and, alongside critical reasoning, to interrogate and judge the ways in which politicians, corporations, the media, and the general public interpret (or misinterpret) the evidence for, and effectiveness of, our actions towards sustainable development.

One of the defining features of education for sustainable development is its *interdisciplinary* nature. While much can be learned from the careful examination of many individual facets of sustainability, complex interactions require specific attention to the "whole" as well as the "parts". For example, the feelings or emotions we experience, when thinking about the planet and our relationship with it, will influence our actions in relation to sustainable development. This *affective* appreciation of our planet largely depends on direct personal, aesthetic, and even spiritual experiences of it. While there are many ways in which such experiences can be enhanced or developed (through prose, poetry, art, music, and media etc.), the basis of such an appreciation must involve sensory experiences and these are richest in outdoor environments. Conceptualizing learning in this holistic and interdisciplinary way requires an educator to focus on the environmental and social *systems* that characterize sustainable development. So, for example, the study of plants and animals, and the relationships between them (e.g., food webs), has broader relevance when considering their role in the planetary flow of energy and cycling of nutrients. In turn, human impact on these systems has implications for global climate change, and then the consequences of such changes on, for example, water availability, agriculture, poverty, and social conflict). Such starting points offer limitless opportunities for integrated classroom and outdoor learning through a wide range of "ways of knowing" (see Chapter 6).

Whilst there is a growing body of evidence that early experiences are significant in developing an ethic of care for the environment (Chawla, 2020; Broom, 2017), modernized society is becoming more urbanized than ever before: resulting in many children experiencing limited informal exposure to the natural world (Chawla, 2020). Consequently, if young people are not experiencing the natural world independently or in the company of family or friends, the role of intentionally facilitated structured outdoor experiences become increasingly significant in developing care for the environment and sustainability more generally (Christie & Higgins, 2020).

## How can teachers incorporate education for sustainable development into their planning?

Sustainable development appears in parts of many curricula but is rarely a central focus. This happens despite it being a concept that, to be properly understood, demands an integrated, interdisciplinary approach. This requirement allows teachers to capitalize on the advantages of learning both inside and outside the classroom, with appropriate locations being chosen to enable the students' learning to be most effective. The following case study focuses on a volunteer-run charity that has worked to develop an area of "left-over" playing field land called "Bat's Wood", behind a local Secondary school in Scotland (young people aged 11–18). Bat's Wood is now a biodiverse wood, an orchard and permaculture area growing food for the local community and school to use, and also hosts a mountain bike track for all ages and abilities. The case study shares the way in which school pupils and Mr. Z, a school teacher, took an experiential, outdoor focused, holistic, and whole school and community approach to working with Bat's Wood to "work with" and learn from an integrated and interdisciplinary approach to sustainability.

## CASE STUDY: Bat's Wood

Mr. Z, a secondary school teacher believes that, "In the Climate Crisis, personal awareness isn't the issue; collective apathy is the issue", and was unwilling to see Learning for Sustainability fight for its place in the Personal & Social Education curriculum, alongside other topics such as road safety, domestic violence, and drug abuse. From long experience in teaching, Mr. Z knows how unethical it sounds to teach pupils that the environment will be *their* problem. This is why he loves LfS, which starts with whole school approaches *now*—not the personal choices of the next generation.

Mr. Z undertakes the task of promoting LfS in his school through an inquiry method that works with the "School Improvement Plan". This approach helps identify a relevant approach that remains true to the "whole school" dimension of LfS and yet works realistically within the constraints of being a classroom teacher. The school identified the need to increase its capacity in Pupil Support, and so Mr. Z, supported by insights from a Masters degree in Learning for Sustainability, convinced management to allocate time for the "sustainable development" of an outdoor learning environment for alternative curriculum provision. Through community engagement, he established a charity to that end and led the campaign as an activist/teacher.

This strategy addressed an issue common to many campuses: The lack of coherence across subject disciplines and difficulty in teaching the value of biodiversity on a grass and concrete campus that discourages biodiversity! As one pupil said, "before we started, there wasn't any nature to respect here". By addressing the sustainable development of a meaningful outdoor learning environment while providing alternative support for pupils, he harnessed the bold, future facing philosophy behind LfS. In building LfS into academic and other awards (e.g., John Muir Awards, Personal Development Awards: Skills for Work and National 4 Rural Skills), Mr. Z is able to offer alternative curriculum provision *for* sustainability.

Mr. Z's pupils are creating an outdoor learning environment which the whole school uses and experiences. Students can now experience deep engagement with the natural world and gain understanding of sustainability through their own special place on campus, and through an alternative curriculum relate better to school, and perhaps like it a little more. The engagement and learning results from building the future outdoor learning environment they want to see. By constantly restoring and enhancing campus ecosystem services, they are leaving behind the barren monoculture of grass mown short 18 times per year. They have planted and now maintain a wood of 9000 trees, an orchard of 200 trees and various ecological and horticultural projects; and they explore opportunities for place-based education by community placemaking and environmental action for regeneration.

By teaching and learning *in, through, about, and for* sustainable development, pupils and teachers see the critical thinking behind environmental action for biodiversity and regeneration. "Planting seeds, plants seeds", Mr. Z says, now "the whole school is experiencing a sustainable development".

Although this case study may seem simply a pragmatic way of engaging learners in issues of biodiversity and sustainability, depending on the age and stage of their students, teachers may consider stimulating them to ask why, if these fundamental processes and related issues are so important, they are not a dominant feature of educational and governmental policy. This "critical reasoning" is what takes the issue into the sort of values discussion that is essential if we are to help students envision and work towards a sustainable future.

Sustainable development is clearly the most pressing and the most problematic of contemporary issues, and according to expert opinion, will have to be addressed on a timescale of the next five to 20 years. As is evident from youth climate activism, such a task weighs heavily on the shoulders of young people, and as Tremmel, Page, and Ott (2009) remind us, "Each generation has the duty not to engage in the wishful thinking that the problem can be left for descendants to solve" (p. 87).

Progress towards sustainable development is problematic as it requires major changes in the policies of governments and in our daily personal decisions. Consequently, students need to develop the critical thinking skills necessary to challenge themselves, their politicians, and others with influence, over what is and what is not valued and promoted within society. This approach is supported by UNESCO's (2017) "Key Competencies" in education for sustainable development, which focus on empowering "individuals to reflect on their own actions, taking into account their current and future social, cultural, economic and environmental impacts, from a local and a global perspective" (p. 7). They suggest eight competencies (UNESCO, 2017, p. 10), framed in three areas which are central to a transformational learning experience:

*Ways of Thinking*: Systems thinking, Future thinking, Critical thinking.

*Ways of Practicing:* Strategic competency, Collaboration competency, Integrated problem-solving competency.

*Ways of Being*: Self-awareness, Normative Competency.

To help students develop these skills, teachers need first to ensure that the selection of skills and the depth to which they are pursued are age and stage appropriate. They can then capitalize on the curricular relevance of the subject matter and take advantage of learning both inside and outside the classroom. The processes of building partnerships and participating in decision-making will require carefully constructed learning opportunities in the school (e.g., through an energy-saving campaign) and outside (e.g., negotiating locally with a landowner to plant trees, or engaging in national or international social justice project). The strength of this approach lies in choosing locations that afford experiences for students to help them find meaning and personal relevance, and in developing the interdisciplinary understanding and skills necessary to address the issue of sustainable development.

## Guidelines

- All species on Earth, including our own, are inescapably dependent on and are a part of global geophysical and ecological systems, and all our futures depend on the balance in these systems being maintained. If we significantly harm these systems, we harm our own species too, and educators must make developing such understanding a priority in their work.

- Education for sustainable development is ideally suited to an integrated mixture of indoor and outdoor interdisciplinary learning experiences close to the school environment.

- Outdoor learning has a key role in educating young people *about* our planet (environmental education) and *for* sustainable development.

- Carefully designed and delivered direct, multisensory outdoor learning experiences can encourage the development of a strong affective relationship with the natural world, and help young people understand the local, international and inter and intragenerational consequences of their actions. In some cases, this may well predispose the student to take action "for" the environment.

## References

Broom, C. (2017). Exploring the relations between childhood experiences in nature and young adults' environmental attitudes and behaviours. *Australian Journal of Environmental Education, 33*(1), 34–47.

Burt, T., & Thompson, D. (2020). *Curious about nature: A passion for fieldwork.* Cambridge: Cambridge University Press, 412pp.

Capra, F. (2007). Sustainable living, ecological literacy, and the breath of Life. *Canadian Journal of Environmental Education, 12,* 9–18.

Chawla, L. (2020). Childhood nature connection and constructive hope: A review of research on connecting with nature and coping with environmental loss. *People and Nature, 12*(3), 619–642.

Christie, B., & Higgins, P. (2020). Educational outcomes of learning for sustainability: A brief review of literature. *Scottish Government.* www.gov.scot/publications/educational-outcomes-learning-sustainability-brief-review-literature/pages/3/

Convention on Biological Diversity (CBD). (n.d.). *Various reports.* www.cbd.int/

Earth Charter. (2021). *Preamble.* https://earthcharter.org/read-the-earth-charter/preamble/

Education Scotland. (2016). *Vision 2030+: Concluding report of the learning for sustainability national implementation group.* https://education.gov.scot/improvement/documents/res1-vision-2030.pdf

Higgins, P., & Christie, B. (2018). Learning for sustainability. In T. G. K. Bryce, W. M. Humes, D. Gillies, & A. Kennedy (Eds.), *Scottish education* (5th ed., pp. 554–564). Edinburgh: Edinburgh University Press.

Higgins, P., & Christie, B. (2020). Environmental and sustainability education. In *Encyclopaedia of teacher education.* Springer. https://doi.org/10.1007/978-981-13-1179-6_356-2

Higgins, P., & Nicol, R. (2011). Professor Sir Patrick Geddes: "*Vivendo Discimus*"—by living we learn. In C. Knapp & T. Smith (Eds.), *A sourcebook for experiential education: Key thinkers and their contributions* (pp. 32–40). New York: Routledge.

Intergovernmental Conference on Environmental Education. (1977). *Tiblisi declaration.* www.gdrc.org/uem/ee/tbilisi.html

Intergovernmental Panel on Climate Change. (2021). *Climate change 2021—The physical science basis. Summary for policymakers.* www.ipcc.ch/report/ar6/wg1/downloads/report/IPCC_AR6_WGI_SPM_final.pdf

Intergovernmental Panel on Climate Change. (2022). *Climate change 2022: Impacts, adaptation and vulnerability, the Working Group II contribution to the sixth assessment report. Summary for policymakers.* www.unep.org/resources/report/climate-change-2022-impacts-adaptation-and-vulnerability-working-group-ii

Intergovernmental Panel on Climate Change (IPCC). (n.d.). *Various reports.* www.ipcc.ch/

International Union for the Conservation of Nature. (1980). *World conservation strategy.* https://portals.iucn.org/library/efiles/documents/wcs-004.pdf

Ives, C., Abson, D., van Wehrden, H., Darninger, C., Klaniecki, K., & Fischer, J. (2018). Reconnecting with nature for sustainability. *Sustainability Science, 13,* 1389–1394.

Jickling, B. (1992). Why I don't want my children to be educated for sustainable development. *Journal of Environmental Education, 23*(4), 4–8.

Jickling, B., & Sterling, S. (2017). *Post-sustainability and environmental education: Remaking education for the future.* New York: Pivot Palgrave.

Kasser, T., Tricarico, E., Boyle, D., & Simms, A. (2020). *Advertising's role in ecological degradation.* http://creativecommons.org/licenses/by-nc-nd/2.0/uk/

Kollmuss, A., & Agyeman, J. (2002). Mind the gap: Why do people act environmentally and what are the barriers to pro-environmental behavior? *Journal of Environmental Education Research, 8,* 239–260.

Lähdemäki, J. (2018). Case study: The Finnish National Curriculum 2016—a co-created national education policy. In J. Cook (Ed.), *Sustainability, human well-being & the future of education* (pp. 397–422). New York: Palgrave Macmillan.

Masood, E., & Tollefson, J. (2021). 'COP26 hasn't solved the problem': Scientists react to UN climate deal. *Nature, 599,* 355–356. https://doi.org/10.1038/d41586-021-03431-4

Odell, V., Molthan-Hill, P., Martin, S., & Sterling, S. (2019). Transformative education to address all sustainable development goals. In W. Leal Filho, et al. (Eds.), *Quality education, encyclopedia of the UN sustainable development goals.* https://doi.org/10.1007/978-3-319-69902-8_106-1

Pisters, S., Vihinen, H., & Figueiredo, E. (2019). Place based transformative learning: A framework to explore consciousness in sustainability initiatives. *Emotion, Space and Society, 34*(8). https://doi.org/10.1016/j.emospa.2019.04.007

Ripple, W., Wolf, C., Newsome, T., Barnard, P., & Moomaw, W. (2019). World scientists' warning of a climate emergency. *BioScience,* biz088. https://doi.org/10.1093/biosci/biz088

Ripple, W., Wolf, C., Newsome, T., Barnard, P., Moomaw, B., Maas, B., & Law, B. (2020). The climate emergency, forests, and transformative change. *BioScience,* biaa032. https://doi.org/10.1093/biosci/biaa032

Ripple, W., Wolf, C., Newsome, T., Galetti, M., Alamgir, M., Crist, E., . . ., & 15,364 Scientist Signatories from 184 Countries. (2017). World scientists' warning to humanity: A second notice. *BioScience, 67*(12), 1026–1028.

Rockström, J., Steffen, W., Noone, K., Persson, Å., Chapin, F., Lambin, E., . . . & Foley. J. (2009). Planetary boundaries: Exploring the safe operating space for humanity. *Ecology and Society, 14*(2), 32. www.ecologyandsociety.org/vol14/iss2/art32/

Salas-Zapata, W. A., & Ortiz-Muñoz, S. M. (2019). Analysis of meanings of the concept of sustainability. *Sustainable Development, 27*, 153–161.

Scottish Government. (2012). *Learning for sustainability—report of the one planet schools ministerial advisory group.* www.gov.scot/Topics/Education/Schools/curriculum/ACE/OnePlanetSchools/LearningforSustainabilitReport

Selby, D. (2015). Thoughts from a darkened corner: Transformative learning in gathering storm. In D. Selby & F. Kagawa (Eds.), *Sustainability frontiers* (pp. 21.41). Toronto, ON: Barbara Budrich.

Sobel, D. (2008). *Nature and children: Design principles for educators.* Portland, ME: Stenhouse.

Steffen, W., Persson, Å., Deutsch, L., Zalasiewicz, J., Williams, M., Richardson, K., . . . & Svedin, U. (2011). The Anthropocene: From global change to planetary stewardship. *AMBIO, 40*(7), 739.

Sterling, S. (2001). *Sustainable Education—Re-visioning learning and change* (Schumacher Briefing no. 6). Dartington: Schumacher Society/Green Books.

Strassburg, B., Iribarrem, A., Beyer, H., Cordeiro, C. L., Crouzeilles, R., Jakovac, C. C. . . . & Visconti, P. (2020). Global priority areas for ecosystem restoration. *Nature, 586*, 724–729.

Taylor, A., & Pacini-Ketchabaw, V. (2015). Learning with children, ants, and worms in the Anthropocene: Towards a common world pedagogy of multispecies vulnerability. *Pedagogy, Culture & Society, 23*(4), 507–529.

Tremmel, J., Page, E., & Ott, K. (2009). Editorial. *Intergenerational Justice Review, 3*, 87.

United Nations. (2015a). *Sustainable development goals.* https://sustainabledevelopment.un.org/?menu=1300

United Nations. (2015b). *Sustainable development goals.* https://sdgs.un.org/goals/goal4

United Nations Climate Change Conference (COP 21). (2015). *The Paris agreement.* https://unfccc.int/process-and-meetings/the-paris-agreement/the-paris-agreement

United Nations Conference on Environment and Development. (1992). *Agenda 21.* https://sustainabledevelopment.un.org/milestones/unced

United Nations Educational, Scientific and Cultural Organization. (2017). *Education for sustainable development goals: Learning objectives.* https://unesdoc.unesco.org/ark:/48223/pf0000247444

United Nations Educational, Scientific and Cultural Organization. (2021). *What is education for sustainable development?* https://en.unesco.org/themes/education-sustainable-development/what-is-esd

World Commission on Environment and Development. (1987). *Our common future: Report of the world commission on environment and development* (The Brundtland report). United Nations. www.un-documents.net/our-common-future.pdf

# 5 | Learning through places

## Chapter aims

● Understand how students can learn about places through a variety of ways of interacting with them.

● Introduce some foundational literature underpinning place-responsive pedagogies.

● Recognize that all physical landscapes have a "story", that this story can be sociocultural or ecological, and that together, these can offer a holistic, cross-curricular way of learning outdoors.

● Explore how students can learn more about their places, but also come to transform and improve them.

## What does "learning through place" mean?

Place-Responsive Education (PRE) aims to respond to the social and ecological challenges faced by individuals and communities in specific locations around the world (Wattchow & Brown, 2011). This approach to teaching and learning aims to "ground learning in local phenomena and students' own lived experience" (Smith, 2002, p. 586). Over the last 25 years, PRE (aka Place-Based Education) has almost become a "given" in the world of outdoor learning. Indeed, any outdoor educator who has read a little about the field would know that they are open to critique if their teaching is not connected to the places in which it is located. As place-responsive teaching practices have become more common and more varied, there is an argument to more deeply understand what PRE is, what its origins and limits are, and what its pedagogical possibilities are for teachers in the 2020s.

Outdoor learning critics have long highlighted how some "traditional" outdoor education programmes focus predominantly on developing intra and interpersonal growth, through taking part in thrilling activities, that may largely ignore the "host" land and seascape (Nicol, 2002). There is a notable shift away from outdoor programmes that focus solely on elements of personal growth towards programmes that deliberately explore how people and places are mutually influenced by each other (Mannion & Lynch, 2016).

Brookes' (2002) stinging critique of programmes that treat landscapes "as empty sites on which to establish social or psychological projects" (p. 405) is as relevant today as it was when he wrote those words. So, too, is Baker's (2005) challenge for outdoor educators to root the contents of their programmes in the place in which they are actually based. To make her point, she identifies the sorts of programmes where participants end up developing no real personal connection to the place in which they are located, to the point that they could be anywhere—or, as she calls it: "Any Woods USA".

## Key ideas within place-responsive education

The following presents some key ideas which will ground our discussion about PRE. First, PRE can take place anywhere from busy urban centres to wild and remote locations, and everything in between. Second, it can consider the past (e.g., from distant to recent history), the present (current uses of spaces), and the future (e.g., what places might look like). We believe that social and environmental injustices can be exposed through critically examining past and present uses of space. It follows that we believe these injustices can be addressed in a way that positively shapes the future of our shared places.

The third key idea is that place can be used to teach across the curriculum. All landscapes are cross-curricular (Smith, 2002; Wattchow & Brown, 2011) and offer educators opportunities to teach science, languages, geography, history, mathematics, the arts, and so on (see chapter 3). This re-emphasizes a point that is foundational to this book: Outdoor learning has to do with how particular educational content is taught and learned.

Fourth, we refer to Mannion, Fenwick, Nugent and L'Anson's (2011) model that helps distinguish between education that is place-responsive and education that is not. The first is called *place ambivalent*, because it completely ignores place. An example of this would be an English teacher holding her poetry lesson—which has nothing to do with the place in which the lesson is physically located—outdoors, just because, for example, the sun is shining. A *place sensitive* poetry lesson might respond to local phenomena in general ways (e.g., the birch trees in the vicinity or the robins that fly by). *Place essential* poetry, however, would draw directly on the specific historical, environmental, cultural events that have defined that place and would almost certainly have required the poet to have first-hand experience of it.

It may be helpful to consider Mannion et al.'s (2011) work on a spectrum with place-ambivalent practice at one end and place-essential practice at the other, with degrees of place-sensitivity in between.

Place-ambivalent ←————————————————→ Place-essential

**Figure 5.1** Adapted from Mannion et al. (2011).

The above spectrum can be used to help teachers and programme planners have more meaningful discussions about how place-responsive their classes actually are. For example, one can ask, "Where on this spectrum would you place the session that you ran yesterday?" or "How could you make your next session a little more place sensitive or even place-essential?" Of course, educators may have certain learning outcomes that are not bolstered by PRE. We argue that if one is aware of PRE then one is better positioned to make deliberate pedagogical decisions about the places through which—and about which—teaching and learning occur.

The key ideas above provide a solid platform from which we can more deeply examine PRE and how it can enhance our outdoor teaching and learning practices. Next, we provide an overview of the roots of PRE, before discussing how PRE has evolved from theory into practice over time. The chapter concludes with a discussion on the limits of learning through place and a case study.

## The foundations of place-responsive education

Place-based and placed-responsive education may be relatively new terms for educational lexicon, but some of the theories that inform them have been around for quite some time. For example, those familiar with theories associated with experiential education will already be familiar with some of its historical roots, ideas, and practices. One example would be "situated learning", which is supposed to take place in the specific social circumstances, and engage with the actual physical context, in which learning occurs. Place responsive education finds its roots in a range of disciplinary and interdisciplinary fields including sociology, biology, ecology, human geography, ecopsychology, philosophy, and Indigenous studies.

Sociologists have for a long time been concerned about rootlessness, and Durkheim's concept of *anomie* is a case in point where he feared that the uprooting of people from their traditional communities would lead to aimlessness and the breakdown of values and morality (see for example Giddens & Sutton, 2021). In the 1970s, geographers such as Tuan, Relph, and Seddon were worried that the modern world was creating societies and communities whose work, travel, leisure, and communication practices were causing people to become rootless, or what they called "placeless". Tuan (1977) explained that places are locations that have been given meaning through human experience and to which people feel particular biological and social attachments. Spaces, on the other hand, have not been ascribed the same sorts of value or meaning by humans.

The problems that these early place thinkers were trying to address were subject reductionism (where school subjects were taught separately from one another);

discipline reductionism (which kept the social sciences, the natural sciences, and the arts and humanities from interacting with each other); and educational isolationism (where curricula were theory-based and abstract, and taught in isolation of the communities they serve). If we see how problems of place are associated with reductionism, then the solutions depend on understanding places in a much more holistic and interconnected way. For example, Gruenewald and Smith (2008) highlight how the social, economic, and environmental issues of a specific location can bring together subject areas, thus facilitating Sobel's (2013) ideas of connecting classrooms and communities. It is therefore important to consider the multidimensional, interdisciplinary nature of places and regard this understanding as a necessary precondition to using them for educational purposes.

Nowadays, urban planners talk about creating a "sense of place" and "sense of community" throughout the design and construction phases of new builds. The term "placemaking" is now in common use as a way of (re)imagining old and creating new places (Derr, Chawla, & Mintzer, 2018). A strong argument for PRE is that people are losing their sense of place because of the modern conditions of rootlessness and placelessness and the purpose of PRE is to restore that sense of place. As Malpas (1999) observes, "it is something of a truism to say that that which is closest and most familiar to us is often that which is most easily overlooked and forgotten" (p. 19). This is why Henderson (2010) draws attention to places as being "storied", because it is easy to pass through "empty spaces" without knowing their stories. Understanding and responding to our places' stories is central to excellent PRE.

The field of Ecopsychology has also been influential, with writers such as Theodore Roszak and Joanna Macy being particularly interested in the emotional connections that humans have for nature. By combining the terms *eco* (planetary) with *psychology* (personal), the Ecopsychologists were "pointing the way toward some new basis for sustainable economic and emotional life, a society of good environmental citizenship that can ally the intimately emotional and the vastly biospheric" (Roszak, Gomes, & Kanner, 1995, p. 2).

Ecopsychologists believe in the need to better develop the connection between people and planet through the development of the affective domain (see Chapter 6). More simply, they insist that direct and prolonged experiences in nature (sometimes referred to by Ingold (2000, 2011) as "immersion" or "dwelling") will first stimulate the emotional wellbeing of people and, second, provide the inspiration to become active in protecting nature. Norwegian Arne Næss (1990) distinguished between shallow and deep ecology, where shallow ecology was associated with the term "anthropocentrism" and its narrow focus on human needs at the expense of the natural world. Deep ecology, on the other hand, promotes the inherent worth of all living beings and asks deeper questions concerning culture and nature. In her seminal book, *Silent Spring*, Rachel Carson (1962) demonstrated the intricate connection between all living things, which served to strengthen the collective response to the rising tide of anthropocentrism.

The counter to anthropocentrism was a nature-centred view, which regarded human existence and wellbeing as completely intertwined with the ecologies that they inhabited. Kimmerer (2015) referred to this rising tide as a crisis of relationship and sought instead to promote relationships based on gratitude and reciprocity. From this perspective, ecosystems should be looked at in their interconnected entirety, with humans as simply one part of them. This point has direct relevance to how we think about curricula because subject specialisms tend to reinforce anthropocentric divisions. Aldo Leopold (1949/1989) drew attention to the limited utilitarianism of a human based value system and wanted to extend it to include the non-human. Leopold did not use the term *place* but instead referred to the *land* in its entirety—including the soil, water, minerals, as well as living creatures and organisms. He also advanced the view that we needed new ways of thinking about the land to understand these implications and so he proposed an ecocentric, or biospheric, land ethic. The heart of this is the statement that "a thing is right when it tends to preserve the integrity, stability, and beauty of the biotic community. It is wrong when it tends otherwise" (Leopold, 1949/1989, pp. 224–225). What this means is that at all levels of society, nature needs to be central when making social, economic, and educational decisions.

In the 1990s and 2000s, educational literature on learning through place came to the fore. This was the beginning of a movement that would bring the philosophical and geographical foundations of what "place" is into the educational domain. In an attempt to try and embrace this emerging ethical position a number of new concepts were introduced, such as "a pedagogy of place" (Haymes, 1995), "bioregional education" (Traina & Darley-Hill, 1995), "place-conscious classrooms and community-oriented schooling" (Theobald, 1997), "bioregionalism" (Snyder, 1990), "ecological education" (Smith & Williams, 1999), and "place-based curriculum and instruction" (Woodhouse & Knapp, 2000). All of these authors shared Casey's (1998) vision of working across subject domains to break down the sorts of reductionism that we outlined above. For Casey, place was the starting point for everything: It is "as requisite as the air we breathe, the ground on which we stand, the bodies we have" (1998, p. ix).

While a number of important books and papers on PRE were published in the 2000s (see Stewart, 2008; Baker, 2005; Smith & Sobel, 2010), two publications in particular stand out. First, Gruenewald's (2003) classic paper, *The best of both worlds: A critical pedagogy of place*, outlined a more critical and more theoretically grounded vision of what PRE could become. Wattchow and Brown's (2011) book, entitled *A pedagogy of place* provides a critique of "traditional" outdoor education practices and shows the path towards a pedagogy that is not only located in a place, but actively *responds* to it. In other words, it is not sufficient to know and acknowledge social and environmental inequalities; rather, PRE takes the next step and initiates action by addressing injustices.

As we saw at the beginning of this section, this rise in PRE has emerged from a concern about how the "cumulative effects of modernity" have altered the ways in which we care for our local places and those "we encounter when we travel" (Wattchow & Brown, 2011, p. 51). From this point of view, PRE has gained traction due to the times in which we live right now. We can see how, in times before the internet and before the industrial revolution, our grandparents and ancestors had much less need for PRE. This is because many people already had connections to their landscapes through their constant interaction with it. An example of this might be where people in many countries depended directly on the land for subsistence and income generation and were therefore much more in tune with the land and its seasonal cycles on a daily basis. Historic senses of place very often developed through life circumstances that were based on necessity and not choice. This would be the case for subsistence farmers who had little other viable alternative than to being deeply aware of natural cycles because of their dependence on the places they lived. This is distinct from contemporary life, where social mobility allows people to move between places, and where there may be opportunities for people to deepen their experiences of places of their own accord, but, for whatever reason, they choose not to.

## The evolution of place-responsive education

Generally speaking, one can say that, over time, PRE has evolved from learning about places to transforming them. Baker (2005) suggests that we can, a) get to know our places by looking carefully around us and become deeply aware of what is around us, who is using the land and for what purposes, and whose habitat it is, and b) try to understand how the place has been environmentally, culturally, and historically shaped over time. Very often, PRE involves learning about the familiar—things that we see and encounter everyday, perhaps—but which are not very well known. Repeated visits have been shown to be very effective in enabling young people to develop special relationships with places and their inhabitants (Harrison, 2010).

A deeper way of conceiving PRE involves adding a degree of criticality, in order to better the lives of the humans and "more-than-human" that inhabit these spaces. A paper that is central to this position is Gruenewald's (2003) *Critical pedagogy of place*, which we noted earlier. Gruenewald proposes two concepts that can be used by educators: *decolonization* and *re-inhabitation*. First, he explains how decolonization involves interrogating our places for instances of oppression and of unequal power and opportunity.

There is a growing literature that explains how the land that many of us inhabit right now, has had its natural resources and indigenous populations systematically exploited (e.g., Veracini, 2011). Indigenous scholars outline how "the uniqueness of place" is central to addressing "different histories of colonization, land dispossession, and treaty relationships, as well as assimilationist policies and practices" (Styres, Zinga, Spencer, & Tomlins-Jahnke, 2019, p. xiv). Even if we acknowledge that people and the more-than-human were horribly treated in the past, scholars claim that most non-Indigenous people who live in settler societies, such as Australia,

New Zealand, USA, and Canada, regard colonization as "something that happened in the distant past" (Tuck, McKenzie, & McCoy, 2014, p. 7) and the purpose of PRE is to bring that past into the present and make it visible. Too often, people:

> do not consider the fact that they live on land that has been stolen, or ceded through broken treaties, or to which Indigenous peoples claim a pre-existing ontological and cosmological relationship. They do not consider themselves to be implicated in the continued settlement and occupation of unceded Indigenous land.
>
> (p. 7)

Alongside this discussion is, of course, the "dark side" to place, which may not be rooted in colonialism, but may be—among other things—highly exclusionary, violent, racist, and misogynist (see Schama, 1995). Or, as Derby (2015) asserts, "as living memory of the carnage, obscenity and unapologetic imperialism of the 'historical genocide' of Indigenous peoples fades, the colonial project mutates and manifests subtler forms of 'historical genocide'" (p. 124). Places are full of beauty and wonder, but they are also framed by economic, systemic, and historical factors, including power differences, that determine people's life opportunities.

Consider, for example, how in many of our cities there are areas of affluence and areas of abject poverty. People usually live in the areas they do because of circumstance, where the act of being born in a certain place and going to school within a certain community strongly influences students' life opportunities. We can ask ourselves how growing up in a particular neighbourhood has shaped its inhabitants' values, attitudes, and actions. Similarly, when we walk through wild places, we can ask ourselves, do we know who owns the land and do we enjoy our access by right or by subservience?

Once a place's history and social and environmental issues have been examined through critical lenses, steps can be taken to confront and address past and current "wrongs". Now the discussion can move from learning about places (which is great), to *changing* places by "re-inhabiting" them in ways that deliberately address the inequalities and injustices that exist there. Gruenewald's (2003) concepts of decolonization and re-inhabitation gives us tools with which we can consider more deliberately how to live better in our places—both socially and ecologically.

More recent work by PRE scholars lies in the ways social theorists have described contemporary society, which has been characterized by the increasing speeds associated with "hyper-modernity" (Virilio, 2000); people on the move, who live "mobile lives", by choice or through oppression (Elliot & Urry, 2010); and the constant change and uncertainty that comes from living in "liquid times" (Bauman, 2007). Scholar Margaret Hawkins (2014) highlights the importance of creating "citizens of the world" (p. 97) by combining locally-situated practices with "global others". What does this look like? It involves sharing critical responses to our places with those in other parts of the city (or the planet), and vice versa.

This process of sharing highlights to pupils how the issues within their places are similar or different to those in other places and may even be related through a complex web of history, geography, politics, and economics. Technology is a big part of how PRE practices are evolving, as meanings constructed by students can be shared through videos, slide shows, interviews, podcasts, Facebook, Twitter, and other social media tools.

---

**CASE STUDY**

Mr. Taylor's grade six class in Toronto is doing a project called "Where our wastewater goes". This project involves the class learning about where their wastewater goes, once it gets flushed down the sink or the toilet. So far, the class activities have involved learning about the City of Toronto's sewage facilities from the government website, and a class bus trip to the North Toronto Waste Treatment Plant. The information gathered online, combined with the audio files from interviews with staff from the Plant and video/photos from their visit, enabled four groups of students to put together audio-visual presentations on how their wastewater is collected, separated into liquids and solids, the solids processed, and the water disinfected and largely recycled. Since this project focused on the very systems used to process the waste in the students' neighbourhoods, it can be considered "place essential"; this was about their waste, and its treatment, as opposed to waste treatment in general.

We can see how the class learned all about key topics which have cross-curricular connections to science, biology, geography, mathematics, and language arts. It also involved class-based learning before and after the site visit, thereby connecting different places. This is an example of excellent first wave PRE. Mr. Taylor's class did not have the expertise, nor did they see the need to improve the state of wastewater treatment in their neighbourhood. They did, however, want to learn about how wastewater was dealt with in other places.

Mr. Taylor has an old friend who is a schoolteacher in Barcelona and he decided to get in touch with Bob during the summer break, when he first conceived the wastewater project idea. Bob loved the idea and decided he would do a similar project with his class. They put dates in the diary and two months later were able to have each other's classes present their work to each other through presentations projected onto large screens, with audio.

This is an example of how learning about faraway places can be done without the time, expenses, and carbon emissions associated with travelling to them.

---

## Limitations and possibilities of PRE

Although we're big advocates of learning through places and landscapes, we're the first to acknowledge that there are choices to be made about the places we choose to use. These choices are also dependent on what it is we want to teach and what we want our students to learn, at which point it becomes clear that some places will be better than others, depending on our teaching intentions.

We have argued so far that teaching and learning through place is educationally desirable and can be a force for positive change. Does that mean, however, that we should only teach about places that we can physically visit? Must we fly to Brazil to learn about biodiversity loss in the Amazon rainforest, travel to the Middle East to learn about the Palestine/Israel conflict, or go to Bangladesh to understand how the country has been terribly influenced by climate change? Do we need to physically visit these places to learn about these topics? Our answer is a forceful "no" to all of these questions. If the answer was "yes", we can see how using hands-on, place-responsive approaches exclusively might actually limit student learning. While it is important to remember that digital technologies contribute to greenhouse gas emissions, they also enable us to "visit" and learn about "far away" places without need for excessive travel and, if it can be organized, with the willing help of students and educators living locally in those places. Throughout this book we draw attention to different ways of knowing (see for example Chapter 6), and how one can come to know places directly through multisensory learning and one can come to know other places indirectly through conceptual understanding. Learning through and about place can be both very physically active and sedentary, contemplative and interactive, outdoors and with screens.

We referred above to Bauman's (2007) notion that we are living in "liquid times", by which he meant we have become like displaced tourists moving from one job to another, one house to another, one city to another, and for the purposes of this chapter, one place to another. This again highlights the discussion above about placelessness and rootlessness and the need for education that is rooted in place.

Strangely enough, some of the ways teachers and students might become better placed is through the very technologies that have contributed to displacement in the first place. The use of technology, in particular personal and portable devices, has precipitated a shift in people's attention from their surroundings to engagement with their mobile, media-driven devices. This is undoubtedly a barrier to the promotion of multisensory and direct experiential engagement with surrounding places, as well as to the interaction between people in those places.

In our own work, we are developing a model of learning that features outdoors, indoors, and online spaces (see Chapter 12). We want to try and break down barriers between indoor learning and outdoor learning and develop programmes that pointedly ask the question "Where is the best place to teach this content?"

It is exciting to think of the digital world as just another space in which teaching happens. Understandably, the first image that might appear in peoples' minds is that of students sitting in a classroom at a row of computers. However, it is now the portability and personal nature of digital media that opens up new opportunities for place-responsive outdoor and indoor learning.

This question about where teaching and learning can most effectively take place is one for educators of all kinds, as there is no assumption that the outdoors provides more educationally appropriate places for teaching than indoors or vice versa. It is important to be aware that outdoor learning is not necessarily place-responsive and place-responsive education does not need to happen outdoors. Great PRE can take place indoors and, as pointed out above, outdoor learning can completely ignore local phenomena.

Foundational to effective PRE is the tenet that us humans are effectively intertwined with our places in "assemblages" that have mutual influence on each other (see Mannion & Lynch, 2016; Ingold, 2000). Building our interdisciplinary teaching and learning through, for and about places can be a simple, yet powerful "engine" for instilling young people with care for the communities and ecosystems that nurture them.

## Guidelines

- All landscapes have a past, present, and future, which are cross-curricular and can be used to teach a wide variety of topics.

- Try to make teaching as "place-essential" as possible.

- Go beyond merely teaching and learning about places: Attempt to respectfully transform them for the better.

- Consider how technologies enable us to access the geological, and cultural history of our places and to exchange knowledge with others.

## References

Baker, M. (2005). Landfullness in adventure-based programming: Promoting reconnection to the land. *Journal of Experiential Education*, *27*(3), 267–276.

Bauman, Z. (2007). *Liquid times: Living in an age of uncertainty*. Cambridge: Polity Press.

Brookes, A. (2002). Lost in the Australian bush: Outdoor education as curriculum. *Journal of Curriculum Studies*, *34*(4), 405–425.

Carson, R. (1962). *Silent spring*. London: Penguin.

Casey, E. (1998). *The fate of place: A philosophical history*. London: University of California Press.

Derby, M. (2015). *Place, being, resonance. A critical ecohermeneutic approach to education*. New York: Peter Lang.

Derr, V., Chawla, L., & Mintzer, M. (2018). *Placemaking with children and youth*. New York: New Village Press.

Elliot, A., & Urry, J. (2010). *Mobile lives*. Abingdon: Routledge.

Giddens, A., & Sutton, P. (2021). *Sociology* (9th ed.). Cambridge: Policy Press.

Gruenewald, D. A. (2003). The best of both worlds: A critical pedagogy of place. *Educational Researcher*, *32*(3), 3–12.

Gruenewald, D. A., & Smith, G. A. (Eds.). (2008). *Place-based education in the global age: Local diversity*. New York: Lawrence Erlbaum.

Harrison, S. (2010). Why are we here? Taking 'place' into account in UK outdoor environmental education. *Journal of Adventure Education & Outdoor Learning*, *10*(1), 3–18.

Hawkins, M. (2014). Ontologies of place, creative meaning making and critical cosmopolitan education. *Curriculum Inquiry*, *44*(1), 90–112.

Haymes, S. (1995). *Race, culture and the city: A pedagogy for Black urban struggle*. Albany, NY: State University of New York Press.

Henderson, B. (2010). Understanding heritage travel: Story, place, and technology. In S. Beames (Ed.), *Understanding educational expeditions* (pp. 79–89). Rotterdam: Sense.

Ingold, T. (2000). *The perception of the environment: Essays on livelihood, dwelling and skill*. Abingdon: Routledge.

Ingold, T. (2011). *Being alive: Essays on movement, knowledge and description*. Abingdon: Routledge.

Kimmerer, R. W. (2015). *Braiding sweetgrass: Indigenous wisdom, scientific knowledge and the teachings of plants*. Minneapolis, MN: Milkweed Editions.

Leopold, A. (1989). *A Sand County Almanac with essays on conservation from Round River*. New York: Oxford University Press. (Original work published 1949)

Malpas, J. (1999). *Place and experience. A philosophical topography*. Cambridge: Cambridge University Press.

Mannion, G., Fenwick, A., Nugent, C., & L'Anson, J. (2011). *Teaching in nature*. University of Stirling, Commissioned by Scottish Natural Heritage. www.snh.org.uk/pdfs/publications/commissioned_reports/476.pdf

Mannion, G., & Lynch, J. (2016). Primacy of place in education in outdoor settings. In B. Humberstone, H. Prince, & K. Henderson (Eds.), *Routledge international handbook of outdoor studies* (pp. 85–94). Abingdon: Routledge.

Næss, A. (1990). *Ecology, community and lifestyle*. Cambridge: Cambridge University Press.

Nicol, R. (2002). Outdoor education: Research topic or universal value? Part one. *Journal of Adventure Education and Outdoor Learning*, *2*(1), 29–41.

Roszak, T., Gomes, M., & Kanner, A. (1995). *Ecopsychology: Restoring the earther, healing the mind*. San Francisco, CA: Sierra Club Books.

Schama, S. (1995). *Landscape and memory*. New York: Vintage.

Smith, G. (2002). Place-based education: Learning to be where we are. *Phi Delta Kappan*, *83*, 584–594.

Smith, G., & Sobel, D. (2010). *Place- and community-based education in schools*. New York: Routledge.

Smith, G., & Williams, D. (1999). Ecological education: Extending the definition of environmental education. *Australian Journal of Environmental Education*, *15*, 139–146.

Snyder, G, (1990). *The practice of the wild: Essays*. New York: North Point Press.

Sobel, D. (2013). *Place-based education: Connecting classrooms and communities*. Great Barrington, MA: Orion.

Stewart, A. (2008). Whose place, whose history? Outdoor environmental education pedagogy as 'reading' the landscape. *Journal of Adventure Education & Outdoor Learning*, *8*(2), 79–98.

Styres, S., Zinga, D., Spencer, L., & Tomlins-Jahnke, H. (2019). Contested spaces and expanding the Indigenous education agenda. In H. Tomlins-Jahnke, S. Styres, S. Lilley, & D. Zinga (Eds.), *Indigenous education: New directions in theory and practice* (pp. xiii–xxix). Edmonton, AB: The University of Alberta Press.

Theobald, P. (1997). *Teaching the commons: Place, pride, and the renewal of community*. Boulder, CO: Westview Press.

Traina, F., & Darley-Hill, S. (1995). *Perspectives in bioregional education.* Troy, OH: NAAEE.

Tuan, Y. F. (1977). *Space and place: The perspective of experience.* Minneapolis, MN: University of Minnesota Press.

Tuck, T., McKenzie, M., & McCoy, K. (2014). Land education: Indigenous, post-colonial, and decolonizing perspectives on place and environmental education research. *Environmental Education Research, 20*(1), 1–23.

Veracini, L. (2011). Introducing. *Settler Colonial Studies, 1*(1), 1–12.

Virilio, P. (2000). *The information bomb.* London: Verso.

Wattchow, B., & Brown, M. (2011). *A pedagogy of place: Outdoor education for a changing world.* Clayton: Monash University.

Woodhouse, J., & Knapp, C. (2000). *Place-based curriculum and instruction.* ERIC Document Reproduction Service No. EDO-RC-00-6. Charleston, WV: ERIC Resource Center.

# 6 Harnessing student curiosity and the role of wonder

## Chapter aims

- Develop theoretical ideas that expand the concept of curiosity.

- Introduce wonder as part of this expansion to show how both can be incorporated into teaching practices.

- Explore how teachers can use curiosity and wonder to direct students' attention towards living and acting in a changing world.

## Curiosity and wonder

In the previous version of this book, we explored theoretical ideas that highlighted the importance of curiosity as an organizing principle for learning. This exploration involved contrasting opportunities for learning indoors with opportunities for learning outdoors to discover the differing levels of stimulus in both contexts, and highlighted the importance of experiential approaches to learning and teaching for engaging different senses. We argued that too much indoor learning "can lead to a suppression of the feelings from which respect, *curiosity*, *wonder* (italicized for emphasis), and awe for the world beyond the classroom grow" (Beames, Higgins & Nicol, 2011, p. 54). This led us to discuss child-centred approaches to learning, which is a theoretical position emphasizing the child's own innate disposition to learn. Since the outdoors provides an endless range of opportunities for students to interact with places on sensory, cognitive, and affective levels, we argued that nurturing curiosity was a central aspect of teachers' roles.

Our presentation of curiosity also showed how theories with which teachers were already familiar, from their teacher education degrees, were equally applicable to the outdoors as the indoors, and that no specialist training was needed to go outdoors in the first place. More important was the way we used these ideas to show how

DOI: 10.4324/9781003010890-6

child-centred theories, when applied to the outdoors, provide a wealth of naturally occurring learning, so long as curiosity is central to the learning and teaching process. This was an invitation to teachers, who would not normally go outdoors, to have the confidence to cross the classroom threshold and see what happens when they applied the theories with which they were already familiar, to learning and teaching outdoors.

As we have argued, curiosity might be thought of as something that fuels the desire to know and learn, and is therefore essential to the development of new knowledge and skills. However, curiosity is not a value-free concept and is not without its critics. Thinking about its role in educational processes Egan (1997) has suggested that it might simply be nurtured for its use as a tool to develop cognitive inquiry skills—to find things out. Opdal (2001) has suggested it might only encourage children to ask senseless questions. This is of course an interesting value judgement, and one wonders whose interests are central here—the adult or the child? This is a point to which we return later in the chapter. Opdal (2001) continues to point out that curiosity "is a motive that can move a person to do all kinds of research, *but within an accepted framework*" (p. 342). The italics have been added to point out that at the level of policy and national curriculum, curiosity does not necessarily lead to the challenge of educational orthodoxies, nor even recognize that such orthodoxies might exist in the first place. This is a problem. When thought of in this way, curiosity seems quite functional and limiting, and might result in maintaining and reinforcing values that support the *status quo*. In many countries around the world, this might mean increasing emphasis on performance, measurement, and standardized educational outcomes (Schinkel, 2017). This is also a problem if schools, national curricula, and international agencies seek to foster the sort of reform pedagogies for teaching, learning, and assessment strategies mentioned in Chapter 3.

## The nature of wonder

Mohr Lone and Burroughs (2016) have identified three primary philosophical activities that may be useful to teachers—wondering, questioning, and reflecting. Wonder, they argue, "leads to a desire to question and reflect about the deeper meaning of ordinary concepts and experiences" (p. 18). It is the manner by which we come to appreciate the limits of our present knowledge and understanding of the world. Opdal (2001) believes this is important because:

> wonder is the state of mind that signals we have reached the limits of our present understanding, and that things may be different from how they look. This could generate a research interest, a probing into the frames that so far have been taken for granted.
>
> (p. 332)

The distinction that we are making is that although curiosity may fuel the desire to know, it can also simply be a tool of inquiry to develop the cognitive domain and might even be curtailed by curricular designs and policy frameworks, making it limiting and functional in practice. On the other hand, wonder starts with the affective domain and the excitement of being at the limits of what we know as individuals, having opportunities to reflect on that, and coming to see the frames (cognitive understanding until this point) that have been taken for granted.

We have purposely contrasted curiosity and wonder in this way for a particular reason. Carl Rogers (1983) has said of children that it is "their eagerness to learn, their ability to make difficult and complex choices that will decide the future of our world" (p. 1). As we have pointed out in Chapters 2 and 4, we cannot wait for young people to grow into adulthood to influence the future of their world, or at least there must be a parallel process going on to ensure that adults, and the teaching profession, are responding to help students directly contribute to the development of their futures, and the future of others, and indeed all species.

For Schinkel (2017), wonder is overwhelming in a way that curiosity might not be, according to the differences we have provided here. These differences are based on our view that if teaching practices treat curiosity as something based mostly in the cognitive domain, then teachers and their students will see the purpose of learning as the gathering of "new" facts. The danger of this is that student learning ends up being solely knowledge-based and something that operates within a dominant worldview, which simply reinforces and does not actually challenge existing values and attitudes. We are seeking to promote teaching practices that draw more on the affective domain and specifically explore the limits of students' understandings in order to extend it. Schinkel (2017) introduces the term "deep wonder" which is based on love, mystery, and the search for meaning in a changing world.

We might move between curiosity and wonder from moment to moment, as we teach and as our students learn new things, because although curiosity and wonder are distinct, they are also in relationship with one another. Both the distinction and the relationship are important because we, the authors, do not wish to engage in idle theorizing so much as develop effective, positive practices that are rooted in both cognitive and affective domains.

## Wandering and wondering

One practice we have been developing for some time is what might be called "wandering and wondering". Dictionary definitions of wandering often suggest that it is an aimless pursuit, but it need not be; in fact, it can be very purposeful. This is because wandering is based on mobility and moving from one place to another. It is no coincidence that some of the most productive writers, thinkers, and activists have been indefatigable walkers. Robert Louis Stevenson (1957) championed walking in his *Travels with a Donkey in the Cévennes*. Rachel Carson, John Muir, Margaret Murie, Arne Naess, and Henry David Thoreau, to name a few, were all enthusiastic walkers with an educational purpose. Walking has also been at the heart of nonviolent civil disobedience from Gandhi's Salt March, the colour revolution energized by Rosa Parks, the civil rights protest marches of Martin Luther King, to the current (2020) protests of Black Lives Matter and Extinction Rebellion. In tracing the history of walking in her book *Wanderlust*, Solnit (2014) has concluded that there has been a link between thinking and walking for the whole of human history. It is worth remembering therefore that schooling and its static and sedentary nature is a relatively modern concept.

Thinking, and its associations with the cognitive domain, is not the same as feeling, which is associated with the affective domain. This is important for the pedagogical purposes we have in mind where the sort of wondering we would like to encourage happens when students walk. For example, the apparently simple act of pedestrianism offers multiple personal benefits associated with physical health (e.g., exercise improves cardiovascular fitness and helps with blood circulation) and mental wellbeing (e.g., the release of endorphins that trigger positive feelings in the body). Rubinstein (2015) reminds us that walking can help with modern personal and social ailments such as obesity, anxiety, and alienation. Walking promotes bodily health, but it also provides the sorts of corporeal conditions that stimulate internal bodily awareness, receptivity, and perhaps even wonder. Although we have highlighted that thinking is different from feeling, it is nevertheless important to remember that as an organism with combined physiological and psychological functions, the human body is a place where thinking and feeling interact. The body is in this sense what Whitehead (1938/1968) refers to as "one centre of experience" (p. 23). This means that thinking and feeling are not separate but related—a point to which we will return in this chapter.

As we have alluded to above, the process of wondering is directly related to the affordances of the spaces and places we wander in. That is to say, the places we educate in provide opportunities for something to wonder about. More precisely, we might ask how human experiences are affected by being in specific places and spaces. This is something that can be associated with situated learning theory, which for Dewey (1938/1963) among others, moves the purposes of education away from simply the acquisition of abstract knowledge to something that is influenced by context-based, place-responsive, social phenomenon. This point has deep theoretical significance, as it involves a tripartite relationship between cognition (and its association with curiosity), affect (and its association with wonder), and places (because our attention to places broadens and deepens the more we pay attention) (Nicol & Sangster, 2019). Thus, curiosity, wonder, and wandering, when combined, create synergistic embodied learning where the moral significance of our relationship with places is based on the attention we pay to them, and to the stories that have been told about them (Nicol, 2013, 2014a, 2014b).

Outdoor places of all kinds are characterized by openness and unpredictability, and therefore provide endless experiential and spontaneous learning opportunities where the stimulus for learning is different from being indoors. For example, moving from the classroom into the outdoors is an act of mobility, and it is purposeful because the teacher has made the decision to mobilize the students. For this pedagogical approach to work well the teacher has to avoid the feeling that they need to teach something according to predetermined learning outcomes. Instead, this is more about trying to open up opportunities for new ways of experiencing phenomena. Wandering as part of a teaching practice could simply be an invitation for students to explore an area by themselves. This could be in any available space, such as a playground, park, or somewhere further afield. For safety purposes boundaries do need to be set, at least in the teacher's mind, but the purpose is to use places and spaces imaginatively in a way that wonder might emerge. Once the safety considerations have been put in place (see Chapter 11 for more details on this), it is often just a case of saying something like, "I want you to go for a wander by yourself and find something that interests you". It is an invitation to lead first, not with curiosity and cognition, but through wonder and affect. This can then lead to conversations designed to help students express their experiences. The same invitation might then be put to pairs, then threes, then fours, and so on—each time reflecting on the similarities and differences between the experiences. Gillian Judson's (2018) book, *A walking curriculum*, is an excellent resource for educators who aspire to "engage the body, emotions, and imagination in ways that can increase students' familiarity with the local natural context . . . " (p. 3).

Returning to "questioning", the second of Mohr Lone and Burrough's (2016) three primary philosophical activities, the teacher could prime these sorts of experiences by setting questions in advance. One example of this is through Outdoor Journeys (2021), which recommends a three-phase process of questioning, researching, and sharing. This phased process would account for a range of different learning needs from students whose sense of wonder is sparked individually, to the sorts of curiosity and wonder that might be found by sharing experiences through group discussion. This articulates well with Mohr Lone and Burrough's (2016) third activity, reflection, where the teacher might lead a discussion on students' experiences.

It could be tempting to think that the simplicity of this process makes it easy, but it is not. It takes a lot of practice for the teacher to learn when to teach, when not to; when to direct their attention, and when not to; when to reign-in the students, when to let go; and so on. However, what is special about these types of educational activities is that they are open to the possibility of planned teaching practices but also the unplanned or spontaneous learning opportunities that arise when students are asked to interrogate everyone and everything around them. We are not suggesting a revolutionary abandonment of the school curriculum; we are simply suggesting that there might be more adventurous ways to interact with it and meet its requirements.

## Sedentary wondering

Another practice would be encouraging students to find their own "sense spots". This can be a solitary activity where each student is asked to wander around until they find a spot that attracts them, and then spend some time alone to see what thoughts or feelings come to mind. This practice can be adapted for pairs or larger groups. After this, it is important to provide opportunities for students to capture and share their experiences. A range of artistic interdisciplinary reflective options can be employed to further enhance learning experience, such as writing, sketching, poetry, song writing, mapping, collecting, photography, and so on.

## The wonder to be found in threshold walks

Another way of encouraging wonder is to ask students to go for a wander and find a "threshold". Thresholds exist and appear in different forms. In physical terms, a threshold is something that takes someone from one place to another, such as a gate that allows one to pass into a garden. However, they also represent an aspect of our consciousness such as the movement from one experience to another. Thresholds can therefore be both physical and experiential, and the key to both is a change or movement from one state of existence to another. These transitions can be smooth or disruptive for the learner. This relates to Dewey's (1938/1963) concept of continuity, where a learner's experiences are like a stream flowing from the past into the present, and also forward into the future, as they influence experiences and decisions.

Through finding thresholds, learners are required to distinguish between the quality of experiences that lead to growth, and this can sometimes mean learning from mistakes and confusing situations. These states present the learner with points of ambiguity and disruption, which often happens when something unfamiliar enters the consciousness of the learner (Nicol & Sangster, 2019). Meyer and Land (2005) refer to these as "stuck places" or "epistemological obstacles" that can at first block new learning (p. 377). In other words, they place the learner outside of Vygotsky's (1978) *Zone of Proximal Development* and students will need help with taking the next steps in their learning. These "stuck places" are not something to be avoided. On the contrary, they should be sought out by the teacher, and learners should be urged to discover principles and concepts for themselves. It is therefore important to remember Bruner's (2006) point that meaningful communication between the teacher and learner is key if this approach to learning and teaching is to work well.

It thus becomes the role of the teacher to plan for blockages, identify them when they happen, and help learners move beyond this to promote new understandings. It is easy in everyday life to cross thresholds without noticing them because they may be subtle and concealed, or even "hidden in plain sight". It is likely that students will need help in identifying these thresholds. When the teacher knows that a student may be approaching a threshold, they can encourage the student to look for it. There are good reasons why teachers might want to pay attention to thresholds. One of those reasons is that interesting things happen. Thresholds become very exciting when students see contrasts, interactions, and synergies: Where shadow becomes light, where grass becomes concrete, where pavement becomes path, where day becomes night, and perhaps even where indoor becomes outdoor. When thresholds are crossed, wondering can provide a way to think about the different qualities of experiences and meanings.

In physics, for example, a student rolling a ball in the playground observes it moving and then coming to a stop. They might wonder, "How did that happen?? In biology, the butterfly fluttering around the playground might be seen as a winged insect, yet it was once an egg, before it was transformed to a caterpillar, and then a pupa before becoming the butterfly—an apparently miraculous movement through different thresholds. A teacher might prompt the student by suggesting, "Let's find out how that is possible"! There is a range of books and resources full of practical activities that help to inspire curiosity and wonder (e.g., Judson, 2018). However, although such books promote the joy of learning, they do not necessarily show how learning is itself a movement through thresholds. Even where they do, teaching practices still need to be taught through the different subjects that come to inform this type of interdisciplinary pedagogy. This way, the mind comes to understand the physical environment as interrelated instead of the fractured understanding that curricular disciplines often promote. The teaching practices shared above, and many more, can be conceived by teachers bringing a courageous and adventurous approach to their own planning.

Teachers are not simply passive deliverers of the particular curriculum provided to them. Often teachers are not required to actually engage with "the curriculum" first-hand; rather they engage with planned schemes of work that meet curriculum outcomes. In order to stay connected with the curriculum, we suggest that the problems of the world require teachers to transcend transmissive and passive processes and instead employ transformative ones. Here we provide a teaching framework intended to help make this happen.

## The four-point epistemology

Heron and Reason (2008) and Reason (2006) promoted the idea of epistemological diversity[1] by providing a framework that moves from individual experiences through to socially transformative learning. These ideas are particularly useful because they provide a teaching framework that can be used as an aid to consciously work through thresholds and provide opportunities for curiosity and wonder to emerge. The framework comprises:

- Experiential knowing.
- Presentational knowing.
- Propositional knowing.
- Practical knowing.

Experiential knowing happens through direct face-to-face encounters with person, place, or thing; it is knowing through empathy and resonance (Reason, 2006). The need for this, as Orr (1992), among others, has stated, is that "education will, first, require the re-integration of experience into education" (p. 18) and more specifically that "we experience nature mostly through sight, sound, smell, touch and taste—through a medley of sensations that play upon us in complex ways" (Orr, 1994, p. 6). Reason (1998) explains that "Presentational knowing . . . emerges from experiential knowing and provides its first expression through forms of imagery such as poetry and story, drawing, sculpture, movement, dance and . . . sharing of the experience" (p. 44). In the above examples, the teaching of experiential and presentational knowing should be evident where direct experience and presentational aspects of knowledge were linked to the promotion of wonder. This follows Vasalou's (2013) view that "wonder has often been cast as the passion of inquiry and connected with the desire to know and understand . . ." (p. 2). Wonder provides an "emotional hook" and is the driving force that makes us want to investigate further.

Experiential and presentational knowing are tied closely to students' immediate sensorial worlds. However, they do not necessarily lead to the sorts of questioning and reflecting that Mohr Lone and Burroughs (2016) identified as essential to learning. This comes from the third aspect of the four-point epistemology, propositional knowing, which involves knowing "about something through ideas and theories and is expressed in abstract language or mathematics" (Reason, 1998, p. 44). This is essential if students are to understand, for example, the science of climate change, and the reasons for biodiversity loss around the planet. In order for this type of knowing to happen, students need to critically evaluate texts, propositions and theories, and look for both strengths and inadequacies in order to develop their own theories. This is often indoor work which can easily be designed to connect with outdoor learning, though there is nothing stopping a teacher from taking literature, textbooks, and other resources outside. The fourth aspect of the four-point epistemology is "practical knowing", which is knowing how to act in the world, through taking the time to right wrongs by making decisions based on knowledge. Heron (1996) suggests that practical knowing "fulfils the three prior forms of knowing (and) brings them to fruition in purposive deeds" (p. 239).

The four-point epistemology shown in the diagram above has many uses. First, it is important to note that the framework can be used in a linear fashion, from experiential to presentational, propositional, and practical as this model shows. Alternatively, any of the four areas can be used as a starting point because the theory behind the model is designed to show they all interact with one another. This is where the power of the framework lies. Second, it can be used as a planning device to develop ideas for learning and teaching activities and making sure that each of the four points has been covered. And third, it can provide a post-hoc means to reflect on learning experiences that occur spontaneously, but which can then be directly linked to the curriculum.

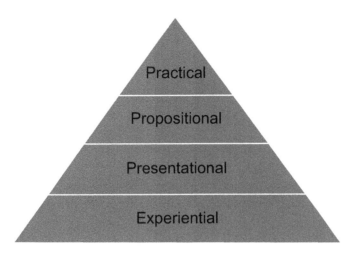

**Figure 6.1** Adapted from Heron (1996, p. 239).

**CASE STUDY: Dear Oak**

*Outdoor Environmental Education: Concept-Based Practice* is the name of a Master's level course run at the University of Edinburgh. It has traditionally been run as a residential course in the Highlands of Scotland within the Cairngorms National Park. Although it is a university course, it is relevant to teaching in schools because the teaching principles that emerge from experiential approaches to learning apply to all people regardless of age. It is also of relevance to the preparation of teachers on Initial Teacher Education programmes.

In the previous section the four-point epistemology was presented in such a way as to encourage movement through, and between, the different stages that link direct experience of nature with different ways of knowing. The following video blog shows the four-point epistemology in use but not with the technical language expressed here. Look closely to identify the four different parts of the framework.

www.teaching-matters-blog.ed.ac.uk/a-video-blog/

The framework is designed to promote the sort of learning and critical awareness that encourages people to be active change agents, not just in the future, but now in their everyday situation at schools and universities. Because of the experiential nature of this epistemology it is not enough to write about how to teach wonder. We invite you to watch this short film:

www.youtube.com/watch?v=tHTuY8UBCCE&feature=youtu.be

The linked films show how the course has tried to capture the students' experiences *in situ* (experiential knowing). It shows deep experiential engagement with an old oak tree. It also demonstrates presentational knowledge because of the lines of poetry shared, but also through the lens of the video camera that makes this available to a wider audience. Notice how the students want to learn more and understand better (the need for propositional knowledge). This is evident where the students seek facts and knowledge about the world's interconnections through the questions they ask. Lastly, there are commitments to action—to actively influence future behaviour—through the different pledges the students make (practical knowing).

Both of these clips started from the wonder the students experienced when they first encountered the old oak tree. They were simply asked to wander in a certain direction, knowing that they would come across the tree, as hundreds of students before them had, and that they would express similar excitement, joy and wonder at finding the tree for the "first" time. What we hope comes through strongly in the video is the deep level of connection and emotion expressed by the students (and staff). The notions of continuity and ecological connectivity with community (including non-human) are strong. We doubt that many indoor experiences could evoke such deep feeling and sense of commitment.

The films and case study purposefully show how rural woodland and city-based experiences can be brought together in the very different ways in which students express themselves. This follows the concentric circles model that is presented in Chapter 1. We encourage movement between the zones when the educational purpose and intention demands it. Thus, it is not just "green", rural, or wild spaces and places that need to be visited. As Duhn, Malone, and Tesar (2017) remind us, "urban environments are key sites for reimagining and reconfiguring human-nature encounters in times and spaces of planetary crisis" (p. 1357). The idea of wonder is important as it levels the playing field between teacher and student. Teachers are not just specialists; rather they can wonder together with their students. We invite all educators to get out there and help make wonder happen for their students and themselves.

## Guidelines

- Invite your students to wander through places and educational sites, and arrive at something that stirs their senses of curiosity.

- Facilitate experiences that allow students to interact with local phenomena through cognitive, affective, and sensory channels.

- Encourage your students to wonder deeply about the social and ecological events that have taken place there, or those that are being witnessed in real time.

- Employ Heron and Reason's four-point epistemology to lend your teaching a certain structure around the different ways that students can come to know something.

# Note

1 The term "epistemological diversity" simply means that knowledge comes in different forms, something commonly taught as part of Initial Teacher Education programmes. One example, but far from the only one, is Bloom's taxonomy which differentiates between the affective, sensory, and cognitive domains (see for example, Bloom, 1956; Bloom et al., 1964).

# References

Beames, S., Higgins, P., & Nicol, R. (2011). *Learning outside the classroom: Theory and guidelines for practice.* New York: Routledge.

Bloom, B. S. (Ed.). (1956). *Taxonomy of educational objectives: Book 1 cognitive domain.* London: Longman.

Bloom, B. S., Krathwohl, D. R., & Masia, B. B. (Eds.). (1964). *Taxonomy of educational objectives: Book 2 affective domain.* London: Longman.

Bruner, J. (2006). *In search of pedagogy volume I.* London: Routledge.

Dewey, J. (1963). *Experience and education.* London: Collier-Macmillan. (Original work published 1938)

Duhn, I., Malone, K., & Tesar, M. (2017). Troubling the intersections of urban/nature/childhood in environmental education. *Environmental Education Research, 23*(10), 1357–1368.

Egan, K. (1997). *The educated mind: How cognitive tools shape our understanding.* Chicago, IL: University of Chicago Press.

Heron, J. (1996). *Co-operative inquiry: Research into the human condition.* London: SAGE.

Heron, J., & Reason, P. (2008). Extending epistemology within a co-operative inquiry. In P. Reason & H. Bradbury (Eds.), *The SAGE handbook of action research participative inquiry and practice* (2nd ed., pp. 366–380). London: SAGE.

Judson, G. (2018). *A walking curriculum: Evoking wonder and developing a sense of place* (K-12). Middletown, DE: Independently Published.

Meyer, J. H. F., & Land, R. (2005). Threshold concepts and troublesome knowledge (2): Epistemological considerations and a conceptual framework for teaching and learning. *Higher Education, 49*(3), 373–388.

Mohr Lone, J., & Burroughs, M. D. (2016). *Philosophy in education: Questioning and dialogue in schools.* Lanham, MD: Rowman & Littlefield.

Nicol, R. (2013). Returning to the richness of experience: Is autoethnography a useful approach for outdoor educators in promoting pro-environmental behaviour? *Journal of Adventure Education and Outdoor Learning, 13*(1), 3–17.

Nicol, R. (2014a). Fostering environmental action through outdoor education. *Educational Action Research, 22*(1), 39–56.

Nicol, R. (2014b). Entering the fray: The role of outdoor education in providing nature-based experiences that matter. *Educational Philosophy and Theory, 46*(5), 449–461.

Nicol, R., & Sangster, P. (2019). You are never alone: Understanding the educational potential of an 'urban solo' in promoting place-responsiveness. *Environmental Education Research, 25*(9), 1368–1385.

Opdal, P. M. (2001). Curiosity, wonder and education seen as perspective development. *Studies in Philosophy and Education, 20*(4), 331–344.

Orr, D. (1992). *Ecological literacy: Education and the transition to a postmodern world.* Albany, NY: State University of New York Press.

Orr, D. (1994). The marriage of mind and nature. *Resurgence, 166*, 6–7.

Outdoor Journeys. (2021). *What is outdoor journeys?* www.outdoorjourneys.co.uk

Reason, P. (1998). A participatory world. *Resurgence, 186*, 42–44.

Reason, P. (2006). Choice and quality in action research practice. *Journal of Management Inquiry, 15*(2), 187–203.

Rogers, C. (1983). *Freedom to learn: For the 80s.* London: Merrill.

Rubinstein, D. (2015). *Born to walk: The transformative power of a pedestrian act.* Toronto: ECW Press.

Schinkel, A. (2017). The educational importance of deep wonder. *Journal of Philosophy of Education, 51*(2), 538–553.

Solnit, R. (2014). *Wanderlust: A history of walking.* London: Granta.

Stevenson, R. L. (1957). *Travels with a donkey in the Cevennes; [and] An inland voyage.* London: Thomas Nelson and Sons.

Vasalou, S. (Ed.). (2013). *Practices of wonder: Cross disciplinary perspectives.* Cambridge: James Clarke & Co.

Vygotsky, L. (1978). *Mind in society: The development of higher psychological processes.* Cambridge, MA: Harvard University Press.

Whitehead, A. (1968). *Modes of thought.* New York: Free Press Paperback. (Original work published 1938)

# 7 Community-based learning

## What is community-based learning?

Community-based learning (CBL) is a form of education that aims to cultivate caring citizens who are both motivated and able to address society's most pressing issues. What we call CBL today vastly predates formal schooling, which rose to prominence alongside the industrial revolution in the early to mid-1800s (see Chapter 3). However, young people have been learning from community members since the beginning of human existence. In this chapter, the focus is on human interaction, as opposed to connections between humans and the more-than-human world.

There are strong philosophical and theoretical arguments and an increasing body of empirical evidence to support the notion of close partnerships between schools and the communities in which they are located. The literature shows how all stakeholders (not just students) can benefit from families, other students, and schools working together with local businesses, social care institutions, cultural and governmental organizations, and colleges and universities (Epstein et al., 2018; Stefanski, Valli, & Jacobson, 2016; NEA Policy Brief, 2008). Indeed, more than 25 years ago, Epstein (1995) argued that a child's education was the product of effective partnerships between the school, the family, and the community.

Three points distinguish community-based learning from other approaches. The first is that organizations and workplaces external to the school become sites for learning (Smith & Sobel, 2010). The second is that community members play more central roles in children's learning. This could mean that everything from law enforcement agencies to food banks to community gardens become sites for cross-curricular knowledge acquisition. Crucially, since it is not possible for teachers to be "content experts" on all of the organizations that are visited, community members become co-educators for children. The third feature of CBL is reciprocity. Reciprocity essentially means that both the community and the students gain from this arrangement (Kendall, 1990). Community-based learning "borrows" the term reciprocity from service learning (see Jacoby, 2003) and from social capital theory (see Putnam, 2000). The term reciprocity is used to describe how pupils, agencies, and the general public can benefit (to varying degrees) from carefully considered educational initiatives that take place in partnership with external organizations and which are facilitated by local experts.

As with place-responsive education (see Chapter 5), CBL often focuses on what is visible and familiar, but less known, such as a corner shop we walk past most days, but about which we know very little. However, Melaville, Berg, and Blank (2006) see a community's history, culture, and present-day struggles as being the basis for developing a relevant and engaging curriculum, which may also serve to shine a light on elements of community life that have been made less visible and less valued by those in power.

Community-based learning, however, is not just about pupils having richer and more authentic learning experiences; it's also about the communities themselves benefitting from schools and pupils being actively intertwined with the agencies that exist to provide goods and services for them. When done well, pupils and "community others" stand to gain from their relationships with each other. While perhaps somewhat idealistic, this win-win notion captures the concept of *reciprocity*.

## Place-based *versus* community-based learning?

Historically, many outdoor adventure education courses have ignored the places and communities in which they take place (Beames & Atencio, 2008). As discussed thoroughly in Chapter 5, there is a body of literature that is very critical of outdoor adventure programmes that are so inwardly focused on personal and social development that they pay scant attention to "place". Brookes (2002), for example, forcefully critiques approaches that treat landscapes "as empty sites on which to establish social or psychological projects" (p. 405).

As discussed previously, all landscapes (urban, rural, and in-between) have "stories" (see Henderson, 2010). Authors such as Molly Baker (2005) challenge outdoor educators to create programmes that reject universalist content that can be taught in any location, and instead focus on what is special and distinct to a given area.

The rise of local, closer-to-home, approaches to outdoor learning has shown how community partnerships have the capacity to benefit students and the communities in which they live and go to school (Maeda, 2005; McKenzie & Blenkinsop, 2006; Stefanski et al., 2016). Indeed, with more than 55% of the planet's population living in cities (World Bank, 2022), it will be increasingly important for educators to develop ways to teach and learn alongside fellow community members within large urban centres. Some suggest that partnerships with families and communities should be a core competency of a professional teacher (Epstein et al., 2018).

Community-based learning and place-responsive education (PRE) are similar but have one principal difference: CBL is, arguably, place-responsive, but not all PRE involves CBL. Consider, for example, an expedition that aims to ski across Antarctica. It is entirely possible to learn about the ecosystems of that place, but, unless one was going to study social interaction within the expedition team or at one of the scientific research bases, there is very little possibility for CBL. Thus, for our purposes, CBL is place-responsive education that is enriched by—and ideally enriches—individuals and organizations within communities.

## Rationales for community-based learning

Now that we have some basic CBL concepts under our belts, we can dig more deeply into the reasons that CBL can be a worthwhile approach to teaching and learning. We know from our discussions in Chapter 5 that students' communities "provide a natural context for learning that matters to children" (Melaville et al., 2006, p. 11). Bloom et al.'s (1956) classic taxonomy is still useful here, as it helps us consider how ways that a pupil's development in cognitive (knowledge), psycho-motor (skills), and affective (attitudes/relationships) domains may be limited by conventional modes of teaching that completely eschew community partnerships.

The students should be the first and most obvious "winners" from CBL. For this benefit to be valued and nurtured over the long term, the communities themselves also need to gain from networks between students, parents, schools, and local businesses, non-profit organizations, and government. Gilchrist (2019) explains how communities can be seen as "the informal interactions and connections that we use to coordinate everyday life" (p. 3). It follows that two reasonable questions to ask would be: *How do schools work more deliberately with community members to help students both contribute to and benefit from their community networks?* and *How do community members and organizations deliberately engage with schools?*

The notion that social networks have value is central to social capital theory (Putnam, 2000; Field, 2017). Essentially, each of us is able to extract benefits from the social networks of which we are a part, and some networks comprise deeper, more trusting, and more reciprocal relationships than others. The argument follows that "better connected people enjoy better returns" (Burt, 2000, p. 3). We can see how social capital theory builds a case for increasing interaction between students and community others—particularly with community members who have different lived experiences to the students. This notion of "bridging" is thus regarded as a way that both privileged and marginalized individuals or groups may gain and learn from relationships with one another. Putnam (2000) contends that all individuals will be more productive in a well-connected society than in a poorly-connected one.

The principal educational and developmental rationale here is that rich social networks enable their members to gain access to resources that they would not otherwise have access to. Without access to these networks, people may be less likely to share information about a job opportunity, the contact details of a reliable plumber, a drill set, or a community group. Following this line of argument, schools have a duty to connect their students with networks that will enable young people to flourish by accessing the knowledge, skills, attitudes, and opportunities held within the community.

Gilchrist (2019) suggests that increasing civic associations and public partnerships might serve to increase social capital within communities. Seen this way, CBL is not just about pupil learning, but broader community cohesion and development. It is these rich networks of people that bring the capacity to increase "democratic renewal, social cohesion, regeneration, and public health" (p. 20). Any outdoor learning programme that ignores these societal imperatives of engaging with "businesses, public services, voluntary groups, and social groups in the communities" (Beames & Atencio, 2008, p. 104) where their schools are located is arguably limiting potential for both student learning and community development.

As this chapter progresses, it should become more apparent that an enlightened kind of CBL involves much more than inviting a guest into the class or having the class visit a senior's residence. While both of these examples could have positive outcomes, CBL has the additional capacity to facilitate deep and meaningful cross-curricular learning.

## Authentic learning contexts

One central reason that CBL can be so powerful is that it's "real". This is a huge oversimplification, of course, as all teaching and learning is real. However, teaching and learning that takes place in a school is deliberately and artificially separated from students' homes and neighbourhoods. Seen this way, the very idea of a type of education that takes place in institutions where students gather to learn standardized pieces of information is rather bizarre! Blank and Berg (2006) explain how their research in both small rural towns and big urban cities showed that student learning can improve when "core academic curriculum is tied to the community" and the "artificial separation between the classroom and the real world" is removed (p. 8).

Community-based learning approaches, by contrast, seek to re-locate education in contexts that are familiar, local, and which have direct relevance with students' everyday lives. Christie, Beames, and Blackwell (2017) refer to these as *authentic learning contexts*, as they are strongly intertwined with students' home and social lives. Authentic learning contexts are powerful because they are real, tangible, and relevant, in the ways they blend "academic content with situations or issues that are meaningful to students" (Imel, 2000, p. 1). Crucially, in contrast to some kinds of adventure-based programmes, learning through authentic contexts does not rely on contested notions of transfer of learning between greatly differing contexts (Beames & Brown, 2016).

This idea of rooting student learning within communities is not a new one. Indeed, about 125 years ago, the American educational philosopher John Dewey, wrote that topics about which students learned in schools "must be derived from the scope of ordinary life-experience" (1938/1997, p. 73). Dewey was firmly against forms of education that involved simply moving from one official educational stage to the next. Rather, he was a champion of education for the here and now—education that was full of meaning in the present, as opposed to some kind of "preparation for the future" (1897). Sue Waite (2013) argues that the "interface" between students' lives, communities, and the school, need to be aligned in order to be productive and worthwhile. This interface is important, as students are not a homogenous group; they are often highly diverse and their individual communities and lived experiences, traditions, and cultures reflect that diversity. Therefore, we need to develop our CBL from our students' vantage points.

While integrating curriculum with the "real world" is a notion that few parents, students, and teachers may argue against, it can be hard work for all parties! Teaching through authentic learning contexts is especially challenging, as it almost certainly won't follow an uncomplicated linear path, the way a series of tightly planned lessons in a classroom might do. As with any lesson plan, intended learning outcomes need to be identified beforehand. The difference, in these most fluid educational environments outside the classroom, is that further learning outcomes may be attained, in addition to the intended ones. Teachers may need to retrospectively connect emergent learning outcomes with what was experienced, by summarizing these and adding comments to their previously prepared lesson plans after the session. Engaging in this process of reflection and forward planning may help when it comes to running a similar session in the future, while demonstrating the responsive educational process of CBL to community partners, parents, principals, and school inspectors.

## Incorporating CBL into existing classroom teaching

Following a key point in the last paragraph, incorporating CBL into existing teaching practice requires much greater time and effort from the teacher than it does to use an "off the shelf" prescribed lesson that has been employed in the past. This is not a slight against teachers who, over the years, have accrued a rich selection of resources and constantly refined their lessons to become more and more effective. However, with CBL there may be an additional level of energy and stress that accompanies the unpredictability of working outside of the classroom with community partners. Communities are constantly evolving, transforming, and experiencing change in a range of ways, so the "field" in that sense is not static. This means teachers must remain especially sensitive to these cultural shifts in relation to the lesson plan—indeed, that's the whole point! Once the community-based teaching has begun, the teacher's role then shifts to one of manager, where they move away from the centre of the stage and invite the co-educators in the community to shine, while maintaining an oversight on transport, food and drink intake, toilets, temperature regulation, and so on.

We hold Smith and Sobel's (2010) book on *Place- and Community-based Education* in high regard. They outlined four ways students can learn through engaging with the people and places within their community. First, cultural aspects of community life can be shared to learn about a broad range of spiritual, religious, and social rituals that have evolved over time. Many of these stories and practices may have been influenced by migration in and out of places—some of which may be due to historical oppression, racism, and forced mobilization from their homelands. Indeed, in some cases, this cultural dilution has come (and continues to come) through highly oppressive forms of imperialism at the hands of powerful entities and policies (Mack, 2011). Learning about the heritage of one's place can help deepen a young person's investment in, and commitment to, making their community a desirable place to live. Learning about place through community members' stories can be especially powerful, as demonstrated by the Foxfire (2018) initiative in Appalachia. In this programme, high school English students interviewed elders in the region and created magazines (and later books) that shared stories of their customs, crafts, and traditions.

The second way to teach and learn through community, involves addressing environmental issues. This might involve conserving a particular section of a park or downtown street, or another nearby site that is familiar to, and valued by, students. Other kinds of environmental initiatives could focus on changing people's patterns of consumption and disposal of material goods, or on how we use natural resources to power many aspects of our lives, such as the fossil fuels heating our homes and fuelling our cars.

Smith and Sobel (2010) argue that "young people must also gain an understanding of what is required to make a living in the places where they live" (p. 51). This focus on business and economic development is their third approach to CBL. They place a high value on working with small and large businesses and non-for-profit organizations, in order to learn about entrepreneurship in more tangible and obvious ways.

The fourth approach to CBL is arguably a nod to Dewey, who we discussed earlier in the chapter. Here, the focus turns to citizenship, where student learning involves increasingly understanding the rights, and taking on the responsibilities, of adulthood. An important element of citizenship involves becoming aware of those who are most vulnerable our communities and who may be less likely, or less able, to advocate and take action for themselves. Following Melaville and colleagues (2006), students learn how to be engaged citizens by "identifying and acting on issues and concerns that affect their own community" (p. 3).

Smith (2002) very clearly articulates how this fourth kind of CBL features first "engaging students in the identification of school or community issues that they would like to investigate and address" (p. 589). The teacher's role then becomes one of helping students to organise themselves in such ways that they can more effectively work to address the issue. Naturally, the teacher also needs to link elements of this initiative to appropriate curricular outcomes, while acting as "manager" of the relationships between the class and external stakeholders.

Billig's (2017) work demonstrates how learning through serving others can yield "academic, social-emotional, and civic outcomes" (p. 76). This approach to education has a particularly strong foothold in American schools and colleges, and Butin (2010) explains that it can connect "classrooms with communities and textbooks with the 'real world'" (p. xiv). As you can see, this language resonates quite clearly with the principles of CBL that we've covered. Crucially, in any kind of service initiative, those being served should have some power to determine the nature of the services provided (Jacoby, 1996; Butin, 2010; Pedersen et al., 2015).

The service element of CBL can bring issues of social justice to the fore and thus make for rich discussions about the kinds of communities young people want to create, rather than simply exist in. Indeed, Sheffield (2011) argues that service learning has the "radical potential to reconstruct individuals, communities and institutional structures that are currently oppressive" (p. 125). This may be especially important for students living in communities with, for example, a history of racial oppression.

Rahima Wade (2000) explains how we must discuss with our students the underlying reasons that a certain "service" is required in the first place. This requires researching the historic, persistent, and systemic issues faced by local communities and, more specifically, marginalized peoples within those communities. In many cases, we may have cultural "blind spots" that can be explained to us by community partners. The onus on broadening one's cultural learning should not be entirely shouldered by others; it is arguable that all human beings need to make efforts to understand their own biases and blind spots. The crucial point here is that the learning comes from understanding the underlying factors that have created the conditions in which some people, for example, don't have enough to eat, rather than from merely handing out food at a soup kitchen.

A final word in this section comes from Wade (2000), who implores educators to ensure that service-learning sessions are not "onetime" experiences. At the risk of sounding "preachy", let us not fall prey to tokenistic approaches, where the service - learning "box" gets ticked by one isolated gesture of goodwill. These actions can, in some cases, perpetuate existing cycles of oppression, and foster mistrust in the wider community. Following Wade, we encourage educators to seek out long-term community partnerships that will benefit all parties over time.

## Challenges of community partnerships

While CBL can be regarded as a desirable, and even enlightened approach to learning and teaching, making it happen in practice can be very challenging. It is perhaps not surprising that forms of education seeking to directly involve young learners in the democratic, economic, and civil processes of society can be a messy undertaking that is full of uncertainties. Luckily, it is not solely up to teachers to implement CBL: It is the responsibility of schools, families, and communities to work together and make it happen (Blank & Berg, 2006). The development of the whole child is facilitated by "bringing together the assets and resources of communities and families at schools to help support students, while ensuring that the school sees the community as an important partner and resource" (p. 11). It is likely that CBL "champions" are needed both within and outside of the school to spearhead initiatives.

In our experience, there are three principal challenges to building community partnerships for educational purposes: Child protection, finding a willing partner, and the additional logistical arrangements.

Since the turn of the millennium, the media gaze focusing on matters of child protection (Furedi & Bristow, 2008) and the research activity on child maltreatment has been steadily increasing (Bullinger, Feely, Raissian, & Schneider, 2020). Furedi and Bristow's research describes how our communities have been weakened by a culture that suspects volunteers, coaches, and other helpful parents as potential child abusers until they have undergone a criminal disclosure (aka police check). Throughout history and across cultures, adults have been largely responsible for shaping the kinds of knowledge, skills, and attitudes that they want their children to develop (Furedi & Bristow, 2008). Late modernity's "risk society" (see Giddens, 1991; Beck, 1992) has served to remove many of the important "influencers" within our communities, as they are seen as a threat to our children's safety, rather than playing an integral role in their educational and developmental journeys.

There is a strong argument for the benefits of including "community others" in educational plans. The risks associated with child abuse or abduction need to be identified and managed, just as with any other hazards that may be encountered (see Chapter 11 on risk management). In most educational settings, it is perfectly reasonable for community adults (even those who have not had a police check) to work with children. What is crucial is that both adults and children are protected by always working in groups (i.e. not one-on-one) that are under the teacher's supervision. In many cases, adults will only require a police check if they will be working with young people on a regular basis and/or being paid for this.

The second challenge when developing a CBL programme is in finding an organization that is willing to work with the class. As noted above, in an ideal arrangement, there is actual reciprocity, where both partners (the agency and the students) benefit. In reality, there will likely be a certain degree of asymmetry, where the organization may feel as if they do not have the capacity to give as much as you and your students might like. There may be an element of educating community organizations, so that schools can highlight to these agencies that they have the capacity (and arguably a civic duty) to bring their expertise and assets to the areas of community development and children's education.

Sanders' (2006) American-based research showed that the biggest obstacles to CBL were school staff not being willing to participate or not having enough time to seek and nurture relationships with partner organizations. Sanders also reported that some communities appeared to view themselves as not being rich enough in collective resources to offer anything meaningful to schools, while some teachers spoke of competition between schools to work with community organizations and individuals who were perceived as having particularly high-value.

Earlier in the chapter, we discussed social capital theory, which focuses on the richness of one's social networks. There is widespread agreement from scholars that building relationships across social divisions is central to building a rich and inclusive community that allows all its members to thrive (see Putnam, 2000; Ife, 2010; Delanty, 2018). One way "in" to CBL, can be to ask parents at the beginning of each year what knowledge and skills they would be willing to share with students, while indicating if their workplaces and affiliate organizations might be suitable for visits.

The third obstacle to CBL lies in the planning associated with the extra logistics of communicating with community partners and arranging transportation, adult helpers, and food/drink/toileting. This additional responsibility is compounded by the non-linear, rather unpredictable path that CBL may take. As mentioned earlier, because CBL doesn't just take place outside the classroom—but has as its central features people teaching who are not school employees; the session often taking place in atypical educational sites—this kind of approach can bring with it additional challenges: First, teachers may find it a more difficult "sell" to parents and school administrators, and second, the learning outcomes may be more difficult to entirely predict at the start and thus "officially" document.

Despite the aforementioned obstacles, more recent research has confirmed that students are highly motivated by seeing themselves as agents of social change (Billig, 2017). This, combined with the pedagogical and philosophical imperatives underpinning CBL, should outweigh the obstacles that present themselves.

## CASE STUDY

Stoney Brook is a fictional middle school in Vermont, USA. The school is located near the fabled "Long Trail", which is 438 kilometres long. Mr. Clément, the school principal, decided that the Grade 8 students needed a community-based, outdoor learning experience. He wanted this to be an adventure-filled, cross-curricular trip. The students, two teachers and four students studying outdoor education at a nearby college, travelled 55 kilometres south by bus, and spent the next three days walking back to school.

The three principles of CBL are apparent in this case study. First, the learning took place in a variety of sites away from the school. Apart from the trail itself, the students visited a ranger station, a community-run coffee shop for seniors, and an organic farm. Second, many of the people from whom the students were learning were not their schoolteachers: The educators included the OE students, the rangers, the volunteers who ran the coffee shop, and the staff at the farm. On day two, the group spent the afternoon working at the organic farm. In return for their help with weeding and clearing out an old barn, they received mini-lectures on bio-dynamic vegetable growing and small business start-up. This exchange reflects the third principle of reciprocity, where both the server and the served benefit from the interaction.

There wasn't time to help at the café, but plans were made for a return trip, where the Grade 7 class would paint the cabin that housed the café in exchange for being able to camp on site for a couple of nights.

The arguments for local businesses, social care agencies, and governmental organizations to become partners in the schooling of society's young people are growing. The National Education Association in the USA, states that "[m]ost school professionals now realize that the job of educating students cannot be achieved by their efforts alone. Rather, it requires a collaborative effort with families, communities, and other stakeholders" (NEA, 2011, p. 6). In its ideal form, however, CBL is more than another approach to learning outside the classroom: It features the promise and possibilities of "civic renewal" (Butin, 2010).

As with place responsive education, CBL is arguably most effective when it is critical and transformative in nature (Jakubowski, 2003). Seen this way, there is a strong imperative to consider the range of knowledges held within community spaces, which might come in the form of stories, cultures, and traditions local to those places and specific to the communities that have lived there over long periods of time. We deliberately use the plural term "knowledges" here to represent our view that "what we know" can be gained in formal spaces, such as schools with "traditional" teacher-learner relationships; passed on through generations by cultural practices; and gleaned through personal lived experiences.

For example, Indigenous knowledges are often understood as ways to "restore, renew and revitalize" connections to people and place (Battiste & Henderson, 2009, p. 9). Often it is this kind of diverse cultural wealth—seen also in immigrant communities—that is under-valued by dominant educational models that privilege "codified Western knowledge", which lends itself to being replicated in standardized tests (Urrieta, 2016).

Some may not share the view that a school's principal mission is to strengthen the communities in which they are located. However, it would seem to be a very limited conception of education that ignores the rich, reciprocal opportunities for growth that can come from rooting teaching within the contexts of students' own communities, as opposed to taking place in some distant and decontextualized location. Chambers (2017) argues that we must examine how and from where we construct knowledge. Powerful, real-world educational experiences that come from "holding a mirror up to ourselves" (p. 50) can thus play a vital role in shaping how our students view their place within their local community and beyond.

All of the sources that we have drawn on to explain CBL are united in their belief that teaching and learning for citizenship and democracy needs to begin at an early age and continue through direct experiences of engaging with pressing local issues. We are convinced, just as John Dewey (1916/2004) was more than 100 years ago, that the primary aim of education is to enable students to become active citizens in a democratic society. Indeed, following Epstein and associates (2018), students need to be placed firmly in the centre of a model that features partnerships between school, family, and community. Community-based learning can require much time and energy to coordinate students, parents, teachers, community organizations, and school administrators, but we are increasingly convinced that this approach to education is one that should become normalized.

## Guidelines

- Teaching is enriched through students engaging with "real world", authentic learning contexts.

- Off campus sites, such as local businesses, government agencies, social welfare organizations, become extensions of the classroom.

- Community members, with their wide varieties of knowledges and skills, become co-educators.

- The strengthened social networks that arise from CBL can benefit all members of the community.

- CBL can be used to expose, understand, and address central issues of, for example, racism, colonization, and systemic poverty.

## References

Baker, M. (2005). Landfullness in adventure-based programming: Promoting reconnection to the land. *Journal of Experiential Education, 27*(3), 267–276.

Battiste, M., & Henderson, J. S. Y. (2009). Naturalizing Indigenous knowledge in Eurocentric education. *Canadian Journal of Native Education, 32*(1), 5–18.

Beames, S., & Atencio, M. (2008). Building social capital through outdoor education. *Journal of Adventure Education & Outdoor Learning, 8*(2), 99–112.

Beames, S., & Brown, M. (2016). *Adventurous learning: A pedagogy for a changing world.* New York: Routledge.

Beck, U. (1992). *Risk society: Towards a new modernity*. London: SAGE.

Billig, S. H. (2017). Implementing service-learning in elementary schools to enhance inclusion. In S. Lavery, D. Chambers, & G. Cain (Eds.), *Service-learning* (International perspectives on inclusive education, Vol. 12, pp. 75–94). Bingley: Emerald.

Blank, M., & Berg, A. (2006). *All together now: Sharing responsibility for the whole child*. Washington, DC: Coalition for Community Schools.

Bloom, B., Engelhart, M., Furst, E., Hill, W., & Krathwohl, D. (1956). *Taxonomy of educational objectives, Handbook I: The cognitive domain*. New York: David McKay.

Brookes, A. (2002). Lost in the Australian bush: Outdoor education as curriculum. *Journal of Curriculum Studies, 34*(4), 405–425.

Bullinger, L. R., Feely, M., Raissian, K. M., & Schneider, W. (2020). Heed neglect, disrupt child maltreatment: A call to action for researchers. *International Journal on Child Maltreatment: Research, Policy and Practice, 3*, 93–104.

Burt, R. S. (2000). The network structure of social capital. *Research in Organizational Behavior, 22*, 345–423.

Butin, D. W. (2010). *Service-learning in theory and practice: The future of community engagement in higher education*. New York: Palgrave Macmillan.

Chambers, R. (2017). *Can we know better? Reflection for development*. Rugby: Practical Action.

Christie, E., Beames, S., & Blackwell, I. (2017). Developing whole school approaches to integrated indoor/outdoor teaching. In S. Waite (Ed.), *Children learning outside the classroom* (pp. 82–93). London: SAGE.

Delanty, G. (2018). *Community*. New York: Routledge.

Dewey, J. (1997). *Experience and education*. New York: Touchstone. (Original work published 1938)

Dewey, J. (2004). *Democracy and education*. Mineola, NY: Dover. (Original work published 1916)

Epstein, J. (1995). School/family/community partnerships: Caring for the children we share. *Phi Delta Kappan, 76*, 701–712.

Epstein, J. L., Sanders, M. G., Sheldon, S. B., Simon, B. S., Salinas, K. C., Jansorn, N. R., . . . & Williams, K. J. (2018). *School, family, and community partnerships: Your handbook for action* (4th ed.). Thousand Oaks, CA: Corwin Press.

Field, J. (2017). *Social capital* (3rd ed.). Abingdon: Routledge.

Foxfire Fund. (2018). *Travels with Foxfire: Stories of people, passions, and practices from southern Appalachia*. New York: Anchor.

Furedi, F., & Bristow, H. (2008). *Licensed to hug: How child protection policies are poisoning the relationship between the generations and damaging the voluntary sector*. London: Civitas.

Giddens, A. (1991). *Modernity and self identity: Self and society in the late modern age*. Cambridge: Polity Press.

Gilchrist, A. (2019). *The well-connected community 3E: A networking approach to community development*. Bristol: Policy Press.

Henderson, B. (2010). Understanding heritage travel: Story, place, and technology. In S. Beames (Ed.), *Understanding educational expeditions* (pp. 79–89). Rotterdam: Sense.

Ife, J. (2010). *Human rights from below: Achieving rights through community development*. Cambridge: Cambridge University Press.

Imel, S. (2000). *Contextual learning in adult education*. Centre on Education, Training and Employment, Practice Application Brief no. 12. ERIC Clearinghouse on Adult, Career, and Vocational Education.

Jacoby, B. (1996). Service learning in today's higher education. In B. Jacoby (Ed.), *Service learning in higher education: Concepts and practices* (pp. 3–25). San Francisco, CA: Jossey-Bass.

Jacoby, B. (Ed.). (2003). *Building partnerships for service-learning.* San Francisco, CA: Jossey-Bass.

Jakubowski, L. M. (2003). Beyond book learning: Cultivating the pedagogy of experience through field trips. *Journal of Experiential Education, 26*(1), 24–33.

Kendall, J. C. (1990). Combining service and learning: An introduction. In J. C. Kendall & Associates (Eds.), *Combining service and learning: A resource book for community and public service* (Vol. 1, pp. 1–33). Raleigh: National Society for Internships and Experiential Education.

Mack, J. (2011). Hoquotist: Reorienting through storied practice. In H. Lessard, R. Johnson, & J. Webber (Eds.), *Storied communities: Narratives of contact and arrival in constituting political community* (pp. 287–307). Chicago: Chicago University Press.

Maeda, K. (2005). Community-based outdoor education using a local approach to conservation. *Australian Journal of Outdoor Education, 9*(1), 40–47.

McKenzie, M., & Blenkinsop, S. (2006). An ethic of care and education practice. *Journal of Adventure Education & Outdoor Learning, 6*(2), 91–106.

Melaville, A., Berg, A., & Blank, M. (2006). *Community-based learning: Engaging students for success and citizenship.* Washington, DC: Coalition for Community Schools.

National Education Association. (2008). *Parent, family, community involvement in education* (NEA Policy Brief). www.nea.org/assets/docs/PB11_ParentInvolvement08.pdf

National Education Association. (2011). *The power of family school community partnerships: A training resource manual.* http://www2.nea.org/mediafiles/pdf/FSCP_Manual_2012.pdf

Pedersen, P. J., Meyer, J. M., & Hargrave, M. (2015). Learn global; serve local: Student outcomes from a community-based learning pedagogy. *Journal of Experiential Education, 38*(2), 189–206.

Putnam, R. (2000). *Bowling alone: The collapse and revival of American community.* London: Simon & Schuster.

Sanders, M. (2006). *Building school-community partnerships: Collaboration for student success.* New York: SAGE.

Sheffield, E. C. (2011). *Strong community service learning: Philosophical perspectives.* New York: Peter Lang.

Smith, G. (2002). Learning to be where we are. *Phi Delta Kappan, 83*(8), 584–559.

Smith, G., & Sobel, D. (2010). *Place-and community-based education in schools.* London: Routledge.

Stefanski, A., Valli, L., & Jacobson, R. (2016). Beyond involvement and engagement: The role of the family in school—community partnerships. *School Community Journal, 26*(2), 135–160.

Urrieta Jr, L. (2016). Diasporic community smartness: Saberes (knowings) beyond schooling and borders. *Race, Ethnicity and Education, 19*(6), 1186–1199.

Wade, R. C. (2000). Beyond charity: Service-learning for social justice. *Social Studies and the Young Learner, 12*(4), 6–9.

Waite, S. (2013). 'Knowing your place in the world': How place and culture support and obstruct educational aims. *Cambridge Journal of Education, 43*(4), 413–433.

World Bank. (2022). *Urban development.* www.worldbank.org/en/topic/urbandevelopment/overview#:~:text=Today%2C%20some%2055%25%20of%20the,world%20will%20live%20in%20cities.

# 8 Integrating mobile digital technology

## Chapter aims

- Articulate the broader educational reasons for integrating digital technology into everyday teaching.

- Understand the pedagogical affordances of using mobile devices outdoors.

- Recognize the pitfalls surrounding using mobile devices outdoors.

- Consider ways to decide when, why, how and in what ways to use mobile digital technologies outdoors and when not to.

## Background

The world experienced a sea change in 1995, with the advent of the worldwide web. Another date associated with society-altering technology/communication advances is 2007 and the arrival of the first iPhone. Featuring a "touchscreen"— alongside easy access to web searches, filming and photography, email and video calls—the smartphone has revolutionized how humans communicate with each other and the world around them. The iPad followed in 2010, and many children born since then have grown-up with mobile, touchscreen technology and regard it as a normal and integral aspect of everyday life. Indeed, in the United States, 84% of teenagers have their own mobile phone (Commonsense Media, 2019), and a 2020 report showed that more than half of British teens sleep with their phones by their side (Childwise, 2020). These statistics are reflected similarly across all continents with little debate as to whether mobile devices are here to stay or not: Evidently, they are.

In this chapter, we are focusing our discussion on mobile, screen-based devices, such as touchscreen phones and tablets, and the ways in which they can enhance and deepen learning. Bolliger and Shepherd (2017) suggest that this kind of

 DOI: 10.4324/9781003010890-8

learning takes place when "learners interact and engage with curricular, pedagogical, and social resources at various locations through portable electronic devices" (p. 182). The topic of incorporating technology into outdoor teaching more generally is receiving increased attention, particularly in terms of how to determine the pedagogical appropriateness of these mobile devices as educational tools (Hills & Thomas, 2020). The suitability of everything from mobile devices, through to drones and weather stations, needs to also be considered as a part of larger, school-wide discussions about teaching and learning. Due to the dominance of mobile, screen-based devices, this chapter is given to considering their pedagogical pitfalls and affordances, and at times expanding thinking to ways in which other pieces of mobile technology, such as drones, might or might not offer further possibilities for broadening and deepening learning.

Before going any further in this chapter, it is important to highlight that we are aware of certain assumptions that are being made. We are assuming that educators working outdoors with young people have the financial resources and communication infrastructure to support the integration of mobile technology into their practices. We do this to hopefully provide a wide range of ideas and applications for mobile technology outdoors. At the same time, we acknowledge that while many students have phones and other mobile technology, including access to the internet, not all students will have the same access—and some will have none. The above notwithstanding, mobile learning in the Global South is gaining tremendous traction as a low-cost, high-yield form of education. *M-learning* can be defined as the "distribution of digitized contents through mobile devices enabling the educators and students to learn anytime and anywhere" (Shukla, 2021, p. 280). Still, many teachers will not have the luxury of a set of tablets for their class, along with access to mobile data. This will require modifications to learning and teaching with technology which reflect the access to technology and internet in each context.

The literature indicates that a high proportion of school aged children are wedded to their mobile phones and these phones play an enormous role in mediating how they gather information about the world, undertake self-directed learning, and communicate with others (Twenge, 2017). Of course, mobile phones greatly influence how people interact with each other in society—whether it is at home, at a cafe, at school, or at work. There is widespread debate regarding mobile phone use in schools, with some claiming they can be used as learning tools, and others highlighting that they are merely a distraction (Oxford Learning, 2019). Similar debates are taking place with regard to the use of school owned tablets in classrooms, with some voices highlighting how some state schools have embraced tablets to a much larger degree than their independent school counterparts (see Rim, 2018). This is partly due to parents of children at such schools wanting to reduce the amount of their children's screen time (Rim, 2018). At the same time, many schools are adopting tablets (iPads and Kindle) to enable students to access a wider range of learning materials (e.g., books, tutorials, quizzes) for students that were not previously available or affordable in hard copy.

Similar kinds of "mobile devices in the classroom" discussions of course take place among educators who work outdoors. Giving educators the tools with which to navigate discussions around when, where and why it may be appropriate to use mobile technology is the aim of this chapter.

## How mobile devices can be incorporated into outdoor learning and teaching

We suggest there are five main ways in which mobile devices, such as tablets and phones, can be incorporated into cross curricular outdoor learning and teaching. These are as tools for gathering information, being a resource of information, geolocating and mapping, remotely supporting and supervising, reflection and sharing.

First, devices can be used to *gather information* about a place, in person. This can be done through typed note-taking, video footage, audio recording, and photographs. The idea is that information is gathered during the outing that can be accessed and/or reflected upon once back in the classroom or base. Once back where there are more powerful computers and stronger internet connections, this information can be recalled, deeply investigated, organized, shared, and expanded upon through accessing additional information about a place online, such as historical information and other people's experiences of places.

A second way tablets and phones can be used is as *mobile libraries*. There are countless apps that can help students to identify birds, flowers, trees, mushrooms, plants, rocks, and animal tracks. Beyond apps, one can also bring electronic books, pdfs of readings and stories, as well as pdfs of larger reference books that might cover everything from local history, field guides, stories of place, to first aid manuals. This significantly reduces the volume of resources to be physically carried in the field.

A third use for mobile devices relates to all things to do with *geolocation, mapping, and navigation*. Granted, at this point in time, schools lucky enough to have tablets may not have them enabled with mobile coverage (e.g., 4G) even in, and certainly beyond, the school grounds. At their most basic level, mobile devices with roaming internet can function as navigational aids for students. Moving beyond following on-screen directions, we arrive at a much more sophisticated educational employment of these devices which enables the first two uses of mobile devices—gathering information and being a source of information—to be attached to a specific place. Thus, these tablets and phones can provide students with the possibility to "story" the places they visit. From this view, mobile devices can become a way to take a popular leisure activity like geocaching and transform it from an electronic navigational exercise into a deeply engaging way to learn about place (see Chapter 5).

Another means of using phones in particular is as a way to *provide safety and support* for students who are travelling more independently. It might be that you are teaching a session in a more urban centre and supervising a Grade 9 class with ten groups of three. As a teacher you could be in touch with the designated "communications contact person" from each group. On a simple level, this arrangement allows students to inform the teacher where they are or if they are going to be a few minutes late. As discussed in the supervising groups outdoors chapter (Chapter 11), having this capacity to communicate is not unproblematic, as phones run out of battery power and students can choose to not communicate with teachers. This latter issue is one of trust and responsibility, and not one that is fundamentally about using digital technology outside. With students on remotely supervised expeditions, for example, mobile phones allow students to confirm their location and wellbeing to the educator who is back at the base. They may also seek advice on route choice, for example, with regard to weather or challenging terrain.

When used well, mobile phones can enable young people to experience more independence than they otherwise might have outdoors. The educator who is not physically with the students can continue to play the important roles of "sounding board", advice giver, listener, and general supporter (see Prince, 2017). Fans of Vygotsky (1934/1998) will also see a familiar assumption here: "What the child is able to do in collaboration today he [sic] will be able to do independently tomorrow" (p. 202). In cases like the Grade 9 class in an urban area and the groups on expedition, phones can play a much more important educational role—one beyond ensuring that people are where they planned to be.

The fifth and final way mobile devices can be employed positively is through *sharing experiences and learning* with peers, family, and the wider community through public online spaces. Initially, this can involve demonstrating learning through online portfolios, posts on websites and social media, and may involve the creative use of photo, audio, music, and film making tools and apps. These shared posts can then feature a wide variety of media, such as art, drama, video, photography, prose, music, and so on—all of which may serve as educational "hooks" that can help to harness curiosity and encourage wonder within students (see Chapter 6). These varied means of expression offer students alternative avenues to learn, and demonstrate their learning, than they might otherwise have.

As a starting point, sharing what one has learned with others is important for the learner and for those who care about the learner. Taking this to another level involves reaching a wider audience of people who do not know the learner, and this involves the learner becoming the educator, such as the eight-year-old who is teaching others on a YouTube channel how to tie her favourite knots. Moving to yet another level can involve engaging in social and environmental justice activities (e.g., #fridaysforfuture), and in citizen science, such as collecting and uploading data for an ongoing bird survey.

Beyond the initial levels of sharing information—which feature a large degree of "look what I have done" and looking at what others have done—mobile devices and digital technology more generally have the ability to enable young people to become contributors to larger conversations. Viewed this way, young people can move away from being consumers of the content available on public online spaces and towards being thoughtful "prosumers". Prosumers not only consume products, but create products for other people as well (Ritzer, Dean, & Jurgenson, 2012). Indeed, we believe there is rich fruit in exploring, more generally, how students can contribute to building knowledge and capacity that can be shared with others for everyone's educational benefit.

## Pitfalls surrounding using mobile devices outdoors

"Generation Z", born between 1995 and 2010, has been the subject of countless newspaper and magazine articles, a number of market research reports, and some books (see Beames, 2020) for some of these). A primary concern of many of these pieces is the effect of mobile devices on mental and emotional wellbeing, brain physiology, and reduced physical fitness and health (Lissak, 2018; Twenge, Joiner, Rogers, & Martin, 2018). There are apps that facilitate increased physical activity and healthy living, and the literature surrounding the wellbeing of today's young people in relation to mobile device use is increasing in size and robustness. However, much less rigorous research has been done in the area of pedagogy. If mobile devices are an integral part of children's out-of-school lives, what role might phones and tablets play in daily learning and teaching?

Writing in 2004, before the advent of touchscreen, "smart" devices, Cuthbertson, Socha, and Potter discussed the "double-edged sword" of using technology in outdoor learning contexts. They warned of gadgets and tools that unwittingly added "membranous layers to our direct encounter with the natural world" and could then "work against the actual goal of the outdoor education programme" (p. 137). Adding extra layers into our interactions with the natural world is a central pitfall of using technology outdoors. Mobile device use has another downside, however, and that is the reduction of face-to-face interactions with others, such as classmates or community members (Beames, 2017), which can in turn complicate the building of strong learning communities. If, as outdoor educators, one of our main purposes is for our students to learn about place and others through community, then it is important to ensure they have direct interaction with place and others (see Sobel, 2013). When taken together, there is an imperative for educators to balance the amount of "head down" time with "head up" time, and thus ask themselves if their students' head down time is proportionate to, and aligned with, the lesson's learning outcomes.

One way to highlight the potential pitfalls through incorporating mobile technology into learning outdoors is to adopt the Puentedura's (2006) SAMR model as a tool for considering ways in which teaching with technology can be optimised. The acronym SAMR stands for *substitution, augmentation, modification,* and *redefinition.* These terms can help educators better understand the nature and purpose of the technology they are thinking about employing in their teaching. When visualized as a continuum that reflects how educational tasks can be altered by integrating technology, substitution can be seen as directly replacing a traditional tool (e.g., bringing a field guide on a tablet), whereas redefinition would involve technology bringing experiences that were not possible before (e.g., interacting with people "back home" or in the classroom while on a trip). One approach is not necessarily better than the other, however, what is centrally important is having a discussion beforehand about the appropriateness of introducing a given piece of technology into the lesson with regard to the intended learning outcomes. In summary, using the SAMR model can assist teachers as they judge how some pieces of technology might serve as a substitution or augmentation of current methods, while those featuring modification or redefinition are actually transforming the learning process (Puentedura, 2013).

We know that some outdoor educators are concerned about the possibility of a student sharing information about health and safety incidents with family and others outside the programme. While this can be disruptive to the learning experiences outdoors, it can also breach the privacy of individuals. This could happen, for example, when an accident occurs and students are tempted to share inaccurate or incomplete information with outsiders, and which may negatively or inappropriately portray individuals, schools, and programmes. Fears of this kind of misrepresentation can lead to personal mobile devices not being permitted in outdoor learning spaces in order to avoid these possibilities. This can be addressed by having a conversation with students about communication policies, just as you might in a classroom setting. Equally, learning how to responsibly communicate with people external to the programme, and considering the benefits of not communicating until they return "home", can provide additional learning opportunities. Of course, as with any teaching tool—whether indoors or out—the use of mobile technology devices needs to be thoughtfully considered and monitored by educators. Ultimately, this example about an accident involves deeper, ethical questions surrounding privacy, which are important for both educators and students and need to be collectively discussed and addressed to ensure the safety, privacy, health, and well-being of all individuals. What is crucial is that the usual "in school" rules and regulations apply equally once outdoors.

All of this points to educators being better equipped to make their own decisions about when to incorporate mobile technology into their outdoor teaching and when not to. If we accept that mobile technology devices offer positives and potential for expanding and deepening learning, it follows that outdoor educators need to be experts at judging how these devices can become more integral to their learning and teaching practices—particularly where they bring opportunities to become more deeply engaged with people and places.

## A decision-making tool

Here we offer a decision-making tool to assist educators as they consider whether or not (and how) to incorporate mobile technology into their teaching. Writing in Australia about all things technological and outdoors (including drones, for example),

Hills and Thomas (2020) contend that educators outdoors need to become much more adept and deliberate about determining what learning might be enhanced or degraded by using or not using a given piece of mobile technology, and in what ways this might happen. What is of central importance is that teachers consider the degree to which using a piece of mobile technology will enable them to better achieve their intended learning outcomes. So many of our pedagogical decisions come back to this simple question of how what we do, or do not do, will enable students to learn more effectively. Pitfalls need to be considered as well, of course, and two big ones include: Privacy and security issues and the impacts of mobile devices on the natural places and their inhabitants that are being encountered. Our three principal questions surrounding mobile device use in relation to the lesson's intended learning outcomes are:

1. What educational possibilities does using the mobile technological device support?

2. What are the pitfalls of using this device?

3. To what degree do the benefits outweigh the pitfalls?

Together, these three questions offer educators a simple decision-making tool for determining what and how mobile devices might benefit learning for individuals and groups. When considering benefits and pitfalls of mobile tools in each given learning situation, it is essential to then weigh up the degree to which the affordances outweigh the pitfalls. A process of learning by doing—trial and error—led by students and educators is important within an authentic learning community. As with risk assessments (Chapter 11), all the decision-making need not be placed in the teacher's hands, of course; it can and should be done in negotiation with students as a part of the learning process, as this can help to build a shared learning community where decisions are made together. For example, learners using their phones to gather information about plants will enable them to quickly find the information they need and permit the teacher to move more freely among individuals and small groups. This allows learners to work more independently and develop further data gathering skills, while shifting the teacher's role from "keeper of all knowledge" to one that is focused on supporting a kind of pedagogy that is more self-directed. Conversely, knowing how and when to decide to not use mobile devices, can allow for very different kinds of interaction between people and place, and between people in a given place.

Even though this chapter's focus is mainly on mobile screen-based devices, the SAMR model and the three questions above are useful for examining any kind of educational tool, prop, or piece of equipment that is being considered. Therefore, in the case study presented below, we bring in a drone to broaden the discussion about how other forms of technology (existing and yet to be created) may offer wider learning opportunities for students present and absent. The case demonstrates how the third question—to what degree do the benefits outweigh the pitfalls?—can be addressed.

## CASE STUDY

A fictional class of Grade 8 students (approximately 13–14 years old) is planning to travel to a nearby castle ruins. The class will travel by public bus and will be accompanied by one teacher and one parent.

The trip's learning outcomes have to do with history and mathematics. The principal questions decided by the students before the trip centred around why a castle was built there in the first place, why it was designed the way it was, and what life might have been like for those who lived in (and nearby) the castle. The students planned to take measurements of the lengths and heights of the castle's walls and areas of the main rooms (which were in ruins), so once back in the classroom they could calculate the volume and mass of the stones, and imagine the kinds of logistics that might be involved in the castle's construction.

The teacher, Ms. Kerrigan, asked a volunteer from the local archaeological group to bring along some big tape measures so the class could measure the dimensions of the castle's interior living spaces. Tape measures are another kind of technology, too, after all.

The class also wanted to gather more information about the history of the castle, and they had found out everything they could about this place through the material they could gather remotely. However, much of the history was not in books or the internet, but was available in the display cases at the castle.

When the teacher ran a planning session on what to bring on the trip, some students suggested all five of the classes' tablets and the new drone that one of the boys had got for his birthday. Ms. Kerrigan used the key questions above to consider each of these pieces of technology.

How will the tablets help achieve the learning outcomes? First, they can be used as cameras to take pictures of information plaques, rooms within the castle, and human influences on the surrounding landscape. Second, they can be information resources and can enable information on web pages and pdf documents to be stored and brought along. The pitfalls associated with the tablets are that many of the students will be so focused on using them that they will not see much of the human story that is contained within the place they are visiting. There might also be some squabbles regarding who gets to use the tablets.

How will the drone help achieve the learning outcomes? The main thing that a drone can do is provide aerial photos of the castle. This might help students with the goal of learning about the building and its measurements. The principal pitfall of the drone is that Ms. Kerrigan suspects it will consume most of the children's attention and thus be a major detraction from the session's intended learning outcomes. Furthermore, Ms. Kerrigan checked the local government regulations on the use of drones, and found that there were restrictions on flying in busy public areas.

The class decided to bring two tablets. These would be kept by the teachers and accessed by students who would take footage of anything that would add to their existing body of knowledge about the castle. Ms. Kerrigan and the class decided against bringing the drone. Even though they were sure it would enable them to make a snazzy video of the field trip, Ms. Kerrigan made the final call, as she felt it would be far too much of a distraction for the students. However, were there students unable to attend the field trip, they may well have taken it and had a group of students dedicated to creating a film of the experience, including drone footage of the site, interviews with students about their learning, with the development of the film undertaken when back at school.

If you were in Ms. Kerrigan's shoes, what decisions would you have taken? Would you have brought more iPads or perhaps none at all? Would you have brought along the drone? What other kinds of mobile technology could have added educational value to this outing?

Thomas and Munge (2017) remind us that the "temptation to adopt new technologies in outdoor education will always be there, as will be the need to question how these technologies will alter student experience" (p. 12). Technology has always existed in some form, of course, and temptations to adopt what is new and exciting will constantly emerge. A key suggestion offered in this chapter is to be wary of uncritically adopting mobile technology; just because one has access to particular mobile technology resources does not mean that one has to use them. Referring to the SAMR model discussed earlier, Thomas and Munge (2017) are particularly wary of introducing technology unless it promises to substantially improve the potential learning outcomes.

Much of our discussion has centred around the mobile tablet or phone, rather than other kinds of portable digital technology. It is important to note that the same pitfalls and affordances exist with other items, such as the drone example in the case study. Sometimes these devices "may add unwanted layers of clutter that reduce direct interaction with geophysical, ecological, and sociocultural elements of the landscape, whilst lessening the quality and quantity of interaction between humans—whether with classmates or community members" (Beames, 2017, p. 4). At other times, they may offer the curiosity and wonder learners are looking for and enable learners to showcase their learning in ways that are transformative for themselves and others, through filmmaking for example.

## Concluding thoughts

We have seen that screen-based mobile devices can be used for five principal ends: Recall, resource, geolocation, independent travel, and sharing. Some examples have been provided regarding how mobile technologies beyond tablets and phones, such as drones, can be employed. As mobile technology is such a pervasive part of childrens' and adults' lives now, we believe there is a certain educational imperative to judiciously incorporate it into teaching in meaningful ways. We propose three questions to assist teachers to arrive at their decisions: What are the affordances? What are the pitfalls? And, to what degree do the affordances outweigh the pitfalls?

It is our firm conviction that in our outdoor classrooms there are times when mobile technology devices are not appropriate, but there are times when they will greatly enhance the acquisition and retention of knowledge and skills. There are no right or wrong answers, of course, as all of our landscapes, curricula, and students will differ. Further, it is our view that setting up a binary between experiencing place(s) and using mobile devices is unhelpful. It is up to educators to ask themselves: What are the most appropriate methods needed to arrive at educational objectives, and in what ways will mobile technology enhance outdoor learning experiences. The time is ripe for educators to explore exciting and deeply meaningful ways in which to incorporate mobile devices into their outdoor teaching in ways that enhance connection with nature and community.

## Guidelines

- Mobile phones and tablets can be used to gather information about places, as mobile libraries, for mapping and geolocation, to provide safety and support, for sharing experiences and learning.

- Keep in mind that using mobile technologies will alter social interaction and interaction with places.

- Employ the three-step decision-making tool when considering the adoption of mobile, screen-based technologies:

  ○ What are the benefits of using the mobile technological device?

  ○ What are the pitfalls of using this device?

  ○ To what degree do the benefits outweigh the pitfalls?

- Mobile technologies offer opportunities to invoke curiosity and wonder and support self-directed learning for individual students.

## References

Beames, S. (2017). Innovation and outdoor education. *Journal of Outdoor and Environmental Education*, *20*(1), 2–6.

Beames, S. (2020). Educating generation Z. *Idrott & Hälsa*, *1*, 16–19.

Bolliger, D. U., & Shepherd, C. E. (2017). An investigation of mobile technologies and web 2.0 tool use in outdoor education programs. *Journal of Outdoor Recreation, Education, and Leadership*, *9*, 181–196.

Childwise. (2020). *The monitor report*. www.childwise.co.uk/reports.html#monitorreport

Commonsense Media. (2019). *The common sense census: Media use by tweens and teens 2019*. www.commonsensemedia.org/research/the-common-sense-census-media-use-by-tweens-and-teens-2019

Cuthbertson, B., Socha, T., & Potter, T. (2004). The double-edged sword: Critical reflections on traditional and modern technology in outdoor education. *Journal of Adventure Education and Outdoor Learning, 4*(2), 133–144.

Hills, D., & Thomas, G. (2020). Digital technology and outdoor experiential learning. *Journal of Adventure Education and Outdoor Learning, 20*(2), 155–169.

Lissak, G. (2018). Adverse physiological and psychological effects of screen time on children and adolescents: Literature review and case study. *Environmental Research, 164,* 149–157.

Oxford Learning. (2019). *Cell phones in the classroom: Learning tool or distraction?* www.oxfordlearning.com/should-cell-phones-be-allowed-classrooms/

Prince, H. (2017). Text messaging as a near synchronous method of remote support in outdoor adventurous settings. *Applied Mobilities, 3*(2), 168–183.

Puentedura, R. R. (2006). *Transformation, technology, and education in the state of Maine.* www.hippasus.com/rrpweblog/archives/2006_11.html

Puentedura, R. R. (2013). *SAMR: Moving from enhancement to transformation.* www.hippasus.com/rrpweblog/archives/000095.html

Rim, C. (2018). *iPads are not the future of education.* www.forbes.com/sites/christopherrim/2018/10/31/ipads-are-not-the-future-of-education/#2c3de8c21f54

Ritzer, G., Dean, P., & Jurgenson, N. (2012). The coming of age of the prosumer. *American behavioral scientist, 56*(4), 379–398.

Shukla, S. (2021). M-learning adoption of management students': A case of India. *Education and Information Technologies, 26*(1), 279–310.

Sobel, D. (2013). *Place-based education: Connecting classrooms and communities.* Great Barrington, MA: Orion.

Thomas, G. J., & Munge, B. (2017). Innovative outdoor fieldwork pedagogies in the higher education sector: Optimising the use of technology. *Journal of Outdoor and Environmental Education, 20*(1), 7–13.

Twenge, J. M. (2017). *iGen: Why today's super-connected kids are growing up less rebellious, more tolerant, less happy—and completely unprepared for adulthood.* New York: Atria.

Twenge, J. M., Joiner, T. E., Rogers, M. L., & Martin, G. N. (2018). Increases in depressive symptoms, suicide-related outcomes, and suicide rates among U.S. adolescents after 2010 and links to increased new media screen time. *Clinical Psychological Science, 6,* 3–17.

Vygotsky, L. S. (1998). *The problem of age* (M. Hall, Trans.). In R. W. Rieber (Ed.), *The collected works of L. S. Vygotsky: Vol. 5. Child psychology* (pp. 187–205). New York: Plenum Press. (Original work published 1933–1934)

# Day excursions and residential outdoor education centers

In the previous version of this book we considered how the provision of outdoor learning could be thought of as taking place within concentric circles. We stated:

Four 'zones' of outdoor learning exist, with the school grounds placed firmly in the centre. Beyond the school grounds is the local neighbourhood, which can be explored on foot or by using public transport. Day excursions ('field trips') often take place a little further away and usually require some kind of group transport. Residential outdoor centres, cultural visits, and expeditions that involve being away from home overnight, comprise the fourth 'zone', and have their own obvious logistical challenges.

(Beames et al., 2011, pp. 5–6)

In 2012, we discussed the first two zones (school grounds and the local neighbourhood) at length. This new chapter builds upon and extends our discussion to

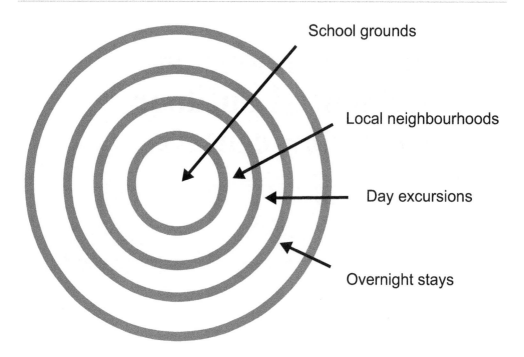

**Figure 9.1** The range of contexts for outdoor learning.
*Source:* (adapted from Higgins & Nicol, 2002, p. 44).

include the third zone of day excursions and fourth zone of overnight stays more generally, and residential outdoor education centres specifically.

We acknowledged at the time that some commentators might have viewed our original focus on the first two zones as an under appreciation of the sorts of learning that takes place in the third and fourth zones. However, there was a very important reason for us taking this approach. At the time we were increasingly aware of various international imperatives, debates, and initiatives related to education, health, and wellbeing, and threats to the provision of learning outside the classroom. We believed that the best way to get more students outdoors quickly, efficiently, and in increased numbers was to support school teachers to further outdoor learning on their doorstep. We firmly believed then, as we still do now, that the vision behind the concentric circles model was not to prioritize one setting over another. Instead it was designed to provide a strategic and integrated overview of how outdoor learning could, and should, be a progressive undertaking involving all of the settings. Our intention is that teachers and their students might move naturally between the zones, as and when their educational purpose and intention demands it. It is from this holistic, progressive, and inclusive position that we now consider the two zones of day excursions and overnight experiences.

# Day excursions (third zone)

The school is the epicentre of the concentric circles model. Typically, teachers and students go there in the morning to start school and, in the afternoon, they leave to go home. For the most part this is a daily routine of school life that is perpetuated day after day, week after week. The Covid-19 pandemic has significantly changed the ways that schooling is happening around the world. In many countries, the dominant shift was to move learning into the online space. While this was an appropriate response, when teachers and children returned to schools, the outdoors offered many a place for learning that was safe and engaging, and which allowed for the rebuilding of learning communities disrupted by Covid-19. Therefore, the third zone offers the opportunity to break from routine and to go beyond the school and its grounds during a school day, which is significant for a number of reasons. Most teachers will already be familiar with the idea of day excursions because of cultural visits to museums, sites of historic interest or other locally significant places. This means the third zone might be more familiar learning terrain for a lot of teachers than the first, second, and fourth zones. However, crossing the threshold into the third zone is significant pedagogically because the experience of time changes (e.g., start, finish, and breaks); experience of space changes (with different learning opportunities in different places); and new opportunities for relationship-building occur (learning new things about, from, and with other people).

One key distinction that separates zone three from zones one and two is the likely need for some form of transport and consideration of logistics. This will require a degree of prior co-ordination and we recommend a simple three-stage exercise that includes mapping, site visits, and tuition, to support this planning process. Educators may wish to add more depth to each stage depending on the site and the specific educational and physical needs of their students.

## Mapping

The first step is to locate the school on a map. Then, use the school as an epicentre and identify as many outdoor learning sites as possible that are within range of the school by foot, bicycle, and/or accessible by public transport. This could be a teacher-led exercise across the whole school, for all ages, or it could be a class-based activity for students and their teacher. It may also be a useful exercise for an entire school to undertake as part of an in-service or "twilight" professional development session. It works well for new members of staff, for students who are looking to orient themselves to their new "place", and for staff who do not live in the communities in which they teach. Internet search engines can be very helpful for this activity, using key terms such as "urban studies centre", "city farm", "urban park", "country park", "green space", "open space", "botanic gardens", "ecology centre", "discovery park", "environmental education centre", "forest school", "bushcraft centre", and so on. It will be necessary to make different combinations of these search terms to allow for the regional, national, and international variations. Naturally, those teaching in languages other than English will need to adapt their searches to include culturally and linguistically relevant words.

We also recommend that teachers encourage conversation and brainstorming with local networks of friends, families, community groups, and colleagues within their school, their school "cluster" and beyond for word-of-mouth suggestions for sites to visit. This process may generate more original, historical, and unusual suggestions than would ordinarily be identified through generic internet searches.

## Site visit

Second, we recommend teachers investigate the sites that have been identified. It is important to consider which of the sites have buildings and shelters, and equally important that educators understand how to access them, as some buildings may have seasonal opening and closing times. These buildings are important for managing bodily needs, such as toileting, having a snack and drink, or taking shelter from the weather. Again, this may require more or less research, depend on climate, season, and the specific needs of the group of students (physical ability, age, size of group, and so on). In addition to this mapping exercise, we believe it is essential for teachers (where possible) to visit these places in person to experience the location, to meet with staff, and to plan the educational experiences possible at each place (see also Chapter 5).

## Tuition

Third, it is useful for teachers to consider whether these sites offer tuition and if so establish if there are associated costs. Here, tuition means teaching offered by in-house educators, guides, or instructors. If this is an option, teachers will need to decide whether they will make use of it or not, and who will pay any associated costs. This is probably the single greatest pedagogical decision the teacher will make because they have to decide whether it is more important for *themselves* to be working with the students, or someone else, or some combination of both. There are relative merits in all three options, which are also addressed in Chapter 7, where we discuss community-based learning. These pedagogical decisions, and how they are informed, also affect how educators can go about choosing an education centre suitable for their classroom's needs. We will leave this discussion, of how to do this and why it is important, for the section on the fourth zone, which is next.

By the end of this three-stage planning exercise (mapping, site visit, and tuition), the aim is to have collated a visual representation of all sites available within a one-day travelling distance of the school. Plotted in one colour will be the routes that connect the school to the sites on foot or by bicycle, then via public transport, and in another colour the sites that need some form of group transport, such as carpooling, minibus, or coach hire. It will then be possible to build up a portfolio of learning opportunities, equipment, buildings and facilities, and plans for each site, which will help teachers make informed choices and connect excursion opportunities to the curriculum. This should not be an onerous task. In fact, it should be exciting because it is an opportunity to explore new places and co-create curriculum with students. Nonetheless, we appreciate that teachers are busy people, and so if a full mapping exercise seems daunting, there will still be much to be gained by initially identifying a single location, and then gradually building a portfolio.

There is pedagogical potential in working through these individual stages with students and colleagues. Doing this could develop a deep understanding of what is topical, current, historical, and of interest in the community being visited (this relates to the "place" discussion in Chapter 5). This process itself can spark a range of lesson ideas and new topics for exploration in the school year that can be woven throughout the four zones.

There is research that supports teachers developing planned, regular, and continuous outdoor learning activity that is embedded within the school curriculum. The most comprehensive body of research with international significance comes from Danish colleagues Mygind, Bølling, and Barfod (2019), who write about *udeskole* (literally "out school"). They explored the motivations and challenges experienced by Danish class teachers going outdoors on a weekly basis over the period of a year. They describe how *udeskole* takes into account encompasses preparation, evaluation, transport, and breaks in learning (Mygind et al., 2019). One of their findings discusses the role of collaboration and teamwork as a motivating factor for teachers when increasing outdoor learning in their schools. This suggests that schools may generate more capacity for outdoor learning by building teams that include teachers, parent helpers, volunteers, and the head teacher/principal.

There is increasing guidance emerging on how to conduct locally based curricular enquiry by using this type of partnering. We recommend the book, *Place-making with children and youth* by Derr, Chawla, and Mintzer (2018) to help with different ideas, frameworks, and the overall planning process. This research and Dewey's (1938/1997) concept of continuity (discussed in Chapter 6 are also consistent with Sobel's (2013) argument to connect classrooms and communities. This kind of place-making is needed for the sorts of transformative pedagogies that are required if the human species are to live more sustainably with the planet (Salonen & Siirilä, 2019).

Given all of this, we do not mean to suggest that if teachers can only visit a place once then they should not visit it at all. We are simply suggesting that curricular embeddedness is more likely when teachers build multiple visits to a particular location into their plan for the school year. This brings with it increased opportunities to understand a place at different times and seasons and for different educational purposes.

# Residential outdoor education centers (fourth zone)

When writing this section, we had two related yet different scenarios in mind. The first is a schoolteacher who is relatively inexperienced in using the outdoors centres, and who is planning an overnight educational experience for the first time, for their class of around 30 students. The second is the more experienced schoolteacher who has previously taken students to residential outdoor education centres, and wants to get more from their future visits. Let's begin with the first scenario: Taking the first step into planning an overnight experience for students.

It is likely that an inexperienced teacher will face barriers if they want to take their students outdoors. Since barriers prevent progress, it is important that they are named as a first step in overcoming them. In the early 2000s, these barriers were summarized by Higgins, Nicol, and Ross (2006) as cost, time spent planning and organizing, student/staff ratio, safety, weather, transport, disruption to classes, and lack of outdoor adventure qualifications. Recognizing these barriers, Christie, Higgins, and McLaughlin (2014) note that there has been very limited high-quality empirical research concerning residential outdoor education centres. Although these studies reflect the situation in the UK, their implications have worldwide relevance. Bourke, Buskist, and Herron (2014) noted that there were over 200 Residential Environmental Education Centres in the United States and their research similarly indicated the need for high quality programme evaluation. In Malaysia, Harun and Salamuddin (2014) pointed out that claims around the development of social skills at residential outdoor programmes needed to be critically examined. Further, in terms of educational benefits, Prince (2020) has pointed out that the majority of research into residential outdoor education has looked at short-term outcomes of less than three months. This suggests that there is still uncertainty over whether the outcomes identified in research up to this point have a lasting impact on participants' lives.

Residential outdoor centres are governed and defined by their funding schemes, which are controlled by a broad portfolio of supply from the public and private sectors. These centres can also be supported by organizations in the third sector, which do not belong to either the public or private sectors, as they are non-governmental or not-for-profit (i.e. charities and social enterprises). Terminology about these sectors and how they interact varies internationally, both across and within, the boundaries of nation state countries. Understanding the nature of funding sources for these centres is an important factor that can help teachers select a suitable one to visit. Some centres require well-documented intended programme outcomes to stay afloat through the public sector, while others rely on generous donations from families, private funds, or charities.

The fluidity of source funding sometimes means that even within individual organizations, there is a blurring of the edges of these sectoral distinctions. A mixed economy best describes the pattern of residential education worldwide, differences in funding streams is a significant reason why the quality of programming (for formal educational purposes) at outdoor centres varies so much. We do not mean to suggest that any one sector is better than the other; we simply mean that quality assurance is likely to be a factor within and between sectors.

Determining the difference in quality between outdoor centres is complex because rarely is there oversight from, or regulation of, specialists, nor a requirement for centres to align directly with curriculum documents. Similarly, it is uncommon for there to be any overall regulation in terms of quality assurance or specialist monitoring of educational outcomes and curricular alignment. Additionally, educational intentions may be better suited to different providers, and the affordances of sites (for fieldwork, adventurous activities, etc.) where the centre is located. The following case study helps to show how to put some of this guidance into practice.

---

### CASE STUDY

Amina is a biology teacher in a secondary school set in a large city in Malaysia. She wants to take her pupils to one of Malaysia's Residential Outdoor Environmental Centres (ROEC) for one week, but is aware of the barriers that she has read about—most of which refer to the lack of evidence on the lasting impacts for students. Amina's Head Teacher is keen to support her but wants to know the educational justification for students being away from school. Amina emails the ROEC manager and requests information about the programmes on offer and how they link with the curriculum. In return Amina is sent several different choices of timetables that list a range of different activities. Amina decides to develop a set of follow-up questions to ask the ROEC manager:

1. What will students learn at your centre that they cannot learn at school?

2. What are the educational purposes of the timetables you sent, in what way are the activities appropriate in achieving them, and what evidence is there for this?

3. Can you tell me about the theories, or educational frameworks, that support learning at your centre?

4. How are the staff who work with the students qualified to deliver these educational aims? (Please don't tell me about their outdoor qualifications—I am sure they are competent and that my students will be safe in their hands.)

5. There is a worry that some aspects of schoolwork may be missed by pupils having a week "out". How can I explain this to parents who might need reassurance that this time out of school will be valuable?

6. Can you explain what the costs are for so I can explain these to parents?

---

It is understandable that the mixed economy of provision we have spoken of might leave schools and their teachers wondering how to make judgments of what they might expect in terms of educational quality and value for money. These are deliberately provocative questions that should be welcomed by all educational institutions. They are not exhaustive, and teachers are encouraged to think of other questions they might want to ask.

## Key research findings

Keeping in mind Prince's (2020) observation above about the shortage of research on long-term impacts, nevertheless residential outdoor education has become the focus of an increasing amount of research. For example, the single largest piece of research undertaken on the impact of residential outdoor education was completed by Kendall and Rodger (2015) in a five-year longitudinal multimethod study based in the UK. The researchers were able to determine educational impacts immediately after, and then at several time points after, the residential outdoor education experience across a range of centres. They found that the most significant impact was on staff-student relationships at both primary and secondary levels. The research identified an influence on student resilience, self-confidence, and well-being. It also found a strong connection between these and the leadership and co-design of learning back at school, particularly for secondary students.

There was a feeling from staff and students that overnight educational experiences had an impact on student attainment levels. Participants identified a positive effect on their knowledge, skills, and understanding, such as being independent learners and working as part of a team. An impact on cohesion was identified as a result of the interpersonal relationships developed through community living. The impact on leadership, co-design, and facilitation helped secondary students to run activities for other students. There was also a positive influence on transitions, where primary students were better prepared for the move into secondary school. Lastly, there was an improvement on pedagogical skills, where new techniques and processes that teachers observed at outdoor centres were adopted afterwards in the classroom. One very significant issue to note is that the research focused on *partnerships* developed between outdoor centres and schools. The impact of the delivered programmes was greater as a result of the integration between the centre and the school's curriculum and ethos. This is a point to which we will return in the summary of this chapter.

These findings provide both experienced and inexperienced fourth-zone school teachers with a range of possible impacts that might occur as a result of a residential outdoor education programme. Although this research can support teachers in their quest to validate reasoning for choosing residential outdoor education experiences, it does not offer them any indications on how to determine the quality of provider. Additionally, this research was based on a funded initiative, so schools trying to make decisions about individual centres within this complex patchwork of provision for the first time still need to consider not just educational quality, but value for money.

Scrutton (2019) provides a categorization to help with decision-making in relation to budget and costings. He suggests that generally, providers offer three different types of programmes that a school might choose from. The first is what he calls the adventure programme. These are the sorts of multi-activity programmes where students engage in a blend of outdoor pursuits such as canoeing, climbing, sailing, biking, team-building activities, and cooperative group work, which are aimed at delivering personal and social development. For example, one paper from the United States said of residential environmental education programmes, that these "settings and situations may be particularly fruitful for engendering and supporting trust and trusting relationships" (Ardoin, DiGiano, O'Connor, & Podkul, 2017, p. 1336).

The second is where the provider offers field studies programmes. These are popular with secondary schools as they directly relate to curricular subjects (such as biology and geography). These might also include centres that seek to foster nature connection programmes as reported by Mullenbach, Andrejewski, and Mowen (2019).

The third is a combination of the adventure course and other curricular components, but is not restricted to the more traditional focus on field studies subjects. In a controlled experiment, Quibell, Charlton, and Law (2017) noted that children "increased their attainment in English reading, writing and maths significantly more than children who received conventional classroom-based schooling" (p. 581). This gives some indication for the potential of cognitive gain in overnight educational settings. In response to this experiment, Loynes, Dudman, and Hedges (2020) conducted a follow-up study that noted a range of cognitive and non-cognitive learning outcomes associated with residential experiences, but they suggest caution in terms of what current research is able to determine in areas such as literacy and numeracy developments. It is Scrutton's (2019) view that it is the exceptionally strong affective learning element, in addition to the cognitive experiential learning process, that makes residential outdoor education so different from the school environment. It is questionable whether it is useful to separate the cognitive from the affective for the purpose of research, when at the level of the human organism they are so purposefully and bodily entwined (Whitehead, 1967). However, it is heartening that the last decade has seen more, and increasingly rigorous, research in what has been a sparsely populated field. Prince (2020) has been able to build on these developments using large data sets to look at long term impacts (more than three months). This systematic review identified "confidence, teamwork, life skills, intrapersonal skills and the take up of new opportunities/activities as the impacts of use in young people's lives since their residential experience" (p. 8).

## Partnerships as the way forward

From our own research and practice, our main historical criticism of residential outdoor education centres over the years has been where the school teachers handed responsibility for teaching and learning to residential outdoor education centre providers (Nicol, 2001, 2002; Christie, 2004; Telford, 2010). This overdependence on providers, and perhaps even deference, lacked the progressive provision that we are promoting through the concentric circles model. Importantly, it raises the need for integration and partnership between schools and providers, as articulated in terms of progression (of experience), connection (to curriculum), and relevance (to home community) (Christie & Higgins, 2012).

In this regard, Kendall and Rodger (2015) found that the need for partnership working, which applies to any outdoor learning taking place with another provider (day trips and overnight stays), is of utmost importance. The project they reported on included 60 schools (primary, secondary, and special) involving 13 partnerships of residential outdoor centre providers and schools. The findings highlighted how the school/outdoor centre partnerships had distinct identities, which were rooted in the "challenges and themes relevant to their particular context, from . . . attainment to community cohesion, from family support and raising aspirations, to cultural diversity" (Kendall & Rodger, 2015, p. i). In a US study, O'Farrell and Hung-Ling (2020) reported on a small-scale study in South Dakota and noted that schools reported many benefits of partnership but at the same time warned of "partnership fatigue" that came from challenges arising from "the result of poorly defined leadership roles, unequal distribution of responsibilities, and a lack of enthusiasm from one or all parties" (p. 4).

If residential outdoor education experiences are to enrich learning and extend the curriculum, the teacher, school, and provider need to work together to set the programme of activities to ensure coherence before, during, and after the visit. This collaborative co-design approach seeks to ensure that the experiences are embedded in the overall school curriculum, along with the culture and ethos of the school. For this to happen authentically, teachers themselves must lead and have an overview of this process. This pivotal role has been noted by Christie and Higgins (2012), in relation to overnight experiences, and more recently by Stern, Frensley, Powell, and Ardoin (2018) in relation to modelling behaviour. The researchers explained how "known adults (parents, teachers, and pastors), rather than more distant adults—such as celebrities—emerged as the role models most consistently linked with positive attitudes and intentions among students" (p. 826). Not only can teachers become role models for encouraging learning, but they maintain an overview of individual and group learning as students move from place to place and back to school. This curricular mobility needs oversight and continuity and the best person to lead this partnership building is the teacher.

Adopting this kind of teacher led partnership approach to planning educational outings can foster a clear and coherent understanding of the value and role of teaching further afield within the school staff culture. In doing so, teachers can feel more confident about the rationales underpinning why they are teaching and learning outdoors through day excursions and residential experiences, and be ready to share this knowledge and enthusiasm with colleagues, parents, providers, and, most importantly, their students.

## Guidelines

- Adopt the mapping techniques described here to help plan outdoor learning activities, and communicate the value of this approach to colleagues.

- Invite your students and colleagues to help with this process as a way of embedding outdoor learning across your whole school.

- Use the concentric circles model to conceptualize, plan and increase the range and scope of your outdoor learning through visiting different places.

- Develop teacher led partnerships between schools, communities, and outdoor centres to maximize outdoor learning opportunities through the power of mutually supportive collaborations.

## References

Ardoin, N., DiGiano, M. O'Connor, K., & Podkul, T. (2017). The development of trust in residential environmental education programs. *Environmental Education Research*, *23*(9), 1335–1355.

Beames, S., Higgins, P., & Nicol, R. (2011). *Learning outside the classroom: Theory and guideline for practice*. New York: Routledge.

Bourke, N., Buskist, C., & Herron, J. (2014). Residential environmental education center program evaluation: An ongoing challenge. *Applied Environmental Education & Communication*, *13*(2), 83–90.

Christie, B. (2004). *Raising achievement in Scottish secondary schools? A study of outdoor experiential learning*. Unpublished Doctoral Thesis, University of Edinburgh, Edinburgh.

Christie, B., & Higgins, P. (2012). Residential outdoor learning experiences and Scotland's school curriculum: An empirical and philosophical consideration of progress, connection and relevance. *Scottish Educational Review*, *44*(2), 45–59.

Christie, B., Higgins, P., & McLaughlin, P. (2014). 'Did you enjoy your holiday?' Can residential outdoor learning benefit mainstream schooling? *Journal of Adventure Education and Outdoor Learning*, *14*(1), 1–23.

Derr, A., Chawla, L., & Mintzer, M. (2018). *Placemaking with children and youth*. New York: New York Village Press.

Dewey, J. (1997). *Experience and education*. New York: Touchstone. (Original work published 1938).

Harun, M., & Salamuddin, N. (2014). Promoting social skills through outdoor education and assessing its effects. *Asian Social Science*, *10*(5), 71–78.

Higgins, P. & Nicol, R. (Eds.). (2002). *Outdoor education: Authentic learning through landscapes* (Vol. 2). Sweden: Kinda Kunskapscentrum. Retrieved from http://www.education.ed.ac.uk/outdoored/resources.html

Higgins, P., Nicol, R., & Ross, H. (2006). *Teachers' approaches and attitudes to engaging with the natural heritage through the curriculum* (Commissioned Report No. 161, ROAME No. F04AB04). Battleby: Scottish Natural Heritage.

Kendall, S., & Rodger, J. (2015). *Evaluation of learning away: Final report*. London: Paul Hamlyn Foundation.

Loynes, C., Dudman, J., & Hedges, C. (2020). The impact of residential experiences on pupils' cognitive and non-cognitive development in year six (10–11 year-olds) in England. *Education 3–13*. https://doi.org.10.1080/03004279.2020.1722199

Mullenbach, L., Andrejewski, R., & Mowen, A. (2019). Connecting children to nature through residential outdoor environmental education. *Environmental Education Research, 25*(3), 365–374.

Mygind, E., Bølling, M., & Barfod, K. (2019). Primary teachers' experiences with weekly education outside the classroom during a year. *Education 3–13, 47*(5), 599–611. https://doi.org.10.1080/03004279.2018.1513544

Nicol, R. (2001). *Outdoor education for sustainable living?: An investigation into the potential of Scottish local authority residential outdoor education centres to deliver programmes relating to sustainable living.* PhD Thesis, University of Edinburgh, Edinburgh.

Nicol, R. (2002). Outdoor education: Research topic or universal value? Part one. *Journal of Adventure Education and Outdoor Learning, 2*(1), 29–41.

O'Farrell, P., & Hung-Ling, L. (2020). Gateway to outdoors: Partnership and programming of outdoor education centers in urban areas. *Education Sciences, 10*(11), 340. https://doi.org/10.3390/educsci10110340

Prince, H. E. (2020). The lasting impacts of outdoor adventure residential experiences on young people. *Journal of Adventure Education and Outdoor Learning*, 1–16. https://doi.org/10.1080/14729679.2020.1784764

Quibell, T., Charlton, J., & Law, J. (2017). Wilderness achooling: A controlled trial of the impact of an outdoor education programme on attainment outcomes in primary school pupils. *British Educational Research Journal, 43*(3), 572–587.

Salonen, A. O., & Siirilä, J. (2019). Transformative pedagogies for sustainable development. In W. Leal Filho (Ed), *Encyclopedia of sustainability in higher education* (pp. 1966–1972). Cham: Springer.

Scrutton, R. (2019). Investigating the process of learning for school pupils on residential outdoor education courses. *Journal of Outdoor and Environmental Education, 23*, 39–56.

Sobel, D. (2013). *Place-based education: Connecting classrooms and communities.* Great Barrington, MA: Orion.

Stern, M., Frensley, B., Powell, R., & Ardoin, N. (2018). What difference do role models make? Investigating outcomes at a residential environmental education center. *Environmental Education Research, 24*(6), 818–830.

Telford, J. (2010). *Meanings, values, and life course: A study of participants' experiences at a Scottish outdoor education centre.* PhD Thesis, University of Edinburgh, Edinburgh.

Whitehead, A. (1967). *The aims of education and other essays.* New York: The Free Press.

# 10 Risk management

> **Chapter aims**
>
> - Understand and be able to define key terms, such as hazard and risk.
>
> - Know how to conduct a basic risk assessment.
>
> - Understand the six elements of a basic risk management plan and be able to construct one for learning outdoors.
>
> - Know how to undertake a risk/benefit analysis.
>
> - Be able to devise ways in which students can be involved in managing the hazards they might encounter.

We begin this chapter with a statement that may be somewhat surprising and perhaps a little provocative: The starting point for any discussion on risk management in education should be a session's learning intentions. Only then can we have a proper discussion about whether the likelihood and severity of being harmed through this educational activity are proportionate to its intended benefits. As educators, it is our job to equip children with the tools to flourish as individuals, contribute to the betterment of society, and care for our ecosystems. If we are going to educate students with lifelong global learning in mind, it follows that students should develop the skills with which to manage the risks they will encounter throughout their lives.

In this chapter, we are focusing primarily on managing risk through measures we can take *before going outside*. The next chapter focuses on managing your groups outdoors.

## What is risk management?

Risk management is a catch-all term for the measures educators can put in place to reduce the likelihood of a student or staff member being harmed—both physically and psychologically. A central element of managing risk involves conducting risk assessments, and a good portion of this chapter is dedicated to discussing how these can be done in straightforward ways, which will help to ensure they are used and not left on a shelf. We want educators to feel empowered to take a balanced, thoughtful, and enabling approach in their practice, in order to facilitate safe and powerful learning experiences for their students outdoors.

It is helpful to distinguish between two key terms: *Hazard* and *risk*. A hazard is anything with the potential to cause harm, such as road traffic or an icy slope. Risk refers to the likelihood and severity of being harmed by a hazard. Risk assessments, therefore, examine the possibility of being harmed by various hazards and judge the seriousness of the associated consequences (Barton, 2007, p. 12).

It should be noted that risk assessment in education is not restricted to going outdoors; all schools and outdoor learning organizations will have risk assessments that cover areas from fires in the kitchen to slippery hallway floors. It may be, however, that a school does not have their own risk management systems for outdoor learning. This is where teachers who are keen to take their students outside may need to create plans and/or revise existing ones.

Many of the conversations around risk management in outdoor learning seem to revolve around ensuring that "bad things" do not happen to the young people we are working with. We argue that this is correct, but only up to a point. As educators, we need to be mindful of the long-term consequences on a child whose schooling only takes place indoors. Prioritizing a culture of "as safe as possible" will inevitably result in greatly limited opportunities to learn in authentic contexts. The paradox here is that there are risks associated with trying to remove as many risks as possible!

All educators (whether working indoors or out) have a duty to provide a *standard of care* similar to what other "reasonable and prudent" educators would do in similar situations. A reasonable and prudent educator would complete a risk assessment for any outdoor learning session taking place in the local neighbourhood, on a whitewater river, or anywhere in between. Once outdoors with learning underway, they may deem it necessary to deviate from that original plan if certain environmental or group conditions have changed. It is important that this potential for flexibility and dynamic application of risk management plans is included in the original design.

As noted in the introductory chapter, the areas of "outdoor play" and "risky play" have seen a lot of research activity—particularly in the early years (e.g., Sandseter, 2009; Lavrysen et al., 2017). We value the rich literature on outdoor play, which helps teachers to understand the importance of young people learning to take risks, however the scope of this book remains on curricular learning from primary school and up. Play pedagogy is one of many approaches to learning outdoors, and Brussoni, Olsen, Pike, and Sleet (2012) in Canada have shown that a large body of research demonstrates how "[c]hildren have a natural propensity towards risky play" and that "keeping children safe involves letting them take and manage risks"

(p. 3134). The philosophical and empirical arguments for young people becoming accustomed to, and overcoming, real world risks are strong. Children's outdoor play specialist, Tim Gill (2010), tells us that:

> A mindset that is solely focused on safety does children and young people no favours. Far from keeping them safe from harm, it can deny them the very experiences that help them to learn how to handle the challenges that life may throw at them.
>
> (p. 1)

While low consequence accidents are bound to happen during outdoor learning programmes, as they are in day-to-day life, the UK Health and Safety Executive (2011) guidance on *Tackling health and safety myths* notes that "fear of litigation and prosecution has been blown out of proportion" (p. 3). As long as steps have been taken to manage risk—such as the steps we outline below—it is highly unlikely that any breach of health and safety law will have taken place.

We will now examine six key tools that can form part of teachers' risk management plan: Risk Assessments, Emergency Action Plans, Consent Forms, Off-site Checklists, Journey Plans, and Incident Reporting. Naturally, these elements will vary between school districts, regions, and countries. Readers are advised to follow guidance within their own jurisdictions, such as governing body regulations, school guidance, and government policies.

## Risk assessments

Risk assessments are a key part of good practice in outdoor learning, and, in many countries, are legally required. They should be completed well before an outdoor lesson begins. A standard risk assessment will identify "the foreseeable risks" that might be encountered during an outdoor lesson or trip. The ultimate aim of the risk assessment is to highlight specific elements of the outing that may need to be managed, in order to reduce the risks to acceptable levels (Going Out There, 2021). In some cases, reducing risks might mean not engaging in a particular kind of activity. Keep in mind that once you arrive at a particular scene (or shortly before that), you may decide to alter your risk assessment due to changes in environment and personnel. Outdoor leaders are encouraged to respond to the immediate conditions rather than rely entirely on an assessment made beforehand.

In basic outdoor learning contexts, two general kinds of risk assessment tend to be used: *Standard* and *dynamic* (adapted from Barton, 2007). *Standard* (also called *generic*) *risk assessments* cover hazards that one can expect to encounter—whether it's taking the bus to the museum or planning a weeklong canoe trip. In local settings, these typically involve the "big three": Exposure (to wind, precipitation, sun, and cold); vehicular traffic (when crossing or walking beside roads); and terrain (e.g., conditions under foot, steep slopes, water features). Other hazards will be added, which are specific to the place and activity. For example, a rock climbing programme will need to ensure the equipment is in suitable condition; an overseas hiking trip may need to ensure that the vehicles being used to transport people to the trailhead are properly serviced and driven by an experienced and qualified driver; and a trip to a large city art gallery will need to have a plan in place for keeping track of students in a crowded, urban environment. Note that in some cases, such as an unusual trip or occasion, it may be appropriate to have an event-specific or site-specific risk assessment created to complement the standard, everyday one (Barton, 2007).

Educators may be intimidated by the perceived complexity of undertaking a risk assessment, but we contend that they are relatively straightforward to create. Note that we used the word "create" here. It is very important that leaders do not uncritically cut and paste from risk assessments they have found on the web or copy directly from those completed by a colleague last year. Risk assessments should be designed to suit the specific people, places, and activities involved and be revised/reviewed regularly before going outdoors.

Risk assessments do not require complex mathematical formulae. Indeed, Gill (2010) notes that quantitative risk assessments with scoring and arithmetic "can be confusing and difficult to apply consistently" and may "struggle to cope with the subtleties and dilemmas thrown up by real-life situations" (p. 16). You may have come across risk assessments which use scores from one to five, where the likelihood of being harmed by a hazard (e.g., two out of five) is multiplied by the severity of being harmed (e.g., four out of five). This would leave a risk rating of eight. The trouble with these kinds of ratings is they add another layer of subjectivity to an exercise that already has a certain element of subjectivity! We advise approaching such forms with caution.

A key part of risk assessments is ensuring they are used. They are "living documents" and should not be kept in a forgotten binder on a dusty shelf. A useful risk assessment needs to be brief and applicable. One tip for keeping your risk assessments shorter is to *only include those hazards your group is reasonably likely to encounter and those hazards likely to cause serious injury or death*. Right away, this rules out minor items such as getting a splinter on a wooden banister while visiting city hall, and permits a focus on more major hazards, such as road traffic, which will be encountered and can very easily injure or kill a student. Focusing on *the serious stuff one can expect to encounter* not only means fewer hazards need to be listed in your risk assessment, but fewer columns will be needed as well, as the likelihood and severity columns are not required.

All standard assessments should be completed well in advance and approved by the head of school, programme director, or designated health and safety advisor. Standard risk assessments should be discussed amongst the staff team at the beginning of the day or before the activity begins, and, if needed, additions made that respond more directly to the environmental conditions, student needs, and intended learning outcomes. All participating staff need to be involved in creating the risk assessment and understand the process of implementation.

In their simplest form, risk assessments include two columns: Hazard and Control measure, plus an area where additional "on the day" items can be added. This way, the static nature of a standard risk assessment can become more responsive to changes in weather, staffing, students, and equipment. This additional area may also be used to highlight foreseen, but unusual, activities. For example, if a class is involved in an environmental project using loppers and secateurs to clear bushes, managing how these tools are handled can be added.

Here's an example of a risk assessment for a town based, outdoor learning session taking place in Scotland, with children that are ten to 11 years old.

| Hazard | Control Measure |
| --- | --- |
| Traffic | Cross roads using crosswalks or use parallel lines/pods, as appropriate. Students all wear high visibility vests. |
| Rain, cold, and wind | Carry suitable warm and waterproof clothing. Consider bringing a group shelter or tarp. |
| Low energy | Carry sufficient food/snacks. |
| Terrain | Wear sturdy footwear. Be aware of uneven terrain (e.g., holes that may not be visible due to long grass/bushes). |

*Additional considerations: Elizabeth has a broken arm, with a cast and sling. She is struggling to put on clothing. Bring an extra, oversized insulated jacket.*

The second kind of risk assessment is dynamic. *Dynamic risk assessments* are ongoing and are usually not written down. In most cases it is a question of having all of your senses constantly alert in order to gather as much information as possible from the surrounding environment. Outdoor educators need to be considering the following:

- Changes in weather.

- Students' physical, mental, emotional condition.

- Terrain "under foot".

- Crossing points for road, rail, or water.

Dynamic risk assessments concern judgments derived from an inner dialogue or from regular check-ins with a co-leader and the students themselves and may demand that plans are changed rapidly. An inner dialogue might be something like, *Harriet looks a little cold, so I'll offer her a wool hat. Mark and Theo are continuing with their play-fighting and seem oblivious to their surroundings. I'm worried they will stray onto the busy road without realizing it. I need to stop this now.* Examples could include altering a cycling route due to roadworks or a ropes course session being postponed or revised due to a staff member being sick.

Two areas receiving increasing attention is the threat of unwanted encounters with people and dogs who are not involved in the learning session. Intimidating teenagers showing up on the school grounds, suspicious-looking adults paying disproportionate attention to smaller children while on outings, and uncontrolled or unleashed dogs are issues that justifiably concern both parents and teachers, and which may require their own space in a risk assessment form. In these cases, the dynamic risk assessment may point towards moving locations, if possible, and perhaps phoning for support.

## Consent forms

Once the risk assessment is in place, you can work on developing the consent forms (also called permission slips). There are two main kinds: "Blanket" consent forms and event specific forms. Schools can use a once-a-year blanket consent form that will cover a variety of low-risk, curricular activities taking place in the school grounds and local neighbourhood. Having this kind of parental/carer permission to teach near the school, but outside the property, is crucial to reducing bureaucratic barriers to spontaneous, serendipitous, and place-responsive teaching.

Expeditions, overnight cultural visits, and stays at outdoor education centres will require their own specific consent forms, as these are not considered to be routine visits. A day trip involving a short boat trip, for example, might also fall under this category and thus require a separate consent form. Keep in mind consent forms are not merely about getting parents' signatures on file; a good consent form is primarily an information form containing a clear and accurate description of the programme to which the guardian is consenting.

Consent forms need to cover the following items:

1. The educational rationale for the activities.

2. The nature of the activities.

3. The experience and competence of accompanying staff.

4. The clothing, footwear, food/drink, and personal effects (e.g., a small rucksack) required.

5. Assurance that a Risk Assessment has been recently conducted and an Emergency Action Plan is in place.

6. Contact details of the person in charge.

7. A place for parents to highlight any concerns (e.g., medical, logistical).

8. A place to sign and date the form.

*Event-specific consent forms will also need to include times, dates, and locations*

So far, we have only discussed parents and legal guardians giving their consent for their child to undertake a certain kind of outdoor learning. Some might ask where the child's voice is in all of this! While we sympathize with this viewpoint, if the consent form is for a school sanctioned activity, the minor's consent to take part is not required; after all, children are not normally asked if they consent to being taught science in a laboratory. An extracurricular trip or activity might be different, as a consent form for the participant could be used to be sure the student was willingly taking part in a charity abseil, for example. To be clear, school based, curricular outdoor learning should not require written consent from students. We discuss the students' roles in assessing risk at the end of the chapter.

## Emergency action plans and incident management

An "emergency action plan" (EAP) is a brief, readily accessible flowchart that can guide action in a time of considerable stress. For local learning outside the classroom with our university students, we use a half page laminated sheet with the emergency action plan on one side and the risk assessment on the other. This is kept in the top lid of our backpacks. A printout in a clear waterproof case works just as well and will leave teachers more likely to revise these documents more often.

For the purposes of our EAP, crises can be categorized as life-threatening and non-life-threatening. Life-threatening injuries are usually time sensitive and thus need rapid evacuation to definitive medical care. So, a traumatic incident involving a boy who had fallen out of a tree and was not breathing would be managed very differently to one where he twisted his ankle and was otherwise fine.

Wilderness medical protocols always place "scene size-up" or "dangers" as a top priority. Thus, when entering an accident site, it is vital to quickly identify any hazards that could pose a danger to you, your group, any bystanders, and, of course, the patient(s) (National Outdoor Leadership School, 2021). Any outdoor educator working in remote locations where access to definitive medical care would be delayed needs to use wilderness medicine guidance to inform their EAP.

In a local, outdoor learning context, it is good practice to have a brief meeting with all staff/adults involved before heading outdoors. Teachers can clarify who will be in charge of first aid, who will manage the group, and what phone calls will need to be made to whom and by whom. This ensures clear allocation of staff roles and responsibilities, which can lead to a considered and professional response to incidents.

A basic EAP for Scottish upper-primary school students going to a local park might look something like this:

**Emergency (life-threatening):** Call 999. Stabilize patient. Manage airway, breathing, circulation. Await arrival of Emergency Medical Services. Alert school office (555 111 2222). Gather group together and manage their primary needs.

    **Non-life-threatening:** Stabilize injured student. Alert colleagues. Gather group and manage their primary needs. Transport to Hospital Emergency or back to school. Alert school office (555 111 2222).

It is plain to see how simple the above steps are. It would be easy to think that they do not need to be written down. However, a release of adrenaline combined with stressful environmental and social factors may greatly obscure judgement in the moment. For this reason, having an established, easily accessible set of instructions or a flow chart will increase the likelihood of leaders responding appropriately to any incident that may occur on a school outing.

Any outing away from an educational setting (e.g., school, outdoor centre) must have a designated "home base" contact. This person is usually an administrator who will be at the office or who can be reached at any hour. Their responsibility is to provide assistance as necessary, which could range from simply being a "sounding board" for how a sensitive incident can be managed, to taking over as an "incident commander" in serious cases. Additionally, they may be able to garner the assistance of community partners and medical/rescue services in the area. A written plan should be provided by leaders prior to departure that includes: Where the group is going, what the group is doing, the details of everyone participating, and the expected time of return.

Cell phones need to be considered in all kinds of incident management. It is advisable to discuss the use of mobile phones with fellow staff as part of the pre-trip EAP creation, and to have a clear understanding of cell phone reception in the areas being visited. This is also a healthy conversation to have with students. It may be advisable to have an agreement in place with students whereby, in the event of a serious accident, no information about the incident is shared with anyone outside the trip until such time as the situation is being properly managed. It is important to ensure that inaccurate information and misleading photographs are not innocently shared with parents and the wider world. The plan for mobile devices should be in-line with the school's policy on phones and social media.

While away from the school, communication with parents and media is best undertaken by the designated and trained home base contact. Particularly serious incidents need to be carefully managed by the designated senior staff member. If a leader/teacher needs to relay information to people outside of the school, it should be kept to a minimum, by focusing on facts and by only identifying individuals involved if absolutely necessary. One way to avoid identification through naming is to create student medical summary lists where each student is allocated a number and only the number is referred to through communications— the school and staff members also having the same list. School districts and regional governments will have guidance for dealing with the media and can advise as necessary. When taking learning outside it is essential for teachers to be familiar with their organization's established incident response processes and policies.

Irrespective of whether the incident is minor or major, it is important for leaders to write down an account of all events and times, as soon as possible, before details are forgotten. Voice memos made on phones are highly effective for capturing rich details of events. This written or audio resource can be particularly useful for any future enquiry or risk management review. Most school districts will have official incident forms that must be completed, and in some countries, organizations are required to report any serious injuries to the government agency responsible for Health and Safety.

## Off-site checklist and kit

The fourth of the six elements of a risk management plan is the off-site checklist and associated kit. It is essential for the educator in charge to have a prepared list of what to bring on any outing. Instructors leading one-off trips and expeditions will make specific checklists for these occasions, but those leading regular outings in familiar territory (e.g., from a school or outdoor centre) can prepare a standard off-site checklist. Apart from the obvious benefit of ensuring nothing important is forgotten, the off-site checklist (and the kit prepared beforehand) affords educators more spontaneity in their teaching—much in the same way a blanket consent form does. The off-site checklist can be a laminated form kept next to the off-site kit, which can be kept handy in a prepacked backpack that any staff member can use.

The following checklists feature tasks to be completed and items to have prepared before leaving the grounds. These are considerations only, of course, and teachers should amend this list to fit their circumstances.

### *Items to consider bringing:*

- Students' medications (e.g., asthma inhaler, EpiPen) and relevant medical information, the risk assessment document, blanket consent forms with parental contacts, emergency action plan.

- Group shelter, insulated foam pad, extra warm/waterproof layers/hats in line with climate, sunscreen, first aid kit (with masks/gloves), hazardous waste kit (with durable gloves for picking up needles or dog feces).

- A "snack bag" with food, drink, cups, plates, and effective hand cleaning materials (soap, antibacterial handwash, and possibly wet wipes), and garbage bag.

- High-visibility vests.

### *Pre-departure tasks:*

- Check the weather forecast and any local traffic/construction reports.

- Notify the office of: Where the group is going, any absences to the class list, which adults are going, planned time of return, and leader phone number.

- Ensure students have the opportunity to go to the toilet before leaving the school.

- Make a toileting plan for the outing—especially for trips to parks and urban centres.

- Ensure children know who are their assigned adult and "buddies" for the outing.

## Incident reporting and monitoring

Accidents do happen, of course—irrespective of how well we have planned and sought to manage all foreseeable hazards (Gill, 2010). It is understandable that some teachers and outdoor leaders are concerned about getting in trouble should a child get hurt on "their watch".

As we have seen, the law is interested in the degree to which the leader with the duty of care has done what other reasonable and prudent colleagues would have done. In the UK, the only way a teacher or outdoor instructor will be prosecuted is if there has been "recklessness or a clear failure to adopt sensible precautions" (Health & Safety Executive [HSE], 2011, p. 3). In a school context, negligence can only be established if:

- The school has not taken care of a child in a way that a prudent parent would have done;

- As a result, the child has been injured; and

- The injury was a foreseeable consequence.

(HSE, 2014, pp. 5–6)

If a horrible accident had taken place on an urban school outing through some kind of freak occurrence, there would undoubtedly be some kind of investigation. As long as schools can demonstrate that they have assessed "risks and put in place proportionate control measures" (HSE, 2018, para 20), there is no reason that a teacher would be prosecuted or lose their job. Precautions might include having conducted a thorough risk assessment before the trip; ensuring consent forms were in place; and confirming the group was managed in a reasonable and prudent manner, in terms of transport, toileting, food, drink, and so on. As the individual responsible for the well-being and safety of others, it is important for teachers to establish what is legally required in their country of practice. These considerations should always be incorporated into the risk management plan.

Any incident that takes place on an outing needs to be reported. Incidents include not just accidents, but illnesses, near misses, and behavioural issues (Barton, 2007). Best practice involves each organization or school keeping a book or list of "near misses", which features locations, weather, events, times, dates, and notable circumstances. Well-documented near misses can reveal patterns of unnecessary exposure to hazards that might otherwise go undetected and thus provide rich learning about risk management practices that may be poor, but have luckily not resulted in any harm. Larger organizations will gather incident data every year and analyze these to identify areas of vulnerability and inform changes in policy and practice.

Incident reporting can be likened to sharing best practices in teaching. Having certain systems in place which enable colleagues to discuss how they can maximise student learning outdoors, while minimizing the likelihood of them being seriously injured, is of paramount importance. It requires a supporting, caring, and trusting community of practice to enable a teacher to say, "We narrowly avoided a serious accident today" and the staff to respond by saying, "Please tell us about this so that we can all learn from it".

The UK's Health & Safety Executive instructs us to focus chiefly on facilitating rich opportunities for student learning, where "mistaken and unfounded health and safety concerns do not create obstacles that prevent these from happening" (HSE, 2011, p. 1). We advise educators to adopt a risk/benefit analysis for their outdoor teaching and learning, and have adapted the following three questions from Education Scotland's (2019) risk/benefit tool:

1. What are the benefits of this experience for learners?

2. What are the risks associated with this learning experience?

3. Are the benefits in proportion to any potential for harm?

If the potential for harm is unreasonably high, then additional measures need to be taken and/or the activity needs to be revised or replaced with something else.

## Journey plans

The sixth and final element of the six-part risk management plan is the Journey Plan. This is a single document that can be completed as much as is possible by the participants and then completed and/or checked by the teacher or instructor in charge. This is an outline highlighting who is involved, where the outing is going, when the group will be back, what the dedicated cell phone number is, and so on. It also has a checklist including, for example: A first aid kit (with any specific medicine), taking a copy of the Journey Plan to the office, extra warm layers, consent forms for all students, and a toilet strategy.

---

### CASE STUDY

Jen and Steve are upper primary teachers in a medium-sized Canadian primary school in an urban area. Together, they decided to develop a risk management plan which would facilitate more frequent, rich learning experiences outside the classroom. This involved putting some systems in place over the summer. There were six main parts to their approach.

First, they identified six principal hazards that were likely to be encountered on a local outing. These included: Weather/exposure; slippery/icy terrain; vehicle traffic of all kinds; the group being separated while getting on/off a bus or subway; reduced energy/dehydration.

Second, they created a simple Emergency Action Plan in the form of a flowchart. This would enable them to follow certain key steps in the event of some kind of incident. This half page document used large fonts and was laminated.

Third, they crafted a blanket consent form for all parents to sign at the beginning of the school year. This would allow them to go outside as often as needed, without seeking permission each time.

The fourth element was an Offsite checklist which could be used to make sure they had done everything they needed to before leaving the classroom, and brought everything with them on the trip they intended. Once they had this one-page document with a list of tick boxes, they laminated it and kept a marker with it, so it could be used over and over again.

Fifth, they drafted a form that would be their Journey Plan. This document would let the school know where the class went, who was with them, when they would be back, and how they could be contacted. On the reverse side of this document, they added a section with the three risk/benefit analysis questions which they considered for each journey.

Finally, they created an online shared document where staff could record any incidents or near misses that took place.

Jen and Steve kept their Risk assessment, EAP, Offsite checklist, and blank Journey Plans in their own risk management folder. This was shared with their Vice Principal, who was able to offer some minor suggestions for improvement.

## Getting students involved

In Chapter 6 of our 2011 book, *Learning outside the classroom*, we wrote about students learning how to take responsibility for themselves and others. Risk management is no different. A risk assessment, in particular, should not be something that is "done" to a group of young people; they need to play a strong role in identifying substantial and foreseeable hazards they might encounter, and in devising strategies to minimize the likelihood of being harmed by them.

We thus advise doing two kinds of risk assessments. The first is to be done by the educator long before the outing. This risk assessment needs to be checked and approved by a line manager. The second kind of risk assessment is one the educator does with their group. This can be a workshop that takes a whole morning or, with a well-practiced class, might only take five minutes. With younger groups, risk assessments can be undertaken as hazards emerge throughout the learning experience; these can be facilitated by teaching students how to identify and then manage risks appropriately. Of course, it is important to avoid generating a culture of anxiety and fear, so this requires a balanced approach.

There should be no ambiguity about the group leader being the person who is legally in charge and who takes ultimate responsibility for the group's safety. Even if there is a two-tiered risk management system, the risk assessment is the defining document. There is no reason, of course, why students cannot be privy to the official risk assessment and all associated documents.

Scotland's *Curriculum for Excellence through Outdoor Learning* states that "Children and young people should not be denied an experience simply because some significant but unlikely hazard could not be completely eliminated" (Learning and Teaching Scotland, 2010, p. 24). It is simply not possible, nor desirable for all hazards to be eliminated during an outdoor lesson (Gill, 2010). In this view, a properly conceived risk management plan will serve to keep staff and students as "safe as necessary", rather than "as safe as possible". Martin, Breunig, Wagstaff, and Goldenberg (2017) remind us that not even the best risk management plan "can address every problem that a leader might encounter" (p. 309). Risk assessments can thus be regarded as consciousness-raising tools that can serve as guidelines to help educators make better decisions about their outdoor teaching.

As a final point in this chapter, we wish to highlight a trend in risk management thinking. While traditional approaches to risk management in the outdoors have tended to focus on the activity delivery itself, research in the last decade suggests that focusing primarily on participants, equipment, and environment can obscure less obvious causes of accidents (Dallat, Salmon, & Goode, 2015). Drawing from data and protocols in, for example, the aviation industry, Dallat and colleagues explain how risk management in outdoor learning needs to become more "systems-focused", where sport governing bodies, regulatory organizations, local governments, and schools can be seen as part of a complex assemblage of intertwined factors that influence outdoor learning programmes (Dallat et al., 2015). Viewed this way, it may be that the cause of an accident can have its roots in banal events such as, for example, a dated verbal agreement between certain key players who are no longer involved, an alteration in the timetable, a staff member being sick, school board policy changes, a crucial external person not being around to share key pieces of local information, or a student's full medical history not being fully disclosed with teachers. There is an increasing imperative for local governments, organization managers, and school districts to adopt a systems approach to risk management, whereby the activity that is being risk assessed is viewed as being influenced by a much larger set of sociocultural and organizational structures. This trend is gradually taking hold in countries such as Australia.

This chapter aims to demystify the complex and somewhat intimidating topic of risk management outdoors. Putting in place the six key pieces of a risk management plan will make it much easier to take children outside more regularly and with a much higher degree of self-assurance. We have strongly argued that the starting point for educational planning needs to centre directly on what students need to learn and the best ways for this to be achieved. From there, risk/benefit analyses can ensure the anticipated hazards inherent within the activity are in proportion to the lesson's intended learning outcomes.

## Guidelines

- Ensure your risk management strategy comprises the following documents: Risk Assessment, Emergency Action Plan, Consent Forms, Off-site Checklist, Journey Plans, and Incident Reports, and meets your country's or region's local requirements.

- Have an Offsite kit that is packed and ready to go.

- Make time for your students to create their own hazard assessments and complete their own journey plans.

- Ensure you consider the benefits as well as the risks, and seek to balance these.

## References

Barton, B. (2007). *Safety, risk, and adventure in outdoor activities.* London: SAGE.

Brussoni, M., Olsen, L. L., Pike, I., & Sleet, D. A. (2012). Risky play and children's safety: Balancing priorities for optimal child development. *International Journal of Environmental Research and Public Health, 9*(9), 3134–3148.

Dallat, C., Salmon, P., & Goode, N. (2015). All about the teacher, the rain and the backpack: The lack of a systems approach to risk assessment in school outdoor education programs. *Procedia Manufacturing, 3,* 1157–1164.

Education Scotland. (2019). *Risk/benefit tool.* https://education.gov.scot/improvement/learning-resources/managing-risk-in-outdoor-learning/

Gill, T. (2010). *Nothing ventured: Balancing risks and benefits in the outdoors.* No City Given: English Outdoor Council.

Going Out There. (2021). *Scottish framework for safe practice in off-site visits.* www.goingoutthere.co.uk/wp-content/uploads/2021/05/GOING-OUT-THERE-PRINT-V3.pdf

Health & Safety Executive. (2011). *School trips and outdoor learning activities: Tackling the health and safety myths.* www.hse.gov.uk/services/education/school-trips.pdf

Health & Safety Executive. (2014). *Health and safety: Advice on legal duties and powers.* https://assets.publishing.service.gov.uk/government/uploads/system/uploads/attachment_data/file/279429/DfE_Health_and_Safety_Advice_06_02_14.pdf

Health & Safety Executive. (2018). *Health and safety: Responsibilities and duties for schools.* www.gov.uk/government/publications/health-and-safety-advice-for-schools/responsibilities-and-duties-for-schools

Lavrysen, A., Bertrands, E., Leyssen, L., Smets, L., Vanderspikken, A., & De Graef, P. (2017). Risky-play at school. Facilitating risk perception and competence in young children. *European Early Childhood Education Research Journal, 25*(1), 89–105.

Learning and Teaching Scotland. (2010). *Curriculum for excellence through outdoor learning*. Glasgow: Learning & Teaching Scotland.

Martin, B., Breunig, M., Wagstaff, M., & Goldenberg, M. (2017). *Outdoor leadership*. Champaign, IL: Human Kinetics.

National Outdoor Leadership School. (2021). *NOLS wilderness medicine*. Lanham, MD: Stackpole Books.

Sandseter, E. B. H. (2009). Characteristics of risky play. *Journal of Adventure Education and Outdoor Learning*, *9*(1), 3–21.

# Supervising people outdoors

**Chapter aims**

- Understand the environmental, human, and external factors that may influence students when teaching outdoors.

- Be able to employ basic strategies for teaching concepts and sharing information with groups when environmental, human, and external factors may be competing for students' attention.

- Understand the difference between a stationary site and a moving site, and strategies for managing each.

- Know principles of and strategies for maintaining consistent levels of energy, hydration, temperature, and hygiene.

- Understand key considerations when working outdoors with people with Additional Support Needs.

In the majority of classroom teaching scenarios, most aspects of the setting can be controlled by the teacher. To a reasonable degree, the physical objects (such as chairs and tables), the environmental conditions (temperature), and the structure of social interactions, can be manipulated by the teacher and the school. Once we move the classroom outdoors, however, many of these fundamental elements are beyond the direct control of the teacher and present different challenges.

Outdoor educators need to employ measures that minimize the harmful influences of events over which they have little or no control. Responding to the environmental factors (e.g., wind, rain, sun), human factors (e.g., physiological changes in body temperature and hydration, additional support needs, group dynamics), and external factors (e.g., people who are not involved in the lesson),

DOI: 10.4324/9781003010890-11

is a central competence that outdoor leaders of all kinds need to develop. Students who are distracted by a cold wind, a busy road, or a grumbling stomach will almost certainly be less capable of fully engaging with any lesson. While careful planning will help outdoor teaching sessions run more smoothly, the constantly changing circumstances of being outdoors inevitably demand a degree of "thinking on one's feet".

Where the previous chapter on risk management was predominantly about what systems need to be in place before a group walks out the door, this chapter focuses entirely on managing groups once they have left the classroom and enter an environment that is fluid and constantly changing. Note that while this changeability can be a little scary and does require skill to manage, crucially, this is also at the heart of what can make outdoor teaching and learning so rich and engaging. While the majority of this chapter concentrates on the outdoor learning contexts of zones two and three (local neighbourhood and day excursions), much of the content will be generalizable to overnight stays, such as at a field studies centre.

We now look at six considerations for managing students while teaching outdoors. They are: Environmental, external, and human factors (the biggest section); staff/student ratios; managing the group *en route*; teaching and sharing information outdoors; toileting, personal privacy, and hygiene; and working with people with Additional Support Needs (ASNs).

## Managing environmental, external, and human factors

Three broad categories of factors need to be managed by educators working outdoors: Environmental, external, and human. These three categories underpin the basis of an overall strategy for leading groups outside—whether travelling together to or from a learning site or when delivering a lesson. The environmental, external, and human categories are approached from a risk management viewpoint (see Chapter 10) but also from the perspective of how best to optimise learning, given the prevailing conditions.

### Environmental factors: Sun, wind, rain, snow, and temperature

Perhaps surprisingly, it is the environmental factors that are often more straightforward to deal with than human factors; we can always have an energy bar if hungry, drink some water if thirsty, and put on a woolly hat and do some exercise if cold.

Hot conditions can demand brimmed hats, sunscreen, and perhaps even long, lightweight clothing. In some cases, it may be necessary to limit the amount of time spent outside during the hottest part of the day. Hyperthermia can be debilitating, but is very avoidable if certain measures are taken. Sun protection and regular hydration are critically important.

**Teaching tips:**

- Ensure that everyone is drinking enough by gathering the group and making "a toast" to celebrate the successes of the last hour or two: Everyone holds up their bottles and has a good drink.

- Dealing with the sun's brightness is also important. Leaders should have the sun in their eyes when explaining something to the group, rather than in the eyes of the students. (As with most teaching or discussion sessions, the group can be organized in a circle).

- If natural shade is limited, put up a tarp (this is also a great team exercise).

- When explaining something, leaders should consider taking off their sunglasses. If the sun is excessively bright, or the content will take some time to deliver, use sunglasses that allow others to see the eyes (rose or orange coloured). Maintaining eye contact is very important.

In windier climates, windchill can quickly cool people down. While being wet cools the body, of course, being wet in the wind can lead to rapid cooling. If teachers are worried about students staying warm, care should be taken to minimize time spent in the wind by carefully choosing lesson location with regard to wind and precipitation, and to limit how wet the students become by ensuring that they have appropriate clothing.

When teaching in cooler climes, there is an increased importance of maintaining core body temperature through having warm and waterproof clothing and boots. In the UK, not having this basic gear is a common reason that teachers decide against taking their classes outdoors (Christie, Beames, Higgins, Nicol, & Ross, 2014). Indeed, young people growing-up in urban centres may have little experience with spending a long time outdoors and will thus need some clothing "coaching". *Goretex*™ and other expensive, specialist materials are not needed for learning outside the classroom in the local neighbourhood. In most cases, long cagoule-type jackets (that come down to the knees) and some rubber boots will allow a teacher to run sessions outdoors in light rain, windy conditions, or when the ground is wet. Long jackets like these are also good for keeping students warmer in cold conditions.

**Teaching tips:**

- Give instructions with the students' backs to the wind. This means that they are more comfortable, and, if they are in a tight circle, teachers will be somewhat protected by the "wall" they have created.

- Carry a tarpaulin/group shelter under which the group can take refuge, have a snack, receive instructions, or discuss plans.

■ Use the lee of topographical features (hollows, rows of trees, and physical features (building walls) to provide protection from wind and rain. These can be incorporated into lesson plans as specific teaching or instruction stations.

There are two principal ways to raise a person's low body temperature. The first (and usually best) way is to have them generate their own heat by moving. When it's cooler outside, just staying still for half an hour will cause us to feel much colder, even if we are dressed appropriately and sitting on an insulated mat. Remaining active is central to staying warm.

The second way to raise a person's temperature is through external warming (ideally under insulating layers) by others. This is more of an emergency procedure, as it means that the person is so incapacitated by the cold (or by injury) they are not able to move by themselves and generate their own heat. Outdoor leaders should monitor their students' wellbeing as a matter of course. Apart from students complaining that they are cold, it is important to keep an eye open for any reduction in cognitive and motor function—both key indicators of someone sliding towards hypothermia.

**Teaching tips in colder climates:**

■ Have a few proven, fun active games at the ready. These can quickly and effectively warm-up and energize young bodies and minds.

■ Have an accessible supply of healthy snacks and hot drinks to help guard against children getting cold. The body needs food energy to warm itself.

■ Have a stash of warm hats, gloves, and socks in a backpack. A set of insulated sit-mats is also a good idea. Remember that hats, in particular, will need regular hot washing for hygiene reasons.

**Teaching tips in hotter climates:**

■ Ensure students are wearing appropriate sun hats and sun protective clothing, and are applying sunblock as necessary.

■ Be sure students maintain adequate hydration before, during, and after the activity. Water is best.

■ Avoid being outdoors when the sun is hottest and most damaging. Use cooler times of day and ensure there is ready access to shady areas.

■ Have available a stash of sun hats, sun protective clothing, and sunblock.

Many schools and education districts will have policies around how certain environmental conditions may limit outdoor activity. This might include guidance on elevated levels of air pollution, high winds, hot/cold temperatures, lightning, prolonged snowfall. Practice needs to be informed by these guidelines.

Just because the wind blows, the temperature drops, or it starts to rain, does not mean the session should be abandoned (unless of course there are obvious safety implications). Teachers should consider these changing conditions not only as ongoing management issues, but as learning opportunities, in the same way that they constantly strive to teach well in the classroom. Important life lessons in self-care can be taught through learning to thrive in a variety of weather conditions.

## External factors: Traffic, water features, terrain, and distracting events

Everything in the "external factors" category refers to those non-environmental features over which one has little to no control. Because a thorough risk assessment would have been completed already, teachers know what kind of terrain (or water features) to expect, where the most suitable places to crossroads are, and what to do if a student finds a discarded syringe or needle, and so on.

If giving instructions on the sidewalk and a street-cleaning machine comes by or a protest march appears from around the corner, what can be done? If a friendly dog comes into the middle of the circle while teaching, how can it be managed? What if the dog is aggressive? What if there is an aggressive person?

Unforeseen events often rely on teachers to improvise and "think on their feet". As discussed in Chapter 10, it is impossible to plan for every conceivable risk. Still, when expected hazards do present themselves, educators are expected to act swiftly and reasonably. Understanding the challenges and affordances of a given site, through a previous personal visit, will pay dividends (see Chapter 9 for more on this discussion).

---

**Teaching tips:**

- If teachers expect some distractions to arise during the outdoor lesson, it may be best to give instructions or have group discussions either in the classroom or in a quieter, less busy area.

- Before venturing outside, teachers should discuss with students the distractions that may present themselves, and how these will be dealt with. For example, if a plane is flying low overhead, teaching will pause until the noise has abated.

---

## Human factors: managing primary needs, group dynamics, and pupil personalities

Beyond addressing individual primary needs by ensuring that pupils have adequate energy and hydration levels, and are suitably clothed, teachers have to manage group behaviour and attend to specific individual needs and dispositions. Just as a classroom teacher might do before walking to another part of a big school, it is wise to discuss with pupils what appropriate behaviours are for getting on and off a city bus, crossing a road, or managing a toilet break at a museum.

Teachers know their students' personalities and should be familiar with their surroundings. It follows that they should be able to foresee many of the events that might influence group dynamics or trigger certain behaviours. Students may behave differently outdoors than indoors and may be triggered in different ways in contrasting environments. Just as students needed to learn how to learn indoors (in their first year of school), they may require similar guidance to learn outdoors. Beginning with short local learning experiences and building skills required to go further afield will benefit students as well as teachers, as shared conceptions of "learning spaces" broaden over time. By planning ahead as much as possible and by identifying the environmental, external, and human factors that might present themselves, teachers will be more able to manage risks and distractions during class outings.

---

### Teaching tips

- If needed, pupils can be reminded that expectations surrounding being responsible and courteous are no different if they are outside the classroom. Agreed "codes of behaviour" that are used in the classroom are just as applicable outdoors.

- Consider dividing journeys into sections or into time periods, at the ends of which pupils will re-group.

- Young people generally respond well to being given positions of responsibility, so think about how individuals can be given leadership positions when it comes to crossing roads, keeping the group together, and carrying group equipment.

---

## Staff/student ratios

Many teachers want definitive rules regarding adult/pupil ratios, and most schools and regions will have specific guidance about this. Of course, teachers need to be aware of any prescribed ratios and incorporate them into their planning. Certainly, in most cases within the school grounds, one teacher should be able to manage a class on their own. After all, break times often have one or two teachers overseeing large numbers of young people running around the playground.

Once away from the school, having two responsible, capable adults accompanying would be considered the minimum. Should any incident need managing, one adult can deal with this, while the other manages the group. Although having a third adult can be seen as a relative luxury, it does mean that in the event of a child not feeling well and having to return to school with one adult (for example), the lesson can continue as planned, as two adults remain to maintain an accepted ratio for effective learning outside the classroom.

Parents, volunteers, and teachers in training are an effective way to increase adult to student ratios. Adult volunteers can play specific roles, as well, which may have to do with the Emergency Action Plan, with crossing roads or travelling to a learning site, or supporting pupils with specific needs. Naturally, advice from the school district or local council regarding helping adults must be followed. In many cases, those who have not been "vetted" should not be left in sole charge of students. As noted in Chapter 7 on Community-based learning, regular volunteers in most regions will often need to undergo some kind of police disclosure/background check in order for them to work with students on their own.

We recommend that teachers decide what might be a suitable adult/pupil ratio for their outdoor teaching session based on the following factors:

- The ability of the group.

- The "reliability" of the group.

- The nature of the activities.

- The nature of the site.

- The number of students with additional support or medical needs.

- The supervising adults' experience in leading groups off-site.

Two items in the above list are worth expanding on. First, note that pupil age is not included. What is much more important than something as arbitrary as age, is that the activity is proportionate to the pupils' abilities. Second, the reliability of the pupils is vitally important. For example, it may be that one lecturer could work with 40 university students in a local park, as she knows that those 40 will generally behave as asked. Conversely, taking 40 13-year-olds outside who have a history of behavioural issues may demand very different supervision ratios! Ratios will also depend on whether or not the teaching site is fixed, with established boundaries (e.g., a courtyard), and if the activities feature multiple sites without obvious boundaries, such as a large park.

Note that ratios can be boosted for a specific section of an outing. For example, a parent or head teacher could join for a specific, more hazardous road crossing, and then leave once your class has arrived at the site. Finally, ratios are not just about safety: Ratios also have to do with what is best for maximizing learning. Each teacher should become the best judge of what is the ideal ratio of adults to children to maximize the learning and wellbeing of their particular pupils, in their particular environment. We recognize that often the "ideal ratio" is not possible, and in such cases the intentions and ambitions of the teacher for the session may need to be adapted.

## Managing the group en route

Several elements should be considered when travelling with a group through a park, on a sidewalk, or across a mountain plateau. There is no "best" way to travel together, but a number of factors will lead teachers to adopt the most appropriate method for their class on the day.

First, it is critically important that teachers carry a class list of all participants and adults, at all times. Counting the number of students before, as often as needed during the outing, and afterwards will be a matter of course. Keeping track of students during outings can take two broad approaches: Students checking on students and adults checking on students. Our favourite approach to counting is the "winger" system, where students make a circle at the start of the outing so that each person has a "buddy" on either side of them. At any time during an outing, a teacher can ask everyone to confirm that their winger is present. Within a few seconds, the names of any missing pupil will be known. When working with young students, teachers will need to take responsibility for manual head counts. With this method, each adult has a smaller group for which they are responsible for supervising and counting.

In terms of how the class travels, there are many variations that each have their own merits. Generally speaking, classes can travel as one big group or in smaller groups, such as twos or threes, or as a larger more independent "pod" of perhaps four to eight pupils. Creative student/student and adult/student check-in systems can be developed for pods and large classes alike.

Teachers can also encourage students to wear identifiable apparel (e.g., vests, hats, shirts). This may be more appropriate in crowded, urban settings. As part of the boundaries briefing, children should be instructed on what to do and where to meet should they become separated from the class. In situations with reliable and relatively experienced pupil groups, more freedom and less close supervision may be appropriate and even desirable. Supervising teachers will need to ensure that:

- The independent group work is aligned with the learning outcomes.

- The group has a reasonable "reliability record" from past outdoor trips.

- Appropriate boundaries have been outlined.

- Hazards that are likely to be encountered have been highlighted.

- The names of the individuals in each group are recorded by the teacher.

- There is a system for checking regularly to verify that pupils are safe (this can be indirect).

- Students are able to contact the supervising adults whenever they want.

- Students have been briefed on what do in the event of an emergency.

In most learning outside the classroom circumstances there will be one dedicated cell phone that one adult will carry on behalf of the group. This is the phone that the school can call if they need to contact the class. If pupils are working in independent groups that are some distance from the teacher, each pod will probably need to have its own phone. In colder climes, it is advisable to bring a power bank that can provide additional charges for batteries that are draining more quickly. There is a fluid discussion about student use of cell phones in outdoor learning settings (see Chapter 8), and the ways in which cell phones can be viewed as everything from a helpful educational tool through to an unwanted and possibly hazardous distraction (because people are not paying attention to their surroundings), and this need to be considered.

The concepts of *stationary* and *moving* sites are particularly helpful when managing groups outdoors. Nicolazzo (2007) explains that stationary sites (e.g., the entrance to the town hall) are generally considered much safer than moving sites (e.g., walking to the town hall), as the "hazards and safe zones are known prior to the activity" (p. 26). Moving sites often involve the group travelling from one place to another. With these sites, not all of the hazards may be known or visible until the moment they are encountered.

Nicolazzo (2007) stresses that teaching should take place in stationary sites. This is because the boundaries are fixed and the hazards can be seen. If a group was walking from one place to another and the teacher wanted the group to stop and discuss a certain phenomenon (e.g., the architecture of a building), the most prudent course of action would be to turn this situation into a stationary site, by first clearly delineating boundaries through imaginary lines between certain objects in the vicinity. For example, a teacher could quickly outline a stationary site as "a triangle, from that blue car to the corner of the building, and back to me". Second, a rapid assessment would need to be done to ensure that the risk of being seriously harmed by a hazard is acceptably low.

---

### Teaching tip: Crossing roads

Anything to do with students and road traffic can be considered higher risk. As crossing roads is something that people do frequently throughout their lifetimes, it is justifiable to do it on a class outing with educational purposes. Crossing roads is a lifelong skill to be learned properly.

Wherever possible, roads should be crossed at a designated pedestrian crossing. Drawing from the above site management terms, road crossings are considered to be "stationary sites". First, boundaries will be fixed (on the "current" side of the road, the other side, and for the actual crossing). Second, instructions will be given regarding when to cross, what to do (and where to wait) on the other side, and perhaps how to travel (e.g., alone, with a buddy, in a pod). Third, teachers will choose a suitable place for them to stand after the crossing. Teachers should be ready to intervene for educational/instructional or safety reasons.

In rural areas, with no designated pedestrian crossings, and less frequent traffic, a different approach to group crossings needs to be used. Rather than travel in a line that cuts across the flow of traffic (as one would at a pedestrian crossing), one effective method is to cross as one group that is arranged parallel to the direction of traffic. First, pupils stand in one long line on the side of the road, away from any bends in the road that might obscure a driver's vision. Teachers placed at each end of the line can give each other the "all clear" signal, after which the group crosses the road at precisely the same speed. This way, any on-coming cars will only be faced with the "area" of one person, as opposed to a road full of people that cannot be avoided, as with the crosswalk method. It is then easier for drivers to adjust their course and hopefully slow down.

## Teaching and sharing information outdoors

What is the best way to teach a concept or share information with a group? If teachers watch any seasoned outdoor educator in action they'll probably see most of the discussions happening in circles. With circles, everyone gets to be in the "front row". Circles maximise the possibility of each student to see and hear what is going on, to be heard if speaking, and to generally feel included in the class.

A rounded horseshoe shape can also be used if more of a stage or "front-of-the-class" approach is required. Huddles with several people deep can be effective in confined spaces and when brief pieces of vital information need to be quickly shared. Cooperative learning strategies also have their place when disseminating information or instructions. Teachers can brief a small group of messengers, who can then go and share information with their peers.

We encourage educators to experiment with some of these strategies for sharing information with others outdoors. Appropriate arrangements for outdoor teaching configurations will depend greatly on the educational aims of the class, the physical constraints of the setting, and the changing external, environmental, and human factors. In most cases, teaching is done at a stationary site, where there are clear boundaries and all of the hazards are identified and managed.

## Toileting, personal privacy, and hygiene

One of the trickiest issues to manage when teaching and learning outdoors is going to the toilet. Even if everyone uses the toilet before a short outing, there is always the possibility that someone will need to use the toilet to urinate, defecate, or manage their menstruation while you're out. We regard knowing how to appropriately urinate, defecate, and manage menstruation outdoors as important outdoor skills.

The privacy needed to take care of personal hygiene needs are just the same as they might be for kids on family trips; educational trips are not unusual in this respect. Still, because bathroom rituals are very personal, it is important for teachers to know their students well and prepare them for the possibility of urinating, defecating, and managing menstruating outside, before leaving the classroom.

Adolescents without much experience of spending extended periods away from toilet facilities may benefit more from predictable access to toilets than those who are older and have developed their own strategies. Students will thus find it helpful to know when and where they will have access to a toilet, or not, so they can plan accordingly.

There are several strategies available for urinating, defecating, and managing menstruation outside. If students feel comfortable enough, they could choose to go behind a tree. For those who want more privacy, we suggest going in a trusted small group to a more discrete location. For those who are deeply uncomfortable in these situations, teachers should have a backup option, such as a tarpaulin or portable toilet tent, indicated in their teaching plan. Keep in mind that adults in the group need a system in place for when they need to go—not least because supervision ratios will be temporarily compromised.

Specific to managing menstruation outdoors, reusable and disposable products require different forms of storing prior to handwashing and disposal. All menstrual products need to be transported with the students themselves, and therefore strategies for doing so need to be taught (e.g., use of paper bags, waterproof cloth bags, and/or biodegradable bags). It is important for all teachers to have with them a selection of menstrual products (e.g., disposable pads and tampons) in case students require them.

There may be instances when someone needs to defecate and there is no possibility of waiting until a proper toilet is reached. In these circumstances, usual guidelines for defecating outdoors apply: A site is found well away from water, a "cathole" is dug that is 15–20cm deep, and used toilet paper is either brought out in a bag or is used and then properly buried in the hole. Just as with menstruation, when away from toilet facilities, a portable handwashing and sanitizing station needs to be made available to students for hygiene management. It is advisable for teachers to be familiar with students' personal hygiene and toileting needs before venturing too far away.

One effective group management approach is to treat the toilet area as a stationary site. First, boundaries are fixed and the group not using the toilet is "parked" in this designated area. Second, instructions are given regarding waiting at the "base", travelling to and from the toilet, and being inside the actual toilet. Third, teachers will need to decide where to place themselves: With the waiting group, *en route* (if the main group is based away from the toilet), or near the toilet entrance. The teacher monitoring the toilet can be outside, or in the case of a large public toilet they can supervise from the inside. This description is not a fixed set of instructions, of course, as teachers will have their own systems for managing toilet use in the school or on field trips. Perhaps most importantly, they will know their students' individual needs. In cases of planned activities that involve changing clothes (e.g., swimming), great care must be taken to arrange appropriate supervision in changing rooms, and to provide adequate assistance for children with Additional Support Needs.

If there is no public toilet available, bringing a portable toilet can be an excellent option. Some small, foldable toilets that use easily disposable clinical waste bags are available. Also consider bringing an old tarp that can be used as a privacy curtain.

Eating and drinking is generally straightforward, in terms of managing hygiene. Students will have their own water bottles and often their own snacks. If snacks are being shared, no hands should go into the container; contents should be poured into hands or bowls. One thing schools will be highly alert to, but students may not, is allergies—some of which can be serious or fatal. Ensuring that any shared snacks are allergen-free requires specific guidance pre- and during the trip, and vigilance.

When working outdoors, it has always been best practice to wash hands before eating and preparing food, after using the toilet, and anytime one's hands are soiled. Antibacterial gel or wipes (ideally biodegradable ones) are an effective complement to handwashing and it is the teachers' responsibility to ensure that there are opportunities to maintain high standards of hand hygiene through washing with soap and water and by using disinfectant.

Teachers need to carry face masks and hypo-allergenic surgical gloves, in case they need to get closer to a pupil for some kind of health check or perform first aid, or in case they need to remove some hazardous waste from a teaching site. Used items and any waste can be put in a dedicated garbage bag brought for this purpose alone. Alongside official guidance from the school district, we recommend following the World Health Organization's (2020) guidelines on hand and respiratory hygiene.

---

**CASE STUDY**

One Thursday morning, Kay's Grade 5 class was taking a trip to a local community garden. The journey to the garden takes about 20 minutes and is mostly on the sidewalk of a busy road. In order to ensure that there was nothing unexpected going on that day (e.g., construction), Kay checked the main part of her route as she drove in that morning.

In her off-site kit, Kay had the students' blanket consent forms (with their parent/carer contact information), a first aid kit with specific medications used by students, her hazardous materials kit, extra food and drink, appropriate spare clothing, and a large lightweight tarpaulin.

Before leaving the premises, two students (Aditya & Marek) took a copy of the class' Journey Plan to the school office. The Journey Plan contained vital information about where the class was going, who was going, what they took with them, their designated cell phone number, and their estimated time of return. Aditya and Marek had completed a blank template during the previous class.

The first site of the day was a moving one, as the class was travelling down the road on the sidewalk. Kay placed herself at the back, while her classroom assistant was in the middle. As usual, the group walked in pairs, so that other pedestrians could pass as needed. The group had been on other outings before and the four pupils at the front knew that it was their responsibility to stop at the crosswalk and press the button.

Once the traffic had stopped at the light, the teaching assistant went across first. It's a busy crossing and Kay felt that it was best to place herself halfway across the road, so that the drivers would be more likely to see her high-visibility vest. Kay then signalled for the pre-arranged groups of four to cross to the designated waiting area that the classroom assistant had organized. Once the crossing was complete, the pupils got back into their line of pairs and continued the walk to the garden. In effect, the road crossing was itself turned into a "stationary site".

When the group arrived at the woodland, Kay and three reliable pupils checked the area for dog poo, branches that had broken off and could fall, and anything else that could be harmful. Of course, the two garden volunteers who the class were meeting had already done this, but Kay wanted to instil this practice in her students. During these few minutes, the classroom assistant suggested that people put on or take off a layer of clothing if they needed to. Kay and the students returned from their "reconnaissance mission" and reported to the group that the area, bound by the garden, posed no obvious risks. They now had a stationary site for teaching and learning.

## Working with people with Additional Support Needs (ASNs)

Following our discussion in Chapter 1 on outdoor learning for people of all abilities, we want to highlight some central considerations for working with students with ASNs. Specialists working outdoors with students with ASNs would be very clear in pointing out the following issues (among others):

- Basic needs such as food and water intake, and toileting, need to be carefully managed.

- Mobility capacity may indicate/contra-indicate certain locations being used in certain weather conditions.

- Mobility differences may affect students' capacity to cope with significantly cold/hot weather.

- Behavioral interactions within the group, with members of the public, may require additional, tactful management.

- Students' sensory abilities may be limited and hence prove challenging to manage, though paradoxically the outdoors may provide stimulating opportunities for such learners through novel textures, smells, sounds, light conditions.

- Learners' responses to certain stimuli may be stressful (e.g., loud noises), or may elicit positive outcomes (as previously stated).

- As staffing ratios increase, the person in charge may need to manage "support staff" as well as the students.

- Different medical conditions will demand specific management and support.

- Transport may be complicated, and require specialized or adapted vehicles.

- Adapted technical equipment may be useful for some activities, but training and skill in its use will be required.

- Consequently, Risk Assessments may have very significant additional considerations and dimensions (see Chapter 10).

- Finally, in light of the above, the outdoor learning ASN specialist may need extensive additional knowledge (e.g., of medical conditions) and to be highly trained in ways not common in other learning environments (e.g., basic sign language).

The above bullet points demonstrate how outdoor learning specialists working with students with ASNs need to have a very particular range of technical (outdoor skills and medical), professional and judgmental competences. While the technical skills (e.g., knowledge of medical conditions, use of equipment) can be regularly updated, it is open and caring communication, deep awareness of an individual student's needs, and using the affordances of the outdoors to provide meaningful experiences that is of greatest importance in fostering student learning and growth.

## Final thoughts

In order to contend with the range of human, environmental, and external factors that might be encountered during an outdoor learning session, teachers' abilities to adapt to these constantly changing circumstances are of paramount importance. Having this "big picture" overview and managing its fluid nature is a meta-skill that involves teachers making decisions, solving problems, and using their judgement within circumstances which are not entirely foreseeable. While some may be, such as route choice, lesson plan, teaching, and learning site, other aspects, such as weather conditions and human behaviour of students and those who might be met along the way, may not be.

As discussed in Chapter 10, the decisions made by outdoor educators will come down to "what a reasonable and prudent person would do" in the same circumstances. The ability to "think on one's feet" and respond to ever-changing conditions is an important part of supervising others outdoors. Outdoor educators need to use their own judgement (Barton, 2007), and should be empowered to do so. If, while on an outing, certain conditions have changed, teachers should not hesitate to take action in order to reduce the likelihood of encountering certain hazards.

The skills required to teach outside the classroom are not so specialized that they are the domain of only a few people who have a range of outdoor activities skills, knowledge of natural history, and have taken technical courses on risk management. As with the acquisition of most skills, outdoor supervision skills are gained over time through careful planning, steady practice, and with the oversight of a caring and experienced mentor. We suggest that those new to teaching outdoors should start with modest ambitions and stay close to the school—even within the school grounds. Normalizing the practice of taking one's class outdoors in the immediate environment, will better prepare teachers and pupils for journeys further afield.

## Guidelines

- Outdoor educators need to be aware of the environmental, human, and external factors that may distract, and possibly harm, students. These three sets of factors need to be addressed before delivering educational content.

- Classes can travel together as one group (usually in twos and threes) or in smaller independent "pods".

- Keeping track of students during outings can be done in different ways. Three common ones are: Students checking on students (the "winger" approach), students shouting out their assigned number, and adults checking on students (e.g., going through the whole roll call or through each pod).

- Educators should classify all activities outside the school as either stationary or moving sites. Stationary sites, where boundaries have been established and where local hazards have been identified, are generally best for teaching, sharing information, and group work.

- Having a comprehensive "off-site kit" at the ready enables educators to be more spontaneous with their outdoor teaching, while ensuring that they have the equipment and administrative items to respond to events, as they unfold.

- Be extra mindful of the ways in which people with different abilities may respond to varying weather conditions and social situations.

# References

Barton, B. (2007). *Safety, risk, and adventure in outdoor activities.* London: SAGE.

Christie, B., Beames, S., Higgins, P., Nicol, R., & Ross, H. (2014). Outdoor learning provision in Scottish Schools. *Scottish Educational Review, 46*(1), 48–64.

Nicolazzo, P. (2007). *Effective outdoor program design and management.* Winthrop, WA: Wilderness Medicine Training Centre.

World Health Organization. (2020). *Clean hands protect against infection.* www.who.int/gpsc/clean_hands_protection/en/

# 12 Evidencing learning and developing a whole school approach

---

## Chapter aims

● Identify ways in which individual teachers can integrate outdoor learning into their own practice.

● Consider ways in which educators can assess and evidence learning against the curriculum (e.g., though reflective journals and portfolios).

● Be aware of key administrative and infrastructure items that should be in place before teaching beyond the school grounds.

● Present ways of designing, creating, leading, and implementing a whole school plan that has outdoor learning as an integral part of the school's teaching and learning strategy.

● Demonstrate how distributive leadership can happen at all levels of schooling, where everyone can have a contributing role.

---

This final chapter focuses on a reminder of key administrative and infrastructure considerations, ways in which to evidence learning, and the epitome of embracing outdoor learning: Developing a whole school approach for taking learning and teaching outdoors. Taking learning outside the classroom requires preparation, just as teaching indoors or online does. There are some practical differences, however, in terms of managing risk, and in some cases, supervising students in public spaces (see Chapters 10 and 11). The affordances of specific places is an excellent way to start thinking about the possibilities for learning and teaching. Once these affordances have been considered and potential learning opportunities identified, these can be directly linked to specific learning outcomes as outlined in teachers' specific curricular documents.

At the same time, we believe it is important to keep learning open, and to be guided by student curiosity and wonder (see Chapter 6). This can be done by either

 DOI: 10.4324/9781003010890-12

including a learning outcome that is determined by students beforehand or through being attentive to unexpected learning possibilities ("teachable moments") that emerge during the outing. We recommend a gradual approach that begins with individual teachers who are passionate about taking their own students' learning outdoors. These educators can then inspire and support colleagues to do the same, and thus take a leadership role as their school develops its capacity to teach more of the curriculum outdoors. This involves developing an organizational culture that supports educational change and the visioning, creation, and implementation of whole school plans.

This chapter is divided into five sections. First, we briefly revisit key risk related administrative and infrastructure elements that need to be put in place before any off-site teaching takes place (see Chapter 10). Second, we underline the importance of making clear links between a teacher's specific learning outcomes for their lessons and the official curriculum (see Chapter 3). Third, we examine the similarities and differences between outdoor, indoor, and online spaces for assessing student learning. Fourth, we provide an overview of how a whole school plan can be organized. And fifth, we discuss how leadership for developing and implementing outdoor learning throughout a school (or any other educational institution) requires leadership from all members of staff.

As outlined in Chapter 5, the places and spaces in which learning happens are integral to student learning. Similarly, the outdoors affords different ways of teaching for sustainability (Chapter 4), ethics, world views, and responsibility (Chapter 2). Outdoor places naturally inspire student curiosity and wonder (Chapter 6), and, when community spaces are used, they broaden the potential for collaborative learning in real-world contexts that are close to home (Chapter 7) and further afield (Chapter 9). The integration of mobile technologies (Chapter 8) offers further potential for broadening and deepening learning in these varied places and spaces. Students can be actively engaged in identifying and managing risks (Chapter 10), and teachers can easily learn to effectively manage groups of students while out and about (Chapter 11). Having come this far in this book, readers now have access to all the parts needed to take learning outdoors. We now attempt to bring these parts together by offering guidance on how to incorporate outdoor learning into existing teaching practices; plan, assess, and evidence learning outdoors; and lead schoolwide change.

## Administration and infrastructure

As we know, countless opportunities exist in local community spaces, urban, and rural, for outdoor learning. Local parks, green spaces, woods, rivers, and beaches offer a range of learning opportunities throughout the year, across the seasons for developing connectedness and environmental stewardship (Schwass, Potter, O'Connell, & Potter, 2021). There are a few key pieces of administration that ideally need to be in place before taking children off-site. If teachers are working solely within the school grounds, then this additional paperwork is usually not needed. This is good news for educators who are looking to "dip their toes" into teaching outdoors, as this can be done in the school grounds with little fuss. Once groups of students are going to leave the grounds, then certain administrative elements need to be present.

First, as explained in Chapter 10, teachers need to ensure that they have completed a risk assessment for straightforward, uncomplicated learning outside the classroom. While this may be a document they completed some time ago, or even in the previous school year, it is important that the document is revisited and updated to reflect current circumstances. These might include specific weather conditions, recent road works or construction site developments, or students who have specific needs.

Second, every child's parent or carer should have signed some kind of consent form that permits teachers to take their students to local places that are perhaps within a specific (e.g., two kilometre/mile) radius of the school. This kind of blanket consent form will allow teachers to work in much more spontaneous and unrestricted ways. One-off trips to further away places will normally require a specific consent form.

Third, it can be useful for teachers to share resources, such as rain boots, rain jackets, group shelters, foam sit-mats, and general first aid kits. Having a storage place where equipment that can be used by all teachers is highly recommended. Too often we hear teachers say that a lack of resources meant they were not able to take learning outdoors. While we agree that having specific equipment for learning and teaching outdoors can make some aspects easier, in our view, very little technical, expensive equipment is required to teach a wide range of aspects of the curriculum outside the classroom. Many activities can be carried out with the pupils wearing the clothes they come to school in, particularly if they are briefed in advance that they will be going outdoors. For any trips farther afield, especially if the weather may be wet, waterproof "wellies"/rubber boots are an inexpensive, basic item of kit that schools may invest in. In some contexts, standard waterproof jackets, to be sure all students are able to stay dry and warm would be the next level of provision.

Finally, it is a good idea to have one staff member as the dedicated coordinator of outdoor learning and teaching. This person can have oversight of risk assessments, consent forms, shared clothing and equipment, and act as mentor for less experienced outdoor teachers.

## Individual approaches to connecting curriculum to outdoor spaces

Before getting to the stage where it feels appropriate to develop a whole school plan, it is likely that individual teachers will have been doing their own outdoor teaching. If schools or educational institutions are not ready to embrace whole scale outdoor pedagogies, it will likely fall to educators to take the lead in developing their own systems and practices.

Rather than beginning with the daunting question of "how can I teach outdoors?", it is probably much easier to start with establishing what a lesson's intended learning outcomes are. From there, one can ask, "Where is the best place to teach this content?" We offer three simple questions to help with this:

1. What do I need to teach?

2. How do I need to teach it?

3. Where is the best place to teach it? Outdoors, indoors, or online? Or some combination of the three?

These questions are relevant for all curriculum areas and topics. We do not position the outdoors as the best place to teach all curricular content, and it is unlikely that any one of the three teaching and learning locations in the third point above will be entirely suitable to thoroughly cover a given curricular area. That is why teachers are encouraged to carefully consider their intended learning outcomes and decide on the most appropriate settings and platforms to maximize student learning.

While teachers will be well-practiced at linking learning outcomes in curricular documents to what they do in class, this skill may be less familiar to those looking to move their practice outdoors. That said, we see this linking of curricular outcomes to outdoor lessons as generally being straightforward, as long as the decision to take the class outdoors has been made for the right reasons. The main difference is that because teaching outdoors brings with it elements of uncertainty, serendipitous opportunities can arise and it is entirely possible that learning outcomes that were not planned can be realized. This allows teachers to retrospectively add to their lesson plans in order to capture how particular "bonus" learning outcomes were achieved through serendipitous encounters (see Krouwel, 2005). Of course, there is a "flip side" to this, which is that care must be taken to ensure that the main focus is not diverted to the detriment of addressing the original learning outcomes.

## Evidencing learning

Classroom teachers are of course required to teach to and through a curriculum, and while we recognize the mentality of this, it is important to keep in mind that not all learning needs to be recorded, evidenced, evaluated, or assessed. However, in formal education contexts around the world, evidencing and assessing learning is a core requirement, and doing so through outdoor experiences students provides opportunities to demonstrate that such learning can fit with the "mainstream" of the formal curriculum.

There are many ways in which teachers already assess and evidence learning (e.g., essays, presentations, reports, and evaluations) that happen indoors. These ways of assessing learning remain as relevant outdoors, as they are indoors and online. While teaching outdoors, whether local or rural, in school, or on overnight stays, however, there is a range of ways in which teachers and students can collect evidence of, and for, learning. In addition to what we might call traditional modes of assessment there are others which incorporate aspects of the more conventional assessments, and go further to include reflection *as* assessment, through such tools as reflective journals, portfolios, and film making. Some of these methods are especially effective for assessing learning in ways that are highly individualized.

**Reflective journals**, teachers will attest, are too often implemented in simplistic ways which result in shallow engagement from students and "dear diary" responses of "what happened". In order to make use of reflective journals meaningfully, it is essential students are taught the skills of reflective thinking and writing, and then how to transform and deepen learning through creative methods, such as podcasts, film-making, drawing, and so on (see O'Connell & Dyment, 2015). To realize this possibility it is important for journals to initially be highly structured, and provide a form of "training" for students to learn about the most effective ways to demonstrate their learning.

Once this initial familiarization stage has taken place, students will become more skilled at creating their own methods to critically reflect on their learning journeys. The structure can be reduced when students are ready to lead their own learning in a manner that is facilitated by the teacher. Increased levels of autonomy can be given to students until many of the decisions about the structure of the reflective journal are eventually handed over to the student. This handing over is individual to each student, as some will require more support than others. We suggest the following four guiding questions for structuring journal entries:

1. What happened? What did you (or others) see, hear, do?

2. So what? How did it make you feel? What did you learn/take away from the experience?

3. Now what? What does this experience make you want to learn more about, or do something about?

4. Now what action? What actions will you now take to address your learning or take action?

Students can be asked to link their thinking, reflections, and experiences to wider contexts, literature (academic and grey—e.g., newspaper articles), concepts, and theoretical models. Doing so enables them to demonstrate their deeper understandings of how their learning fits into wider social and ecological contexts. Of course, depending on the grade/age of students, teachers may choose to use only the one, two, or three of the four questions; it may also be appropriate (and indeed encouraged) for students to design their own questions for reflection.

When supporting students in writing their journals, the guiding questions posed by a teacher should focus a student's thinking, while being open enough for them to feel it is *their* focus, to be able to share what they have learnt and how it is relevant to their learning. It is important to remember that the teacher plays a central facilitatory role, guiding the learning. Left alone, in the absence of reflective thinking and writing skills, students may revert back to "dear diary" responses, which lack critical introspection.

Written text is a great starting point for sharing reflections of learning, however reflection can be greatly expanded by adding creative pathways (O'Connell, Dyment, & Smith, 2015). By asking students to add photos and images that help to explain their thoughts, feelings, and experiences, the reflection process shifts from the cognitive to the affective domains. By challenging students to consider different modes of presenting their reflections—through images, film, podcasts, drawing, painting, sculpting, modelling, and so on—the depth of reflection increases and individualized ways of learning can be realized. However, this freedom in the absence of clear guiding questions to direct reflection, may lead to students getting lost and producing shallow responses that too often fall into the "writing for the test" variety (O'Connell et al., 2015).

It is also possible to facilitate group reflective journaling where a small or large group collaboratively creates a reflective journal of their individual and collective experiences (Asfeldt, Hvenegaard, & Purc-Stephenson, 2017). A group reflective journal can take the pressure off individuals and invite more risk taking in terms of presentation due to the responsibility lying with the group, rather than one student. It can also guard against "journaling fatigue" from overly frequent journaling tasks.

While we have provided four generic questions that we have found to be useful in a range of situations, we also use more specific questions and prompts to match specific aims of the learning experience. We also recommend that teachers develop their own questions that suit their own teaching approach and intentions. Like any assessment *as* or *for* learning, it is important to have helpful prompts to enable students to demonstrate their learning. Equally, as with writing an essay, the teacher typically provides the question (or list of questions to choose from), and then invites students to write their own questions, negotiate these with the teacher, and then respond to their own question. With reflective journals, the handing over of structure to the student is no different. Facilitating this process with the student is important to ensure the student is meeting the assessment requirements and also has something that will be helpful for them to respond to.

Grade appropriate assessment criteria need to be provided to students prior to beginning the task, with the focus on reflective writing depth, and supporting ideas with experience(s) and literature. Journals are often graded as pass/fail, however they are widely used as legitimate assessment tools in all kinds of educational programmes.

***Portfolios*** offer an established way of evidencing learning in education (Jones, 2012). Whether led by teachers or students, portfolios have been central to teaching for some time—whether in hard copy or more recent electronic or e-portfolios (Johnson, Mims-Cox, & Doyle-Nichols, 2010). The portfolio approach to capturing student learning places responsibility on the learner to direct their own personally relevant construction of knowledge (Hascher & Sonntagbauer, 2013) and evidence this through a process of inquiry, reflection, and interpretation (Strudler & Wetzel, 2005). Totter and Wyss (2019) explain that e-portfolios are particularly effective, as they are "easily accessible, time and place independent, can integrate multiple media, are easy to update and can more readily reference the work of learners" (p. 70).

They are particularly useful for capturing the embodied learning experienced by students outdoors. Portfolios are now typically created online, with many options for software (paid and unpaid) on offer. These can range from specific purpose-built e-portfolio software, through to free website building sites, and more generic word processing/software suites. All that is required is an imagination for finding ways in which students might evidence their learning across the curriculum outdoors, indoors, and online. Supporting students as they make their own decisions about evidencing learning, and by what means it will be presented, encourages creativity, independence, and self-regulated learning (Glaser-Zikuda, Fendler, Noack, & Ziegelbauer, 2018). The portfolio offers opportunities for collaborative learning between students and environment/places/spaces, students and other students, and students and teachers.

Many of the online platforms and software make evidencing learning outdoors easy, where tablets and phones (and other technology, such as camera equipped drones) can be used to capture learning, afford reflection material on return to the classroom, and foster creativity through the creation of online portfolios, hard copy portfolios, films, books, and websites. The options are as wide as one can imagine and are only limited by students' and teachers' collective imaginations. Portfolios are already being used in schools in a range of ways, led by teachers to evidence student learning, particularly in the younger years, through to later years in schooling where students submit a portfolio as assessment which demonstrates their learning across the school year. The internet houses a myriad of examples, books, and supporting resources which are ever evolving. The reflective journal and skills learned through completing a reflective journal, can be a stand-alone assessment piece, form a part of this portfolio, and or may in some instances provide the structure for the portfolio.

A key message in this section is that just because some teaching and learning is taking place outdoors does not mean that radical new ways of assessing need to be devised as mainstream methods for capturing student learning, such as essays, reports, creative writing, reflective journals, and portfolios, are as applicable to outdoor learning as they are to indoor learning. However, there are of course specific subject areas for which time in the outdoors, to both learn and conduct assessed individual projects generally considered essential. These include studies in biology/ecology, geography/geology where students collect data for projects that are evaluated as part of formal curriculum assessments.

## Developing a whole school approach

A whole school approach is essentially a considered and progressive curriculum that begins in the first year of schooling and continues through to the final year. When deciding to develop and adopt a school wide approach to outdoor learning, this task can seem rather daunting. This challenge can be tackled by involving other schools, community organizations, and families (see Chapter 7). It is essential, of course, that school wide strategies are directly linked to, and embedded within, the official curriculum.

A number of countries, districts, and regions around the world are already adopting outdoor learning as a core part of how the curriculum gets "delivered" (e.g., Scotland, New Zealand, the province of Ontario, the state of Victoria). While the explicit inclusions make the process easier, teachers should not be deterred if their curriculum does not make an overt mention of outdoor learning. Indeed, naming Outdoor Learning in a School Plan can be the beginning of it being incorporated into curricular activity. In many cases, teachers have been taking learning outdoors and linking this to curriculum requirements for decades—before outdoor learning was even a field.

When properly embedded within a school, outdoor learning is not something that is "sprinkled on" existing teaching practices, like some kind of optional, extra seasoning. Indeed, trying to squeeze outdoor learning into existing teaching structures will likely prove difficult. As noted in the previous section on administration and infrastructure, some topics lend themselves more readily to particular spaces and methods (e.g., outdoors, indoors, and online).

Engaging in the development of a whole school approach offers rich opportunities to examine and revise school values and priorities. It enables teachers, parents, administrators, and students an opportunity to deeply consider why certain settings and methods are being employed to arrive at particular desired learning outcomes. A logical progression and integration of learning in outdoor, indoor, and online spaces can be developed, as students journey through their school career.

## Taking personal responsibility for leading curriculum change

All schools need designated leaders and managers whose work allows teachers to get on with the job of teaching. In schools where there is no history or culture of learning outside the classroom and senior management does not appear to support it, trying to initiate changes to the ways people teach and learn can be very daunting. This is possible, however, as Shamir and Eilam (2005) highlight instances of individual educators initiating programme change and, through this process, inspiring "onlookers" to follow suit.

In our view, leadership is about working with a "community of interest" to develop a shared vision and then supporting that community on the journey towards achieving it. This approach to leading is contextual and specific to working towards collective aims. Further, it acknowledges the importance of "followership"—being willing to "follow" others who are taking leadership roles when appropriate. In schools such "contextual leadership" might, for example, involve two classroom teachers working with other teachers, parents, administration, and students to create a shared vision for incorporating the outdoors into all student learning, while and ensuring that staff have the resources they need.

Ideally, this kind of initiative taking is supported by school managers who, following Gurr, Drysdale, and Goode (2022), focus much attention on supporting the personal and professional development of teachers and other adults in the school. Throughout this process it is profoundly important to recognize that in all instances we know, schools need to work within the context of a "school plan". This addresses issues such as student numbers, staff complement and recruitment, buildings and infrastructure, etc. The development of the plan is generally led by senior leaders, and has to be negotiated with and approved by an overseeing authority—in the state system this may be an "education authority" or board. For outdoor learning to be integrated effectively, committed teachers will need to contribute to and then work *with* the plan.

This kind of "authentic leadership" has, as one of its defining features, leaders who "walk their talk" (Avolio & Gardner, 2005). In our case, this would mean, for example, teachers who value learning outdoors both teaching outdoors themselves, and leading curriculum change. While some earlier models of leadership remain important as we consider alternative ways of leading, we invite you to adopt a combination of contemporary leadership theories to underpin your own style which embraces transformation through embracing Indigenous knowledges/ways of being, and feminist and ecological approaches, where leadership responsibility lies with each individual, rather than designated leaders (e.g., Principal and school leaders). Earth Leadership (Smith, 2021) is an example of such an approach, as it draws on multiple models/theories of leadership to empower all of us, as individuals and collectives, to take responsibility and lead reforms in how and where we teach/lead, regardless of named leadership roles, and by valuing the more-than-human, as much as the human.

## CASE STUDY

At Big Mountain School, the Principal led a process of evaluating schoolwide teaching and learning, with a specific focus on individual teachers using the school grounds and local spaces; incorporating outdoor learning throughout the range of school years; and featuring overnight and expedition components.

The first task was to put together a summary of the opportunities for and barriers to incorporating outdoor learning into Big Mountain School, and the affordance of the local area. This was then presented to all staff (administrators, support staff, and teachers), where a process of "blue sky thinking" was undertaken to collect ideas about what kinds of teaching and learning might be desirable. This was then collated and presented to the same group, along with key stakeholders (parents, local politicians, community organizations), to gather further information and give additional shape to the ideas being discussed. The results of this process were then collated again and a whole school programme was developed.

Year 1—Planting the Seed (School Gardening Project)

Year 2—Sprouting Connections (Taking gardening into the community and working with, and learning from, elders)

Year 3—Budding Place Dwellers (Visiting and re-visiting local places)

Year 4—Growing Ideas (Understanding sustainability and local actions)

Year 5—Exploring Places (Weeklong overnight excursion)

Year 6—Expanding Activists (Leading whole school initiatives for sustainability and community actions)

Year 7—Future leaders (Working with Years 1 & 2 in the Garden; weeklong overnight excursion focusing on connection and leadership of self, before learning to lead others)

Year 8—Living a full life (Focus on self-care, and care of environment—local, community, and wider)

Year 9—Alive and Active (Expedition programme with focus on living and learning in brave communities)

Year 10—Sustainability and World Issues (School-based projects, led by students)

Year 11—Leading Change (Students leading their own expedition programmes)

The gardening project begins in Year 1 and is a thread that runs through students' time at the school. In the final years, with guidance from teachers, students can design some aspects of their own learning outcomes, and then develop their own outdoor learning programmes. Central threads of the whole school plan can include social and environmental justice, leadership development, community engagement, and health and wellbeing. The four zones of outdoor learning (Chapter 1) are also used to full effect over the years. Learning, teaching, and assessment is led by a group of teachers, student representatives, and parents, which meets regularly.

This is of course an idealized programme, and we are well aware that few schools will have the flexibility and resources to develop this in all years. If such coherence and progression is not possible in your school, remember it is better to develop some pro-vision than none, and work gradually to develop further across all years.

Evidencing learning across a whole school programme affords opportunities to develop a range of ways in which learning might be assessed. This could involve, for example, a reflective journal which is highly structured and facilitated by the teacher in Year 1, through to students developing their own focus for Year 11, with a reduction in structure across the years. Similarly, a portfolio might be a more suitable way in which to capture such reflections, through the written word, drawings, artwork, photos, film, and music. It may also be suitable to use inclusion criteria that students are required to meet each year, and which changes as their programme evolves and their learning widens and deepens with experience.

The good news within this chapter is that incorporating outdoor learning into existing classroom teaching practices, and across an entire school, is less complicated than one might think. Drawing on Michael Fullan's (2013) work, it is often the social chemistry of getting individuals and groups working well together that is central to effective whole school culture change. Fullan (2006) is a realist, however, and states that whole school change needs to be "cultivated over time" (p. 11), happens in "a thousand small ways during the journey" (p. 14), and demands tremendous resolve.

As we can see from the case study above, it can be a very useful exercise to imagine a long-term view that captures what teachers and students might do for their initial forays outdoors, right up to what a fully realized vision of combined outdoor, indoor, and online education might look like. Mapping out "where we are now" to "where we want to be", and the steps along the way, can be a powerful way to start developing a whole school plan.

A second key point in this chapter is that teachers already possess the assessment tools that they need to capture learning that takes place outdoors. Many teachers reading the above sections on journals and portfolios will be thinking, "well, I already do that". We hope so. We have highlighted these methods in particular, as we find them especially suited to helping students show what they have learned outside of the classroom. Just because an activity took place in a certain environment (e.g., outdoors) doesn't mean that it has to be assessed there (though it may well be). Assessment is an inescapable part of any programme of formal education and readers are encouraged to draw on the methods they are comfortable with, while experimenting with new ones as well.

## Guidelines

- Teachers draw on existing pedagogies and assessment strategies they are familiar with, and embrace new contemporary, multimodal ways of teaching and assessing.

- Start outdoor teaching practices gradually—in one corner of the school grounds for short periods—and expand into surrounding areas and further afield.

- Create a framework for reflective journals and portfolios. Empower students to be innovative and creative in the ways in which they evidence their learning for assessment within the curriculum.

- Be a leader of outdoor learning at your school/organization. Do not wait for someone else.

- Develop a whole school approach that incorporates other schools, individuals, and community organizations into a coherent and progressive plan for outdoor learning.

- Build a community of like-minded educators, locally and globally; support each other by sharing resources through physical and online networks.

# References

Asfeldt, M., Hvenegaard, G., & Purc-Stephenson, R. (2017). Group writing, reflection, and discovery: A model for enhancing learning on wilderness educational expeditions. *Journal of Experiential Education, 41*(3), 241–260.

Avolio, B. J., & Gardner, W. L. (2005). Authentic leadership development: Getting to the root of positive forms of leadership. *The Leadership Quarterly, 16*(3), 315–338.

Fullan, M. (2006). *Change theory: A force for school improvement* (Paper no. 157). Australia, VIC: Centre for Strategic Education.

Fullan, M. (2013). *Change: Making it happen in your school and system.* https://michael-fullan.ca/handouts/

Glaser-Zikuda, M., Fendler, J., Noack, J., & Ziegelbauer, S. (2018). Fostering self-regulated learning with portfolios in schools and higher education. *Orbis Scholae, 5*(2), 67–78.

Gurr, D., Drysdale, L., & Goode, H. (2022). An open systems model of successful school leadership. *Journal of Educational Administration, 60*(1), 21–40.

Hascher, T., & Sonntagbauer, C. (2013). Portfolios in der Lehrer/innenbildung—Bilanz, Rahmung und Ausblick. In B. Koch-Priewe, T. Leonhard, A. Pineker, & J. C. Störtländer (Eds.), *Portfolio in der LehrerInnenbildung. Konzepte und empirische Befunde* (pp. 287–298). Bad Heilbrunn: Klinkhardt.

Johnson, R. S., Mims-Cox, J. S., & Doyle-Nichols, A. (2010). *Developing portfolios in education: A guide to reflection, inquiry, and assessment* (2nd ed.). Thousand Oaks, CA: Sage.

Jones, J. (2012). Portfolios as 'learning companions' for children and a means to support and assess language learning in the primary school. *Education 3–13, 40*(4), 401–416.

Krouwel, W. (2005). The value of serendipitous learning: Part 2—a way forward through self-development. *Pathways: The Ontario Journal of Outdoor Education, 17*(3), 28–32.

O'Connell, T. S., & Dyment, J. E. (2015). *Theory into practice: Unlocking the power and the potential of reflective journals.* Charlotte, NC: Information Age.

O'Connell, T. S., Dyment, J. E., & Smith, H. A. (2015). Students' appropriation, rejection and perceptions of creativity in reflective journals. *International Journal of Teaching and Learning in Higher Education, 27*(1), 1–13.

Schwass, N. R., Potter, S. E., O'Connell, T. S., & Potter, T. G. (2021). Outdoor journeys as a catalyst for enhanced place connectedness and environmental stewardship. *Journal of Outdoor and Environmental Education, 24*(2), 215–231.

Shamir, B., & Eilam, G. (2005). "What's your story?": A life-stories approach to authentic leadership development. *The Leadership Quarterly, 16*, 395–417.

Smith, H. A. (2021). Leadership theory: From effective to extraordinary. In G. Thomas, J. Dyment, & H. Prince (Eds.), *Outdoor environmental education in higher education: International perspectives*. Sydney: Springer Nature.

Strudler, N., & Wetzel, K. (2005). The diffusion of electronic portfolios in teacher education: Issues of initiation and implementation. *Journal of Research on Technology in Education, 37*(4), 411–433. https://doi.org/10.1080/15391523.2005.10782446

Totter, A., & Wyss, C. (2019). Opportunities and challenges of e-portfolios in teacher education. Lessons learnt. *Research on Education and Media, 11*(1), 69–75.

# Afterword

## Next steps

We believe outdoor learning is not just about the outdoors: It is primarily about innovative teaching that occurs in places and spaces which best support learning, attends to local and global issues, and leads to individual and collective action. We recognize that there are many purposes to education that range across the instrumental, practical, pragmatic, and philosophical. However, it is our contention that a core purpose must be to educate the whole child to become an agent of change—one who has learnt from experiences beyond the classroom walls, feels able to "act", and may be motivated to help forge a world that is ecologically and socially just. If educators are serious about doing so, then an approach to learning that depends almost exclusively on them being indoors and working in front of various screens is morally unacceptable, and practically ineffective.

The affordances offered by the outdoors are essential, now more than ever, for our young people's education. The ability to negotiate risk, evaluate multiple sources of information, be mindful of the power of social media (both positive and negative), and have the knowledge, skills, and dispositions to be a catalyst for change through social and environmental action are essential for youth who are navigating their way through a world where the future is increasingly uncertain, complex to understand and difficult to navigate.

The conclusion of this book can be seen as only the beginning of a much broader, richer, deeper educational enterprise that may engage readers further. We hope inclusion of references to the literature we have used to broaden our perspectives will be of use to you, as you broaden your own. Equally, we hope the practical applications will inspire you to expand the time you spend teaching outdoors and stimulate you to do so in new ways.

We have been shaped—both as human beings and as educators—through rich and powerful experiences on lands and seas that have experienced vast human-induced ecological changes over the millennia, and some of which have borne witness to atrocious social events. We offer our collective experience and knowledge to the body of constantly growing and evolving literature on how to teach in, through, about, for, and indeed from such places, and to help those we teach (as well as ourselves) learn more effectively, and in ways that will lead to socially just societies and thriving ecosystems. We have gleaned much of what appears in these pages through working with students and teachers and, to those who have influenced us, we are forever grateful.

We invite you to be courageous with your teaching and go outdoors. It is up to each of us as individual influencers. If we are to address the current climate crisis and biodiversity loss, then we have no time to waste. Begin today. Ask, *where can learning best occur for my students, as I teach across the curriculum in interdisciplinary ways?* Act in ways that support the people around you to become positive agents of change for the planet.

It is now over to you, to bring to life whatever this book has inspired in you, and to play your part in helping your learners to maximize their potential as lifelong learners and active citizens, who can also contribute to the future of a healthy planet and the wellbeing of all (human and more-than-human) who live here.

# Index

Note: Page numbers in *italics* indicate a figure on the corresponding page.